W9-AEJ-981

GOOD MORNING, MONSTER

ALSO BY CATHERINE GILDINER

Too Close to the Falls
After the Falls
Coming Ashore
Seduction

GOOD MORNING, MONSTER

MONSTER

A Therapist Shares

Five Heroic Stories of Emotional Recovery

Catherine Gildiner

ST. MARTIN'S PRESS
NEW YORK

First published in the United States by St. Martin's Press, an imprint of St. Martin's Publishing Group

www.stmartins.com

Library of Congress Cataloging-in-Publication Data

Names: Gildiner, Catherine, 1948– author.
Title: Good morning, monster : a therapist shares five heroic
    stories of emotional recovery / Catherine Gildiner.
Description: First U.S. edition. | New York : St. Martin's Press,
    2020. | Identifiers: LCCN 2020019305 | ISBN 9781250271488
    (hardcover) | ISBN 9781250272263 (ebook)
Subjects: LCSH: Psychotherapy—Case studies.
Classification: LCC RC465 .G55 2020 | DDC 616.89/14—dc23
LC record available at https://lccn.loc.gov/2020019305

Our books may be purchased in bulk for promotional, educational, or business use. Please contact your local bookseller or the Macmillan Corporate and Premium Sales Department at 1-800-221-7945, extension 5442, or by email at MacmillanSpecialMarkets@macmillan.com.

Book design by Leah Springate

Originally published in Canada by Viking Canada

First U.S. Edition: 2020

10 9 8 7 6 5 4 3 2 1

To the five heroes in this book

CONTENTS

AUTHOR'S NOTE

I would like to express thanks to the patients I describe in this book. The five patients featured here had very different social backgrounds, came from different cultures, and, most importantly, had very different temperaments. Laura and Madeline, from opposite ends of the economic spectrum, were both pure pluck. Danny impressed with his stoical nature, Peter with his forgiveness, and Alana with her endurance. Each had heroic qualities I longed for. I learned an enormous amount about different coping strategies from them and use their lessons often. Each one of them altered my psyche for the better.

There is no greater generosity than sharing your life story, and I am enormously grateful to these patients. In return, I worked hard to maintain their anonymity. It was crucial that they not be recognizable.

This is not a book for academics, but for the general public. Although I wanted the book to be inspirational, I also wanted it to be a learning tool. I have reconstructed our conversations from my session notes with each patient. But in order to clearly delineate the psychological truths that I wanted to illustrate, and to camouflage the identity of the patients, I made some people composites by including certain details from some of my other cases if I felt they made a psychological point more clearly. Each case has been shaped into a narrative, so some details are accentuated while others are dropped for the sake of clarity.

I thank them all for sharing their battles with me and with others. I'm sure Peter, the musician, spoke for all when he said, "If sharing my story helps even one person who is suffering, it will have been worth it."

Gratefully,
Catherine Gildiner

LAURA

My heart is not a home for cowards.

D. ANTOINETTE FOY

SURROUNDED BY THE VILLAGE IDIOTS

THE DAY I OPENED my private practice as a psychologist, I sat smugly in my office. Fortified with the knowledge I'd acquired, taking comfort in the rules I'd learned, I looked forward to having patients I could "cure."

I was deluded.

Fortunately, I had no idea at the time what a messy business clinical psychology was or I might have opted for pure research, an area where I'd have control over my subjects and variables. Instead, I had to learn how to be flexible as new information trickled in weekly. I had no idea on that first day that psychotherapy wasn't the psychologist solving problems but rather two people facing each other, week after week, endeavouring to reach some kind of psychological truth we could agree on.

No one brought this home to me more than Laura Wilkes, my first patient. She was referred to me through a general practitioner, who in his recorded message said, "She'll fill you in on the details." I don't know who was more frightened, Laura or I. I was newly transformed from a student in jeans and a T-shirt to a professional, decked out in a silk blouse and a designer suit with linebacker shoulder pads, *de rigueur* in the early eighties. I sat behind my huge mahogany desk looking like a cross between Anna Freud and Joan Crawford. Luckily I had prematurely white hair in my twenties, which added some much-needed gravitas to my demeanour.

Laura was barely five feet high, with an hourglass figure, huge almond eyes, and such full lips that had it been thirty years later, I would have suspected Botox injections. She had masses of shoulder-length blond highlighted hair and her porcelain skin contrasted sharply with her dark eyes. Perfect makeup, with bright red lipstick, set off her features. She was chic in spike heels, a tailored silk blouse, and a black pencil skirt.

She said she was twenty-six, single, and working in a large securities firm. She'd started out as a secretary but had been promoted to the human resources department.

When I asked how I could help her, Laura sat for a long time looking out the window. I waited for her to tell me the problem. I continued to wait in what's called a therapeutic silence—an uncomfortable quiet that's supposed to elicit truth from the patient. Finally, she said, "I have herpes."

I asked, "Herpes zoster or herpes simplex?"

"The kind you get if you're totally filthy."

"Sexually transmitted," I translated.

When I asked whether her sexual partner knew he had herpes, Laura replied that Ed, her boyfriend of two years, had said he didn't. However, she'd found a pill vial in his cabinet that she recognized as the same medication she'd been prescribed. When I questioned her about this, she acted as though it was normal and that there wasn't much she could do about it. She said, "That's Ed. I've already ripped a strip off him. What more can I do?"

That blasé reaction suggested that Laura was used to selfish and duplicitous behaviour. She'd been referred to me, she said, because the strongest medication wasn't limiting the constant outbreaks and her doctor thought she needed psychiatric help. But Laura was clear about having no desire to be in therapy. She just wanted to get over the herpes.

I explained that in some people stress is a major trigger for attacks of the latent virus. She said, "I know what the word *stress* means but I don't know exactly how it feels. I don't think I have it. I just keep on keeping on, surrounded by the village idiots." Not much had bothered her in her life, Laura told me, although she did acknowledge that the herpes had shaken her like nothing else.

First, I tried to reassure her by letting her know that one in six people aged fourteen to forty-nine has herpes. Her response was "So what? We're all in the same filthy swamp." Switching tacks, I told her I understood why she was upset. A man who purported to love her had betrayed her. Plus, she was in pain—in fact, she could barely sit. The worst part was the shame; forever after she'd have to tell anyone she ever slept with that she had herpes or was a carrier.

Laura agreed, but the worst aspect for her was that although she'd done everything possible to rise above her family circumstances, she was now wallowing in filth, just as they always had. "It's like quicksand," she said. "No matter how hard I try to crawl out of the ooze and slime, I keep getting sucked back in. I know; I've almost died trying."

When I asked her to tell me about her family, she said she wasn't going to go into "all that bilge." Laura explained that she was a practical person and wanted to decrease her stress, *whatever that was*, so that she could get the painful herpes under control. She'd planned to attend this one session, where I'd either give her a pill or "cure" her of "stress." I broke the news to her that stress, or anxiety, was occasionally easy to relieve but could sometimes be intransigent. I explained that we'd need to have a number of appointments so that she could learn what stress is and how she experienced it, uncover its source, and then find ways to alleviate it. It was possible, I told her, that so much of her immune system was fighting stress that there was nothing left to fight the herpes virus.

"I can't believe I have to do this. I feel like I came to have a tooth pulled and by mistake my whole brain came with it." Laura looked disgusted, but she finally capitulated. "Okay, just book me for one more appointment."

It's difficult to treat a patient who isn't psychologically oriented. Laura just wanted her herpes cured and, in her mind, therapy was a means to that end. Nor did she want to give a family history, since she had no idea how it would be relevant.

There were two things I hadn't anticipated on my first day of therapy. First, how could this woman not know what stress is? Second, I'd read hundreds of case studies, watched lots of therapy tapes, attended dozens of grand rounds, and in none of them did the patient refuse to give a family history. Even when I worked the night shift in psychiatric hospitals—where they warehoused the lost psychological souls in back wards—I'd never heard anyone object. Even if they said, as one did, that she was from Nazareth and her parents were Mary and Joseph, they gave a history. Now my very first patient had refused! I realized that I'd have to proceed in Laura's weird way, and at her own pace, or she'd be gone. I remember writing on my clipboard, *My first task is to engage Laura.*

Freud has a concept called transference—the feelings a patient develops for her therapist—that he said was the cornerstone of therapy. Countertransference is what the therapist comes to feel for a patient. Over my decades in private practice, I've found that if you don't honestly like your patient, if you're not rooting for her, the patient senses it and the therapy flounders. There's a chemical bond between patient and therapist that neither of you can will into being. Other therapists may disagree, but I think they're fooling themselves.

I was in luck. I related to Laura right off the bat. Her plucky stride, her emphatic speech, and her no-nonsense manner reminded me of myself. Despite her sixty-hour work week, she was going to university at night, crawling ahead course by course. At the age of twenty-six, she was moving toward a degree in commerce.

At our next session Laura came in carrying four books on stress; they bristled with yellow Post-it notes. She was also lugging a huge flip chart on which she'd drawn an elaborate color-coded graph. Across the top she'd written "Stress??????" Below this were several columns, the first colored in red and titled "Dealing with Assholes." A number of "assholes" were listed in subcategories. One was her boss, Clayton; another was her boyfriend, Ed; a third was her father.

Now that she'd read the books on stress, Laura told me, she was trying to locate the cause of it in her life. She'd worked all week on the chart. When I commented that no women had been included, she looked at it carefully and said, "Interesting. That's true. I don't know any asshole women. I guess if I meet any, I just avoid them or don't let them get under my skin." I pointed out that we were coming closer to defining what the word *stress* meant to her, and asked for an example of what qualified these men to be on her list. "They're people who don't follow any rules and really don't give a shit about making things work," she told me.

I said I'd like to construct a history of her life to date, especially since her father was on the list. When Laura heard this, she rolled her eyes almost into her head. I plowed on, asking Laura what her most vivid memory of her father was. She immediately said it was when she'd fallen off a slide when she was four years old and slit her foot on a sharp piece of metal. Her father tenderly picked her up and carried her to the hospital for stitches. When they were in the waiting room, a nurse remarked on the terrible gash Laura had and how she was being a real trooper for not whining. Her father put his arm around Laura, hugged her, and said, "That's my girl. I'm proud of her. She never complains and is as strong as a horse."

Laura was given a powerful message that day, one she'd never forgotten: a declaration of love and affection that depended on her being strong and not complaining. When I pointed out that double edge, Laura said, "Everyone is loved for something." Clearly, the notion of unconditional love—the idea that your parents would love you no matter what you did—was a foreign concept to her.

When I asked about her mother, Laura said only that she'd died when she was eight. Then, when I asked what she was like, Laura said only two words, ones that I thought were a bit unusual: "remote" and "Italian." She could not retrieve a single memory of her. After I'd pressed a bit, she said only that when she was four her mother had given her a toy stove for Christmas and had smiled when Laura opened it.

Nor was she sure how her mother had died. I actually had to suggest that she elaborate. "She'd been fine in the morning. Then my younger brother and sister and I came home from school and there was no lunch, which was strange. I opened the door to my parents' bedroom and she was sleeping. I shook her and then rolled her over. I can still visualize the marks on her face from the chenille bedspread. I didn't call my dad because I didn't know where he worked. I told my brother and sister to go back to school. Then I called 911."

The police found her father and brought him home in a police car. "They covered my mother's face with a blanket that was stamped *Property of Toronto East General Hospital*. I have no idea why I remembered that," she said. "Then the men carried her on a gurney down the stairs and my mother's corpse disappeared."

"Wasn't there a wake or a funeral?"

"I don't think so. My father went out and then it was dark, past suppertime, and there was no food made." Laura figured out that it was her job to make the dinner, and to let the younger siblings know that their mother had died. When she told her six-year-old sister she cried, but her five-year-old brother had no reaction other than to ask if Laura was going to be their mother now.

Her mother's family didn't come to the funeral, nor did they help their grandchildren. "My mother had never talked about it, but I gathered from my dad's snide comments that they'd basically disowned her," Laura explained. She said they were "real Italians—you know, the kind that wandered around Little Italy in black outfits mourning someone for most of their lives. My mother was the only girl in a family of five boys, and she wasn't allowed out of the house past the age of ten. She had to stay home and cook and clean. She could go shopping with her mother but she could never go out alone. One of the brothers had to walk her to and from school every day."

Despite the strictness of her upbringing, Laura's mother managed to become pregnant at sixteen. Laura's father, a Canadian of Scottish descent, was, according to the Italian family, a young hoodlum who impregnated her mom when he was seventeen. Her mom's brothers beat him to a pulp and said they would kill him if he didn't marry her. After the wedding day, not one of her family ever saw her again.

Laura was born five months after the wedding, her sister was born twenty months later, and her brother arrived one year after that. When I asked Laura if she ever went to Little Italy to visit her grandparents, she said she had no interest in them.

I wondered if Laura's mother had been clinically depressed and therefore emotionally unavailable. Who wouldn't be depressed, if not traumatized, having had an overprotective childhood dominated by violent males and then marrying a man who didn't want to marry her, who was himself inadequate, possibly emotionally and physically abusive, who resented and ignored her? Her parents had disowned her, never forgiving her for shaming them. She had nowhere to turn. When I questioned Laura about her mother's death, suspecting a suicide, she said she had no idea what had happened. As far as she knew, there was no autopsy.

Unbelievably, for the duration of her four years in therapy, being given the toy stove would remain Laura's only memory of her mother. Over that time I had her free-associate, write a journal about her mother, go visit her grave—and still there was only a blank.

We returned to Laura's father in the following session. He'd been a car salesman, she told me, but had lost that job when she was little. There were always problems with alcohol, gambling, and "misunderstandings." Despite being a handsome blue-eyed blond, quite smart and charismatic, he'd become downwardly mobile.

The year after the mother died, the father moved the family to Bobcaygeon, an area northeast of Toronto. Laura thought he was avoiding men in Toronto who were pursuing him, but she wasn't sure. To make money he opened a chip truck serving the summer cottagers. The sister and brother played in the parking lot while Laura opened the pop and served the fries. Her dad called her his "right-hand man." They lived in a small cottage outside of town owned by a family who had a number of modest cabins scattered in isolated spots throughout the woods on their property.

The three siblings began school there in September, when Laura was nine. The chip business dried up when the cottagers left. They bought a small heater for the one-room cottage and huddled around it. Laura recalled that two men appeared at their door on one occasion, demanding money for the chip truck, but her father hid in the bathroom. It was Laura's job to get rid of them.

Then one day in late November, her father said he was driving into town for cigarettes. He never came back. The children had no food and only two sets of clothes. Laura expressed no fear or anger, or feelings of any sort, when relating this story.

She didn't want to tell anyone they'd been abandoned for fear of being placed in foster care, so she just kept to their routines. The cabins, deep in the forest in lake country, were owned by a family who had three children. The mother, Glenda, had been nice to Laura when she'd played with their daughter, Kathy. The father, Ron, was a quiet man who had often kindly taken Laura's six-year-old brother, Craig, fishing with his own son.

Tracy, Laura's younger sister, "whined all the time," Laura said with much annoyance. Tracy wanted to go to Glenda and Ron's house to say that someone had taken their father and to ask if they could live with them.

Laura, unlike her younger siblings, knew that her father had abandoned them. "He was backed into a corner, owing money and God knows what else," she said. When the children misbehaved after their mother died, the father had threatened to leave them with an orphanage, and Laura realized that it wasn't an idle threat. All she knew was that it was her job to make things work. When I asked how she felt about being abandoned, Laura looked at me as though I were being melodramatic. She said, "We weren't exactly *abandoned*. My dad knew I was there to deal with things."

"You were nine years old, penniless, and alone in a forest. What would you call it?" I said.

"I guess technically it was abandonment, but my dad had to get out of Bobcaygeon. He didn't want to leave us. He had no choice."

At that moment I realized how bonded Laura was to her dad and how carefully she had defended herself from any feelings of loss. Bonding is the universal tendency for animals and humans to attach—to seek closeness to a parent and to feel safe when that person is present. Laura didn't remember having any "feelings" at the time; all she had were "plans." In other words, she'd let her survival instinct take over. After all, she had two little children to feed and clothe over a Canadian winter in the wilderness. Laura would go on to deride my constant inquiring about her feelings, indicating more than once that feelings are luxuries for people who live a cushy life and don't have to, as she put it, "use their wits."

I could relate to what Laura said about plans versus feelings. When I'd experienced a reversal of fortune in my own life, I had no time to explore my feelings; I had time only to act. I'd grown up in a well-off family, but when I was a young teenager my infinitely sensible father, who owned his own business, began acting mentally ill. We discovered that he had an inoperable brain tumour. When I called his accountant, he revealed that my father had since lost all his money. I had to stay in school and get two jobs to help support the family. I, like Laura, honestly have no memory of any feelings of any sort. My mind was totally occupied with what had to be done to make ends meet.

Early on in Laura's therapy, I joined a peer supervision group—a group of psychologists who get together to discuss cases and try to give one another pointers—and was surprised when the majority of them thought I wasn't accessing enough of Laura's feelings, that I was "buying into her defences." I realized that I had to investigate my own mind to make sure that my reaction to trauma hadn't coloured our therapy. On the one hand, my peers may have been right; on the other, I wanted to ask them if they'd ever been up against the proverbial wall, when without a 24/7 focus on their circumstances they could come to serious harm. Nothing concentrates the mind like the need for survival.

However, there is no denying that not having access to Laura's feelings made therapy difficult. I quickly realized that my first job wasn't to interpret her feelings, but to access her feelings. Later I'd interpret them.

When I wrote in my notes that first month, I summed it up this way: *I have a client who does not want to engage in therapy, does not clearly remember her mother of eight years, which is unheard of in the literature, has no idea what stress is but wants to get rid of it, and had no accessible feelings when she was abandoned. I've got a lot of work ahead.*

As Laura continued to describe her ordeal, it was evident that she'd kept a clear head. She realized that most of the cabins had already been cleaned for the winter, so she and her siblings moved to one of the remotest, not likely to be opened till spring. They took the heater with them. She knew they had to keep to their routines or they'd be detected. So they'd walk down the road nearly a mile every day to take the school bus. Laura would talk about her dad to the outside world as though he were back at the cabin and instructed her brother and sister to do the same.

"So, you were left alone to live in a cabin at the ages of nine, seven, and six," I said. "If you're looking for stressful events, that could go on the list."

"First of all, it's over, and second, I'm still standing," Laura countered. "Nine really isn't that young."

"How long did this go on?"

"Six or seven months."

At the end of our session I summed up how I viewed the situation. "You have been brave. Your life sounds like it's been difficult and at times frightening. You were abandoned, alone in the woods, and responsible for two younger children whom you were too young to parent." I said, "It has all the perils of Hansel and Gretel without the breadcrumbs."

She sat there for a full minute before replying. In what would be almost five years of therapy, it was one of the few times that her eyes filled with tears, albeit angry tears. "What are you saying *that* stuff for?" she demanded.

When I said that I was empathizing with her, she rebuffed me. "That's what you say to people when someone dies. Listen, Doctor, if I'm ever to come back here, I never want you to do that again, or I'll walk out. Keep your empathy or whatever it is to yourself."

"Why?" I asked, genuinely puzzled.

"When you say things about feelings, I see a door opening that's full of hobgoblins and I am never going to enter that room," she said emphatically. "I have to keep going. If I ever started to wallow, even once, I'd drown. Plus, it doesn't make things any better."

While I was nodding, she added, "Before I leave today, you have to promise you will never do that again. Otherwise I can't come back."

"So what you're saying is that you never want any kindness, empathy, or sympathy from me?"

"Right. If I want sympathy, I'll get it from Hallmark cards in a dose I can handle."

Remember, Laura was my first patient. I didn't want to make this bargain with the pathological needs of my client. However, I could see that she was serious about leaving therapy. A tiny shred of empathy from me was too much for her—it terrified her. And it was a deal breaker.

If I hadn't been a new therapist, I would have presented the conundrum to her just as I felt it. We could, as Fritz Perls, the founder of Gestalt therapy, would have suggested, deal with this in what he called "the here and now." Perls believed that the dynamic set up in the session between the therapist and patient is the same dynamic the patient sets up between herself and the rest of world. I could have said, "Laura, you're demanding that I act like the parent you had, the man who was uninterested in your pain. You're used to no one responding to your sadness, but I don't want that role. Right now I feel in a bind."

Instead, I said, "I agree to respect your wishes, since clearly you're very determined, and I want to make you comfortable so that we can work together. However, I will not agree to do that for the entire duration of our therapy."

The next week Laura arrived armed with her books again and identifying her workplace as the cause of her stress. "There's a lot to do, but my boss, Clayton, comes in late and then takes a two-hour lunch with the secretary he's having an affair with," she explained. "He goes home at five, so I come in earlier and leave hours later than he does."

"Have you ever talked to Clayton about this?"

"*Of course!* I even yell at him. But he doesn't give a shit."

"So you're taking on too much work."

"I really don't have a choice. I have to do his work and mine."

"Feeling you don't have a choice is stressful," I concluded.

We spent a great deal of time going over how to deal with Clayton. Deep down, Laura didn't see him changing. As her boyfriend Ed said, "Clayton's got a good thing going. Why should he change?"

"That's interesting, coming from Ed," I said.

"Why?" she asked.

"Well, Ed drops things on you as well. While Clayton dumps work, Ed dumps herpes. He just left it for you to deal with. When you got angry with him, he denied knowing he had the virus, and when you caught him with the herpes medication, he made the feeble excuse that he thought it wasn't contagious. You'd have to be from another planet or else in deep denial to think that."

"At least Ed was sorry. He sent me two dozen roses at work and the card said *Because I love you.*"

Did she think that made up for herpes? What I said was, "Doesn't Ed work for a Jaguar dealership? You told me that whenever a woman comes in to test drive a car, he sends her roses the next day. It's not that hard to do."

"Are you trying to piss me off?"

I assured her that it wasn't my intention to anger her. I said I was just wondering how she felt about Ed's behaviour.

"What am I supposed to do? Never forgive him?"

I pointed out that our conversation had started with what Ed, who's somewhat irresponsible, said about Clayton, who's also irresponsible. I wanted Laura to see the irony of Ed's remarking that Clayton didn't have to change because she did all the work. Laura turned her hands palms-up, indicating that she didn't get the point. Finally, I asked her who did the work in her relationship with Ed. When she acknowledged that she did, I was silent. Finally she asked me what tree I was barking up.

"You forgive Ed for being chronically late, for suspected philandering, and for giving you herpes," I clarified. After a long silence, I asked her why she didn't expect decent, adult behaviour from men.

"At least he says he's sorry. That's more than my dad ever did." Then she looked out the window and said, "Actually, he wasn't that bad of a dad. He kept us after our mother died. A lot of men would have called child services."

"Well, he did leave you up north in Bobcaygeon to freeze in a tiny cabin."

"I told you, we managed." She said this in a dismissive tone, as though I were harping on picayune details. She was using a psychological technique called reframing: taking a concept and relabelling it so as to alter its meaning. She reframed what I perceived as neglect and labelled my concerns "overprotective."

"When you first came here, you talked about the 'assholes in your life.' Can we make that more specific?" Laura looked confused, so I refined the question. "Is an asshole, as you're using the term, someone who takes from you but doesn't give back? Someone who's only meeting his or her own needs?"

"Everyone is out for himself; that was one of my dad's mottoes."

"He was normalizing his behaviour. How many dads go out for cigarettes and then keep on going?"

"There must be dads like that out there. I mean, there *are* orphanages. How do thousands of kids wind up in Children's Aid? Parents leave them, that's how!"

"How many people have bosses who slack off and still keep their jobs because their assistants work overtime to cover for them?" I asked.

"Yeah, well, if I push Clayton too hard he could fire me."

"How many people are lied to by their boyfriend about something as dire as herpes?"

"Probably as many as spend useless money on shrinks."

As Laura angrily packed up to leave, she shook her head and breathed heavily, saying, "Sorry for the attitude, but I can't believe I have to go over this useless crap." Then she added that, other than "a few lapses," her dad had been present in her life. In fact, as she vociferously pointed out, she saw and talked to him often.

Laura was still the reluctant patient defending against the therapy, and I was still the new therapist chipping away too hard at her defences. I was beginning to see that it didn't matter at all if I knew what was wrong with a client. The art of therapy is getting the client to see it. If you rush it, they'll snap shut. It had taken Laura a lifetime to build up those defences, and it would take time to peel them away, layer by layer.

I had my own psychological quandary. I needed to exercise patience as a therapist, but buried within me was a Type A personality. There are two types of personalities, Type A and Type B. Whereas Type B's are laid-back and non-competitive, Type A's are characterized by ambition, aggression, and a need for control. (This is a broad generalization and many people lie somewhere between A and B.) Type A's are champing at the bit, and that drive can translate to stress; indeed, these traits are often associated with stress-related ailments. For example, Laura's stress had exacerbated her herpes outbreaks.

Many social psychologists believe that character type is hardwired, meaning a child is born with certain propensities that don't change as the child grows up. Certainly birth order, parenting, and social variables can soften the edges of whatever type you are, but not by much. In other words, once a Type A, always a Type A. Both Laura and I are Type A's. The good part is we work hard and accomplish things; the bad part is we lack patience and empathy. We tend to mow others down while driving toward our own ambitions. So I had to be careful not to get into a Type A faceoff with Laura. If I wanted to be a good therapist, I'd have to learn to dial back those traits. Patience, a trait in short supply in the Type A personality, would be critical.

2

INTO THE WOODS

PATIENTS OFTEN BRING cultural references to their therapy appointments—they'll recount dreams about television characters, say, or they'll identify with political figures or situations in the news. Their normal assumption is that I'll have shared in this social fabric. However, I often had no idea what they were talking about: for two decades, throughout the seventies and eighties, I barely watched TV or listened to radio. When I went to university I didn't own a television, and was too busy working at various jobs while studying to have watched one. Then, while I was doing my Ph.D., I gave birth to a son. Within two years, I had twin boys. My husband, also a student, and I lived above a store with our triple stroller and three car seats. I also had to finish my Ph.D. by a certain time, so I used to set my alarm for four-thirty a.m. and work around the babies' schedules. Neither my husband nor I had time for television or radio; we used every spare second to take care of our children or work. I was in the odd position of knowing quite a bit about nineteenth-century science, specifically about Darwin and Freud, but nothing about the popular culture I actually lived in. And after many years, I found I didn't miss it anyway. I read instead.

But I did make an annual pilgrimage to the Museum of Television & Radio in New York City, which had copies of every television program ever made (in those days, of course, there was no YouTube). The public could select and watch shows in viewing rooms, where I could catch up on all the programs that my patients had talked about and see the characters that had helped to form them. It was fascinating to watch a TV show in the context of how it had affected a specific patient. Many patients were missing the adequate guidance of parents, so they were dramatically influenced by how people interacted on television and in movies.

Laura was a perfect case in point. Her television dreams opened up a whole new vein in the therapy. As usual, it had been hard for me to engage her in reporting the dream process; when I'd asked about her dreams, she said she never had them. Yet she couldn't help but be a hard worker. She arrived at our next session, teetering on spike heels, with a handwritten account of her latest dream with key phrases highlighted in yellow. She flopped into a chair and said, "This dream is about Colonel Potter."

"Do you have a relative in the army?" I asked.

She said, "Oh, for Christ's sake! You must know he's the colonel on the TV show *M*A*S*H*." When I looked blank, she said, "Don't tell me you don't know Colonel Potter. I hope I'm not seeing a psychologist from Uranus?"

She explained that the show was a situation comedy about an American medical team in the Korean War. Colonel Potter, a career army officer, was the head of the outfit and himself a surgeon. Laura described him as kind, and said that no matter what kind of idiot he was dealing with, he never judged.

"So he was honourable and dependable." I noted two traits that were missing in her boss, her boyfriend, and her father.

"In the dream, Colonel Potter is wearing one of those hats that fly fishermen wear that have lures hooked all over them," she said. "I was limping down a hospital corridor in a hospital gown and he came up to me dressed as he was in the show in his army fatigues, except for the fishing hat. He put his hand on my shoulder and squeezed it as I limped along, but he didn't say anything. I woke up feeling really good."

"What does Colonel Potter mean to you?"

"Oh, I don't want to talk about that, for Christ's sake! I'm ashamed of my behaviour when my father was gone, and this has to do with that time."

Knowing that Laura liked clear, practical solutions, I said, "I thought you wanted to get better in the least amount of time. Shame is like napalm: it's sticky and it burns you and then clings forever. It's best to pick it off piece by piece, if you can."

"Is shame the same as stress?" Laura asked. She was still on the practical track of labelling her stress so as to get rid of her painful herpes.

"I would say that shame could certainly cause stress," I responded. "Shame is a painful feeling of humiliation or distress caused by behaviour that is somehow taboo in our society. Freud says shame makes you feel you won't be loved. Shame is much more pernicious than guilt. While guilt is a painful feeling about your actions, shame is much more psychologically destructive because it's a bad feeling about yourself as a person."

Laura lifted an eyebrow at that, and then nodded, as though she realized she had to investigate it.

"Okay," I continued, "let's go back to the cabin where you, as a nine-year-old, are living with your eight-year-old sister and six-year-old brother."

She said, "This is like the freezing cold water at the lake. It's best to just dive in and swim. So don't interrupt me, just let me spill it out. When you hear this you'll say, 'No wonder she has herpes, she deserves it.'" Her last sentence was a classic combination of guilt and shame, resulting in self-loathing.

Laura looked out the window, avoiding eye contact, and began her tale in a monotone. "A few days after my father left, I realized we had to eat. Plus, Craig's teacher came to my class and asked why he had no lunch." She described how Craig had begun weeping. The other students donated some lunch, and the teacher noticed that he put crackers into his pocket. "She asked me if things were all right at home. I said everything was fine and that my dad was getting his paycheck that day. She wanted to call our home, but I told her we didn't have a phone." The teacher asked her to have her mother call the school.

"That's when I stole money from the milk collection box," Laura went on. "It was passed around and everyone was supposed to put his or her money in, but I took money out. Not a lot or I would have been caught. Then after school I gave my sister Tracy the money to buy some penny candy at the grocery store, and while she was distracting the clerk, I stole canned hams and all kinds of food. I was really good at it. I went all over town to different stores so no one would suspect me."

Then Laura described how she managed to keep her siblings in clean clothes, without a washing machine. "Our favourite TV program was *The Wonderful World of Disney*, so on Disney night I made everyone take a bath and throw out their clothes. I went to the Giant Tiger store every Friday before the weekend and stole new outfits for Monday. I was an incredible thief, just like my father. I guess it's genetic. I once saw this movie called *The Bad Seed* with Patty McCormack, and I knew that was me—pretty and nice on the outside but sneaky and bad on the inside."

I was careful during these disclosures not to interrupt with interpretations. I just listened, as Laura had requested.

"Tracy cried what felt like all the time. Craig never said one word other than that he was hungry. He wet the bed. At first I yelled at him, but then I just ignored it and let him sleep in it. Finally, I did things like say I was going to leave them if they didn't stop complaining or didn't do what I said. It worked. I was the mom."

I was shocked that no official had intervened other than Craig's teacher, who never followed up.

Laura looked at the floor, and I could feel her shame. She didn't usually look pained, but I could tell that what she was about to say profoundly affected her. "I wasn't a good mom. I wouldn't allow anyone to talk about Dad or his leaving. If they started to get blubbery, I said we had to keep going. So I hit anyone who whimpered."

What helped Laura become more compassionate toward her siblings was what she learned from the *M*A*S*H* Christmas special on TV. "Colonel Potter said that gifts weren't important as long as they had each other." Out of desperation, Laura started listening to Colonel Potter as he gave advice to Radar, one of the young soldiers in his command. "He was like Radar's dad. I pretended he was our dad as well. I pretended he was away at war and we had to watch him on TV to get his messages. I told myself that whatever he said, I would do. I got to know him inside and out so that I could say to myself, 'What would Colonel Potter do in this situation?'"

Laura applied this technique to Craig's bedwetting. "I pretended Craig was Radar and I was Colonel Potter. I said, 'So son, what's ailing you?'" When Craig didn't answer, she put her arm around him and told him it would be okay. Within a few days, the bedwetting stopped.

"Then I started talking to Colonel Potter myself about my stealing and he would say things to me like, 'When this war is over, you can pay back all that you stole.' He would tell me that I wasn't a bad person. It was war out there, and we did what we had to do. He also said that 'One day this will all be over, and we'll go back to our homes, where our loved ones await us.'" Laura began repeating the same reassuring words to Tracy and Craig. "I told them that we would all grow up and we would be married to someone just like Colonel Potter who would love us and always want what was best for us. It got us through." Laura still dreamt of Colonel Potter, mostly when she felt alone or backed into a corner.

She sat back and looked at me. "Well, you're the only person who knows this whole wacky saga. I know it means that I'm a thief, but does it mean that I'm crazy?" she asked. "Whenever I read that crazy people hear voices, I always get scared. Thinking Colonel Potter is your father and imagining his voice is too close to crazy for comfort."

Now it was time for me to reframe. "I would say that you're far from crazy. In fact, I would say you're resourceful. You did what you had to do to stay afloat. You wanted to keep your family together, and you did more than most nine-year-olds could have ever done. I think you were heroic."

Laura ignored me. When I didn't continue, she said sardonically, "Stop Mr. Rogering me." Patients who are rarely praised as children often distrust the positive things people say about them as adults. A child's concept of self is formed in childhood and it takes a long time, with many affirmative examples, to turn that self-concept around.

"I can still feel the terror of stealing those canned hams. I can still smell the wet cardboard the owner of the store put on the floor to soak up the slush," she admitted.

"You did it for the survival of your sister and brother. I think Colonel Potter was a perfect father, and we all learn from role-modelling. In fact, it's stronger than any other form of learning.

You were wise enough to choose a role model that worked for you and your sister and brother."

"I was mean to them, though."

"You were realistic. You couldn't have too much crying and whining or you all could have gone under. You ran a tight ship, but look at how kind you were about Craig's bedwetting once you had the tools from Colonel Potter."

Laura wasn't having it. "I wasn't really a good mother. Tracy and Craig are screwed up. Tracy never finished high school; she lives in some godawful place in the country and works pulling apart turkey guts in a factory. She's hooked up with a handyman named Andrew. Both of them are pretty basic. They have no idea how to have a relationship or even get along.

"My brother, Craig, has a kid already. He doesn't live with the mother and is a deadbeat father. He works seasonally, snow plowing, and basically smokes a lot of pot."

"Are you aware that you were only nine years old when you were expected to become a parent?"

"So what? A lot of girls have to parent at nine. They manage."

Evidently the profound shame Laura felt was based on the delusion that she could have been a good mother at the age of nine. Often people's worst pain is built on a false premise. I said, "Not without help. You were forced to do a job that you couldn't possibly have known how to do. Failure is built into that plan."

Sadly, one of Laura's issues that never fully resolved was her delusion that she hadn't been a good parent to her brother and sister. She was unable to accept that she'd been a little girl and was not equipped for the job.

Over the years, I've found that in cases where a child has been handed an adult responsibility at too young an age and they inevitably fail at it, they will forever be anxious about that task as an adult. They never seem to accept that they were too young to manage the task; instead, they internalize their failure in accomplishing it. Laura had focused on her failure to parent and rarely mentioned the trauma of being abandoned. She never once suggested that her father had been neglectful; she laid all the blame on herself.

To illustrate how young Laura had been and how unrealistic she and her father's expectations were, I took her to see nine-year-olds in a school setting. A friend of mine, a school principal, arranged a field trip for us to a grade three class. When Laura observed a group of eight- and nine-year-old girls in their little tights and smock dresses, she was shocked. But when we left she didn't say she'd been hard on herself, as I'd expected. Instead she said, "Jesus, *they* were immature." I took her to three different classes. Finally, on the way home in the car, she said, "Eight and nine is a lot younger than I remember it."

I think her rock-hard defences cracked slightly after that visit to the schools. In her faulty memory of life in the cabin, she was an adult; now she realized what a young child she'd actually been. It was an illustration of how unconscious needs can creep in and alter memory. Her father led her to believe that she was an adult because he needed one in his life, so she thought of herself as one.

It was my first case and we were in the middle of the first year of therapy; slowly, Laura was beginning to see that her life had been very different from most people's. She once described getting an invitation to a birthday party where everyone in grade three was invited. She told the birthday girl that her father was taking her to a baseball game instead. Of course, there was no baseball in the winter in Canada, so the girl's mother likely sniffed trouble. The day after the party, the woman came to the school and brought Laura a piece of cake, a helium balloon with her name on it, and a treat bag full of small gifts. It had been placed on her desk before she'd arrived. Laura said she was amazed at the effort but felt uneasy about it. She didn't experience the gesture as kindness until years later. Whenever she saw the mother waiting near the playground to pick up her daughter, Laura would hide in the bathroom until she left. When I asked why, she said, "It just seemed too weird. I had no idea what she wanted from me." Clearly, Laura functioned well in survival mode, but human kindness threw her for a loop.

Instead of gaining major insights, it seemed that Laura had a big jigsaw puzzle in front of her, and every once in a while, a piece would drop into place. But it wasn't enough for her to see the big picture.

In our next session, Laura described how their frightening fairy-tale existence in the cabin ended. "I screwed up. I got caught stealing underpants for Craig at Giant Tiger." It was April, and the children had been on their own for six months.

Reframing what she portrayed as a "screw-up," I defined it as a success. "So, you managed to survive alone in a Canadian winter from November to April as a nine-year-old with two younger siblings."

"When the police picked us up, they took us back to the cabin," Laura recalled. "They were pretty shocked. They just shook their heads. They knocked on Glenda and Ron's door, the people who owned the cabins, and asked if they could keep us until Children's Aid could be contacted, or until they could find our father and make arrangements." (It would be four years before their father resurfaced, but more on that later.)

Ron and Glenda had three children of their own. Laura could tell that Tracy and Craig were happy to be there, and that upset her. "I thought we'd been all right on our own. Plus, I wasn't used to being told what to do. Of the three of us, I was the one who had adjustment problems."

They stayed for four years. Hiding my amazement that this family had taken in three children, I asked what they were like. "Nice, I guess" was Laura's answer. They had discipline and order, she said. "Tracy and Craig still think of them as their parents and visit for Christmas. I don't. Glenda, the mother, had a lot of rules and she wanted things done her way."

When I asked why her sister and brother adjusted better than she did, Laura said that she'd been her father's favourite. "Dad had never been mean to me. I was the most loyal to him. He ignored Tracy, but he was mean to Craig." Her father had called Craig, who was slight and fragile, "a mommy's boy."

Meanwhile, the man who'd taken them in treated them far better. "Ron, the man who owned the cabins, was a quiet guy but kind. He continued to take Craig fishing and never tried to rush his stutter." (Craig had developed a stutter after his mother's death.) "All of Craig's troubles stopped when we were there. And I'll admit that it was a relief to have food on the table."

I asked Laura about her relations with Glenda.

"Tracy and Craig think Glenda walks on water, and she devoted an enormous amount of time to Tracy's insecurities," Laura said, but admitted that her own feelings were different. "You see, it was always me and my dad."

"Never you and your mom?"

"No, never, so I guess I didn't have any idea what it was to be mothered." Then Laura paused, laughing, "Hey, listen to me! I'm turning into you—interpreting myself!"

Laura described how she resisted Glenda's attentions. "Glenda would say things like 'It's cold out; you need a hat.' I didn't get it. I still don't. It was too late for me to be treated as a kid. I'd already run a house. We were at each other's throats in a quiet way."

But she was grateful to Ron. "He used to take the boys fishing all the time. He had one of those fishing hats with all the lures pinned on them. He never said anything encouraging to me, but once in a while he'd say to Glenda, 'Let Laura alone, Glenda. She's doin' it her way.'"

I pointed out that in her dream, Colonel Potter wore a fisherman's hat with lures. "Could the man in the dream be part Colonel Potter and part Ron—a composite of kindness?"

Laura looked astonished. "Yes, could be. It is exactly Ron's hat in the dream, now that I think about it." She smiled and said, "Sometimes I have a fantasy that I'll grow up, be wealthy, and buy Ron a big boat that always starts, something he longed for but couldn't afford."

Our first year of therapy was drawing to a close. I needed to fully flesh out my treatment plan for Laura and map out ways to accomplish it. She was strongly attached to her father, but that attachment was fraught. She took care of him, forgave him his trespasses, and basically acted as a parent to him. She didn't hold him responsible for his negligence or selfishness. Laura had already been abandoned once; she clung to him for dear life. Her role in that relationship was to be the saviour. With no responsible adult in the family, she'd taken on that role so that they could function. The mother was dead, and the father's arrested development had left him at the irresponsible adolescence stage. She had to shore him up. What did she get out of it? *Survival.*

Laura was a true hero in her family, but the problem was that she assumed that same saviour role in her relationships with other men. She thought it was normal, and it had, in fact, been adaptive behaviour. She allowed Ed, her boyfriend, and her boss, Clayton, to be irresponsible; it was her job to rescue them, just as it had been with her father. It was my job to get her to recognize her deeply buried unconscious need to be the saviour and how she had subconsciously chosen weak and selfish men, like her father, who need saving.

It is the task of the therapist to point out patterns; in Laura's case, the weak—possibly psychopathic—man scenario was an obvious one. But opening Laura's eyes to it was going to be difficult for several reasons. First, she had entered therapy as a way to deal with her herpes, not to resolve childhood issues. Second, she was single-mindedly devoted to her father, so much so that she had refused to engage with kindly foster parents. Despite the fact that her father had disappeared and had made no contact with his children for four years, she was bonded to him. And in return for her saving the family, he gave her what little love he had. It would be a hard dynamic to disrupt, since people do almost anything for love. Whatever role we are loved for in our family, we will continue to enact it, despite the toll it takes.

Although Laura thought she was in charge of her life, in reality she was a motherless child who'd been abandoned, betrayed, and used. Clearly, both Laura and I had a lot of work to do.

3

WHAT THE CAT DRAGGED IN

AS LAURA'S SECOND YEAR in therapy began, so too did my second year as a therapist. I was learning a lot about the ad hoc nature of therapy. Before entering private practice I'd had no idea how many theoretical deviations were required to keep up with a patient. I was quickly realizing that theoretical purity was strictly an academic extravagance. As a psychologist, I would use any weapon from whatever discipline I could find.

Yet even with the necessary intellectual training, at the practical level, I sometimes struggled. Laura had a lot of anger to expel, and would spend an inordinate amount of time expressing exasperation without gaining insight. I'd have trouble subtly guiding the session, which is an acquired skill. In *Blink: The Power of Thinking Without Thinking*, Malcolm Gladwell describes how intuitive judgment is developed over years of experience—learning that's unavailable in any book. And as I became more seasoned as a therapist, I did learn how to zero in on what was necessary for healing.

It was soon after the Christmas season and Laura told me that Ed had given her black satin sheets as a present. When I questioned the psychological significance of Ed's gift, she said, "You know, you're pretty hard on good ol' Ed," adding that he was a great sexual partner. "Sometimes I come home from work and he has candles set up around the room. He buys me lingerie, and we dance. And he really cares that I have a good time."

"It's an interesting gift, since it's sexually tinged," I countered. "It's through sex that Ed has hurt you the most by giving you herpes and by betraying your trust."

"Wow, do you *ever* put stuff behind you? Like, when do you ever say, 'Hey, that was yesterday. Why cry over spilled milk?' I've chosen to cut the guy some slack. He felt awful about the herpes thing."

When Ed lost his job at the Jaguar dealership, Laura defended him, saying he was fired because another salesman, who couldn't compete, had framed him. Then, in order to stay in his luxury apartment, Ed began to sell cocaine until he got another job.

Laura and I talked a lot about psychological boundaries—the limits people create to identify safe, reasonable ways for others to interact with them. The stronger a person's boundaries are, the healthier that person is; he or she is able to signal to others what's acceptable and what's not. Clearly, Ed had crossed a personal boundary of Laura's. She didn't approve of excess drinking, selling drugs, and having no job. Yet she couldn't say, "Ed, you've crossed a line with me with the herpes, the drugs, and unemployment. We're finished." Although Ed's behaviour caused her psychological pain, she had no idea that she had the right to demand he change. As the months passed, Ed didn't get another job. I didn't mention it again, hoping that as we talked more about boundaries, Laura would establish some of her own.

Laura had a triumvirate of inadequate males in her life to whom she was devoted. I decided the weak link in the chain was her boss, Clayton. If she could assert herself and break away from the saviour role with anyone, Clayton was our best bet. She couldn't change him, but she could change her behaviour toward him. She began to focus on her own work and stopped covering for him.

Clayton applied pressure on her, and since Laura had never learned to establish psychological boundaries, his psychological manipulation made her feel anxious and guilty. She unconsciously believed she should have done Clayton's work. She wondered if she was being cruel. She didn't know the basic rules for appropriate social engagement. Normal behaviour, in which there's an equal give and take among people, seemed artificial and saccharine to her.

When I asked why she had no rules of her own, she expressed bewilderment: "Why have boundaries if everyone is going to drive through them, leaving nothing but rubble? No one's going to do what *I* want. Why should they?" Laura had just perfectly defined powerlessness, and powerlessness in a relationship is one of the main causes of stress or anxiety.

Making psychological changes also provokes anxiety. It's very hard to break a habit, especially when you've adapted yourself to a particular pattern that, however maladaptive, has kept you alive. The unconscious is powerful, and it will fight to the death to keep an old pattern in place.

Laura disrupted her pattern by refusing to do Clayton's work. It was further disrupted when Clayton was fired for being the department's lazy, overpaid manager. Laura was promoted to his highly paid position. "They actually blamed *him!*" she said in gleeful amazement. It was a great learning experience for Laura, and gave her a sense of power.

Around the same time, Laura attended a wedding, where she had a startling encounter with a tipsy bridesmaid during the reception. "I see you're with Ed," the woman said. "Did he give you herpes as well?"

After Laura reported this, I just looked at her and raised an eyebrow. By now, she knew what I was thinking. "I know you want me to leave him," she said, "but who would have me? Some nice guy isn't going to put up with someone with herpes."

She had a point, but I suggested that perhaps it was a strange blessing in disguise. "You've always been beautiful and enjoyed sex, but you've been afraid of intimacy," I pointed out gently. "Now you'll have to develop an intimate emotional relationship and wait to have sex. The guy who accepts you for all your flaws before you have sex will be a special person."

"Dr. Gildiner," she replied, "do you *ever* get out into the real world?"

A month later, Laura arrived for her appointment and announced, "Well, I did it. I knew Ed was cheating on me, but I had no idea he'd given herpes to half the city. I told him we were through." When I asked about his reaction, she said Ed had cried. "He said he was sorry, and then said he wanted to marry me. I told him, 'Ed, why would I want a husband who lies, cheats, gives people diseases, and whose full-time job is dope dealing? A boyfriend like that was bad enough.' Am I cleaning house or what? I'm shedding every asshole from my life." She was proud of herself, and I was proud of her.

The only person left in "the asshole triumvirate," as Laura termed it, was her father. That was much trickier. He was her greatest attachment, and unlike Clayton and Ed, he would always remain important in her life.

It was Laura's dreams that revealed how her emotional relationship with her father was changing. Freud said that our unconscious drives or instincts, such as sex and aggression, are blocked from our conscious mind, that civilization doesn't want us to see them. Therefore, those drives are protected by such defences as repression, denial, and sublimation. One of the ways unconscious drives sneak into the conscious mind is through dreams, with the unconscious material camouflaged by symbols. But Freud argues that if you interpret and free-associate to these symbols, it's possible to figure out what the unconscious is trying to impart. If the dream is too well camouflaged, the meaning may be lost; if it's not camouflaged enough, it will be a nightmare. Freud was right when he said, "Dreams are the royal road to the unconscious." And as such, they're indispensable in therapy.

Laura and I had been making headway by interpreting her dreams. One day she held her dream journal close to her chest and said, "Although Freud was a dick in a lot of ways, he was really on to something with dreams. I had one that was so vivid I woke up with a pounding heart and thought for a few minutes that it had actually happened.

"*I was on stage and there were hundreds of people in the audience. I was in ragged clothes with no lipstick, which embarrassed me. On the stage was a gigantic black cat made out of paper mâché. While the band Poison played their new song "Look What the Cat Dragged In," I kicked the cat in the mouth until it began to crack and fall apart. Some people in the audience clapped, but I felt bad and wondered why I was doing this, although I just couldn't help it.*"

In analyzing this dream, Laura said it wasn't hard to figure out the origin of the soundtrack, because she'd recently heard it at her sister's house. I asked what the saying "Look what the cat dragged in" meant to her. Her face darkened. "My father said that to me when I went to prison to visit him."

I was surprised by the newsflash that her father had been in prison. Reading my facial expression, Laura cut me off, saying she never knew why he was in jail. "The prison was thirteen hours away by bus. I was fourteen years old and I'd saved my money for months for the trip. When I walked into the prison, men whistled and my dad just laughed and said, 'My, my, look what the cat dragged in.'"

"As though you were the problem?"

"He just kept laughing. I wanted to be angry with him, but what was the point? He was already down and out, so I swallowed my pride and tried to make things work. Besides, there wasn't another bus until the next day. When I told him that I had to sleep at the bus station, he said, 'Well, you're dressed for it.' I was wearing stone-washed jeans when they were the fad. He didn't like them. That was my last visit to him in jail."

"I guess you were angry. In the dream, you were irate enough to kick that cat in the mouth."

"I wanted to say, 'I'll show you what a cat can drag in'; I destroyed that paper mâché cat in my dream." Laura's face darkened again. "What a selfish prick. Plus, the other inmates were sort of ogling and leering, and he didn't say, 'This is my daughter you're looking at, so fuck off.' He was showing off, in his two-bit way, to a bunch of losers. How the mighty have fallen."

"You experienced him as mighty, and it must have been hard for you to see him so diminished."

She sighed. "I guess he was never mighty. I just thought he was."

This was the first time she had expressed real anger and disappointment in her dad, and it was an important moment in the therapy. A large piece of the puzzle was falling into place.

"So, you go to see him in jail, pay for a bus ticket from your after-school job, travel hours alone at the age of fourteen, and then he insults you, laughs at you, and doesn't protect you from the other inmates. You feel dishevelled, and the inmates are lecherously eyeing you. In the dream, the 'lack of lipstick' and 'the audience' stand for the other inmates seeing you exposed without your father's protection. In the dream, you're angry and kicking the cat that is your father, yet *you* feel guilty. Some applaud and some don't. What is that about?"

"When I get mad at him, I feel guilty. But I know you want me to be mad at him. In his defence, that jail episode was the only time he ever criticized me."

I countered that I wanted her to see him realistically. That way she could develop a relationship that would work for the two of them. I told her that they were doing an unconscious tango—he being irresponsible and she being overly responsible.

"You, like every other daughter in the world, are bonded to your dad. Darwin points out that bonding happens in all species. Your bond with your dad was perfectly normal and necessary. However, I think you've mistaken bonding for love. Bonding is not a choice; it's a biological imperative, necessary for survival. Love is a choice. When you meet an incompetent man who needs you to care for him, you immediately feel warm toward him because you're bonded to that behaviour. You've honed your role of taking care of a man, and have been loved for doing it. But love is where you mutually care for one another. You want to admire your lover's characteristics, not protect him from the ravages of the real world. Your dad loved you, as best as he could, for taking care of him. But some man will love you for all your characteristics, not just the ones that will cover for his mistakes."

Laura took that in, seeming to relax. "That used to sound like Mr. Rogers to me, but in the last few months there's a little spot in my heart that actually longs for that."

In therapy, when pathological defences start to crumble, the patient lets in more material from their background that they've been defending against. Suddenly, memories emerge that were unavailable at the beginning of the therapy. When Laura had been intent on defending her father, she'd blocked many of her negative memories of him; but now, after two years of therapy, those painful memories began to flow like hot lava.

When Laura and her siblings lived in Bobcaygeon, Glenda and Ron and the child services agency had tried to locate Laura's father without success. Finally, they gave up and Glenda and Ron fostered the children. Those were good years, as Laura, Tracy, and particularly Craig flourished. Craig was at his best with Ron and learned how to be a handyman. He began to talk more, and would wait patiently at the window for Ron to come home at night.

On a cold winter night, four years into their stay, there was a knock on the door. Ron opened it, and there stood the children's father, who came in and, according to Laura, said, "'Hi, kids! I've remarried, and it's time to pack up and come home.' When no one moved, he said cheerfully, 'You have a new mom!'"

Suddenly, Laura looked sad as she recounted that her siblings had wanted to stay in their foster home. It was Laura who insisted that they leave Ron and Glenda. "I realize now that it was such a bad decision for my sister and brother. It ruined their lives. My dad never liked either of them. Craig was doing so well with Ron as a consistently kind dad." Her eyes welled up for the second time in therapy.

They moved to Toronto. By now their father was down and out, a chronic, barely functioning alcoholic who lived above a sleazy bar in a bad area. As they walked up the dank, unlit stairwell, there stood a young woman less than a decade older than Laura. She was a skeletal figure, who had bleached blond hair with dark roots; she wore a polyester gold lamé see-through blouse over a black lace bra. Linda was twenty-one and Laura's dad was in his thirties, although Laura noted that he was beginning to look older than his years. When they went to places as a family, people thought Linda was the fourth child.

Linda tottered toward them in heels and said in a baby voice, "Hi, darlings, I'm your new mommy." Both Tracy and Craig said hello, but thirteen-year-old Laura just glared at the twenty-one-year-old rival and went into her room. She had to share a bedroom with her brother and sister and there was no door, only beads hanging from the water-stained ceiling.

Linda was drunk most of the time over the next two years, and unlike the silence that had prevailed with Laura's mother, Linda was a mean drunk. She would yell and scream that she could be with any man in the world but was stuck with an old loser. Laura's father would also get drunk and beat Linda up; Laura would get the ice for her lip or eye.

One night, at the culmination of a three-day drinking binge, Laura's father had an argument with Linda. Laura described the predictable pattern in which her stepmother would taunt her father with sexual comparisons to other men. "She knew he would go ballistic and then, like clockwork, he always did," Laura recalled. "She never knew when to put a sock in it, and she paid for it. He kept telling her to shut up, or she'd be sorry."

Laura remembered that she was in her room reading *Are You There God? It's Me, Margaret* when she heard punches and things breaking and then a commotion in the stairwell. Tracy and Craig stayed in the room, but Laura went out and saw Linda lying in a heap at the bottom of the stairs. Her father, sweating and out of breath, was sitting in a torn shirt at the kitchen table with his head in his hands. She ran down the narrow tunnel stairs. "Linda was lying there crumpled into a little pile. She was unconscious, and her neck was at an odd angle." Laura couldn't find a pulse and ran upstairs to call 911. Then she looked at her dad and realized that he might have pushed Linda down the stairs. "I told him to take off his shirt; I hid it in my room and got him another one to wear. I dried off the blood on his arm where she'd clawed him. I told Tracy and Craig to say there was no fighting when the police came."

"What was your father doing all this time?" I asked.

"He was dead drunk."

When the emergency crew arrived, they pronounced Linda dead from a broken neck. Laura told the police that she'd fallen down the stairs. When they asked why she looked so beaten up, Laura explained that she'd hit her head on every stair. "Linda was a local drunk who caused problems when she drank in bars, so she was just carted away and no one ever saw her again," Laura said matter-of-factly.

"The next day my father, who'd sobered up by then, said that we should be careful on the stairs because they were dangerous—some of the treads were loose. Craig got a hammer and fixed the rubber treads, and the family legend is that Linda fell down the stairs."

"Legend?" I asked. I wondered if Laura was acknowledging that her father had pushed Linda down the stairs.

"To this day, I'm not sure whether he pushed her down the stairs or if she fell. No one saw it."

"Yet she flew with enough velocity to kill her," I pointed out.

"True," Laura said, and then added, "But she was a tiny thing who weighed about eighty-five pounds. Besides, people fall down the stairs all on their own and die. It happens all the time."

"How did you feel about Linda's death and the circumstances of it?"

"Truthfully, I never liked Linda. She was selfish, high maintenance, and a mean drunk. She never made a meal, and she was just another difficult person for me to deal with."

"Still, it must have been fairly traumatic. This was the second time you'd called 911 for a dead wife of your father's. One a mother and one a stepmother."

Laura said she hadn't felt traumatized, that it was just one more thing to be handled.

"All in a day's work? Were you suspicious of, or angry at, or frightened of your father?"

"I know you'll think I'm strange, but I blamed myself. The real trauma for me, since you like to use that word, is that I dragged Craig and Tracy back to Toronto when it was such a bad time for them. My dad couldn't handle any of it. I should have known that and not laid such a burden on him."

"So you blamed yourself for putting too much pressure on him, not him for possibly murdering Linda?"

"I know enough now after two years of therapy that there's something wrong with that logic, but that is honestly how I feel."

What surprised me as a new therapist was the tenacity of Laura's denial. No matter how much she knew what her dad was capable of, she was still unwilling to make him responsible. I was beginning to learn that I was chipping away not at a block of ice but a glacier.

We were at the end of our second year of therapy and were making progress, but we still had to delve more deeply into Laura's relationship with her father. Certainly the "kick the cat" dream was a start at viewing him more realistically. I feared that until she gave up protecting him, she'd keep repeating that role with other men.

On a practical level, I began to wonder if the father, who was clearly more of a psychopath than a hapless alcoholic, had murdered both Linda and his first wife. I wondered if Laura's blockage of all memories of her mother was a means of protecting her father. Did she know more about that death at an unconscious level than she was aware of?

4

REVELATIONS

THERAPISTS CAN DEPLOY a variety of methods, based on certain psychological theories, to treat their patients. During the early years of my practice I relied mostly on a Freudian paradigm, which assumes the unconscious exists. I became more eclectic as time went on. I incorporated Gestalt techniques, such as role-playing and focusing on what was happening in the present, between therapist and patient, as a reflection of how the patient deals with conflicts in the outside world. I also employed Carl Rogers's client-centred therapy whereby the client is considered to be an expert on her own difficulties, with the therapist acting mostly as a sounding board.

In short, I'd found that being wedded to only one orientation was limiting. I needed to think about each case and weigh what was best for each client. Sometimes patients weren't particularly introspective and had trouble accessing their feelings in the Freudian style of free association. So I'd switch from that insight-oriented approach to the immediacy and shock of the role-playing method, where the patient was thrust into a role and had to respond. For example, if she was angry with her boss, I'd pretend to be that boss—and the patient's true feelings would usually emerge during the exercise. Or, if someone was extremely deprived and hadn't been listened to in childhood, I'd use the Carl Rogers approach—simply listening as a way to provide the nurturing needed to grow. Each case required frequent reassessment, and if no psychological progress was happening, it was necessary to try a different technique. As Einstein reputedly said, "The definition of insanity is doing something over and over again and expecting different results."

Sometimes it was helpful to use a sociological model instead of a psychological one. Redefining Laura's case in sociological terms, her father belonged to a group, namely alcoholics, while Laura belonged in the "adult child of an alcoholic" group. The Alcoholics Anonymous organization posits that alcoholics have certain traits, and that their children have developed their own particular traits in response to the parent's alcoholism. In fact, groups exist around the world specifically to help adults who've grown up in an alcoholic home.

So I gave Laura the book *Adult Children of Alcoholics* by Janet Woititz. I wanted her to see the list of characteristics many adult children of alcoholics have in common, especially the eldest daughter, who is usually a substitute parent.

Laura arrived at our next session unnerved by having discovered that she exhibited every trait on the list. She'd created another flip chart, and now read out each trait as though she were an army sergeant doing roll call. "Adult children of alcoholics do the following," she began:

1. *Guess at what normal behaviour is.*
   "I had no idea it wasn't normal for nine-year-olds to have to act as a parent."

2. *Judge themselves without mercy.*
   "I hate myself for having been a bad parent and having herpes."

3. *Experience difficulty having fun.*
   "Fun? What am I, in kindergarten? I work."

4. *Take themselves very seriously.*
   "I'm criticized at work and by my dad for not taking a joke."

5. *Have difficulty with intimate relationships.*
   "Won't let you close to me and won't let you empathize. After all, it could lead to what this book calls *intimacy*—whatever *that* is."

6. *Overreact to changes over which they have no control.*
   "Why wouldn't I? All change is bad. It's murder or the police telling us to move or running from debt collectors."

7. *Constantly seek approval and affirmation.*
   "Will work for Ed, for my dad, and for Clayton to get their approval even though they're assholes. Well, my dad's not a total asshole, but he can be."

8. *Feel that they're different from other people.*
   "I *am* different. Everyone else is still in the sandbox. I've done stuff they couldn't imagine."

9. *Are super responsible.*
   "I'll kill myself to get the job done and then never think I did it well enough. I wake up in the night worrying about what I have to do the next day at work."

10. *Are extremely loyal, even in the face of evidence that it's undeserved.*
    "Well, that's too obvious to even discuss. I was loyal to

Clayton, Ed, and my dad, all men who should get the asshole-of-the-year award in their age groups."

For Laura, the book and the symptom list were a lightning bolt. She felt that they described her as though the author had peered into her soul.

She had no idea until she read the book that she wasn't unique. As she finished her list, she raised her voice in revelation: "*I'm just a product of an alcoholic home. I get that now.*"

One week Laura revealed that her grandmother had died. When I expressed my condolences, she said it was unnecessary since both of her grandparents had been "cretins." She waited a few minutes and then said, "I ought to know. I lived with them. After Linda died, my dad got involved in some petty crap and was imprisoned. We were shipped off to Owen Sound to live with his parents when I was fourteen or fifteen."

Her grandparents lived in a trailer park; they were, she said, "as stupid as posts, and gave white trailer trash a bad name. It's amazing they found each other, because one was as batshit crazy as the other. If you didn't do some stupid thing they wanted, they flipped out." Once, when Laura came home from the store with creamed corn instead of niblets, she was beaten with a belt and then locked in a closet for twenty-four hours. (Confined spaces and the smell of mothballs still made her short of breath.) There were many other examples of this kind of behaviour. And, during the beatings, she was told that her father was no good and nor was she.

Laura hadn't been used to physical cruelty and verbal abuse. Even when her father lived with Linda, he was never cruel to Laura, nor was he ever a disciplinarian. In fact, he often praised her. His modus operandi was neglect.

She mentioned that her grandfather had been "oddly sexual" toward her. When I asked her to clarify, she said, "He would say that I looked like 'a wop whore' like my mother, and that their son would have been successful if she hadn't trapped him and ruined his life. Whenever I came home from a date, he said he was going to check my virginity. Just once I held up a knife and said that if he ever touched me, I'd call my foster parents, Ron and Glenda, and then the police would come and he could join his son in jail. Grandpa was too stupid to know I meant it, but Grandma knew which way the wind blows, and said, 'Leave her alone, we don't want her cooties.'"

That was the first time Laura had ever mentioned improper sexual behaviour. And when this happens, there's often more that the patient isn't revealing.

"Can you tell me more about the sexual talk of your grandfather?"

She shook her head dismissively. "He never did anything. He was a coward underneath. Grandma was the one who had the power of her sick convictions."

I tried to tread carefully, to not plant any ideas, but I did finally say that people who've had chaotic lives are more often sexually abused because, without a parent's protection, they're more vulnerable. Also, they have no idea about normative behaviour, or that they have the right to say no.

"Not me. I would have slit anyone's throat who came near me, and I think guys can pick up on that kind of thing."

Laura had been victimized, but she never took on the victim role. That was what was so heroic about her. Even though she'd been fighting for many years, she got up every day determined to better herself.

But although she was a hero in one way, psychologically denying her pain had its drawbacks. Instead of experiencing her real, buried feelings—fear, loneliness, and abandonment—she felt only anger. Anger is not a feeling; it's a defence. When you can't acknowledge your true feelings because they're too excruciating, you defend against them with anger. It was my job to get Laura to attach real feelings to what had happened to her.

One thing I learned from Laura's case was that a psychologist cannot judge. Everyone is judgmental to some degree; it's how we humans sort and assess situations. I could have labelled Laura's father as "an alcoholic sociopath who had arrested development at the adolescent stage" or, in layperson's terms, just called him selfish. However, once I'd heard about his sadistic mother and perverted, unemployable father, I realized he'd had an uphill battle. No one had prepared him for adult life. He, in fact, was better at parenthood than his own parents had been. Only he knew what his parents did to him in his childhood. He had no role model, therapy, or tools of any description, but he did keep trying, in his limited way, to reconnect.

During the latter half of our third year together, some information from the past surfaced to impact the therapy. Laura's sister, Tracy, hadn't been doing well over the last few years. She had a two-year-old son who in the previous year had contracted encephalitis, been in a coma, and was now mildly brain damaged. Recently she'd had twins. Her husband was ineffectual and a low-functioning depressive. Laura had travelled to Tracy's rural home on several weekends to help with the new babies.

Then Laura learned that Tracy's husband had committed suicide by hanging himself in the bathroom. In the aftermath of this terrible event, Tracy confessed that she couldn't handle the twins on her own.

"What is Tracy asking you for?" I tried to clarify.

"Help. I'll give it. I'll go every weekend to her godforsaken falling-down farmhouse and offer a set of hands. Man, when I'm there I'm busy every minute. I had to pay for diapers since she was trying to ration them. Jesus, she really isn't coping."

"I agree she needs your help. She's lucky to have you; no one can organize or work harder than you." I tentatively inquired, "But what about emotional help?"

"All she does is cry when I don't discuss concrete things."

I reminded Laura that her sister had experienced the same losses as she had: their mother's death, their father's abandonment, Linda's violent death, their father's incarceration. I pointed out that Laura had been their father's favourite while he'd ignored Tracy, calling her "Mrs. Whiner." Laura was the smart, pretty sister who had the admirable will of iron. Tracy had none of those gifts. I gently suggested that she might need Laura's emotional support.

"I do what I can. I already told her that we'd get through this."

What Laura was describing was encouragement, not intimacy. I decided to introduce the topic again. We'd bandied about the word *intimacy* and she'd read about it, but I still didn't think she'd internalized its true meaning. I knew I had to proceed gingerly, given that her underlying feelings were so well defended; when she closed a door, it slammed. I suggested that perhaps Laura might want to share her inner feelings with her sister. I pointed out that she'd had three years of therapy and Tracy had had none. "Have you ever told Tracy that you're in therapy?"

"Jesus! *No.*"

I reminded her that she'd come into therapy to learn how to handle her stress and anxiety, and it had worked well. Not only had her herpes attacks diminished; she'd also learned much more about herself and how to improve her quality of life. But she needed to delve deeper. "There's that concept called intimacy you've read about, where people share their feelings," I ventured.

"I *know* about it. I'm not from Ork."

And yet Laura looked confused. So I said, "Intimacy is when you're familiar with your emotions, then share your feelings, your fears, your shame, your hopes and joys with another person."

"Christ! Why not just dance naked in the streets?"

I ignored that. "It will be hard for you to do it at first, since no one expressed feelings to you in your childhood," I said. "In fact, you had to block your feelings just to handle your life. No wonder it's hard for you to learn." I explained that speaking intimately is like learning another language. The more you do it, the easier it becomes.

Laura was fixated on the practical, and demanded that I give her an example.

"When you shared with me that the herpes caused you profound shame, I was able to empathize with your feelings." I reminded her that when she first came to therapy, she forbade all empathy.

She nodded and laughed as though that had been in another lifetime.

"What if people use it against you?" she asked.

"That's always a possibility. You should express intimacy only to people you believe you can trust. It's a building block for more trust. You're going to have to take a bit of a leap of faith on this one."

"Honestly, it sounds dicey, but I get it. It can make you closer or blow up in your face."

"When people share their feelings, they feel better, less stressed and less anxious. If you plan on having a life partner, it's emotional intimacy that will be the glue that holds you together long after the physical intimacy fades." She made a face indicating she found that concept a bit far-fetched.

Laura and I rehearsed how to have an intimate conversation. I tried to give her some vocabulary to use. I said, "Possibly Tracy doesn't know how to be intimate any more than you do. Maybe she uses whining as you use anger—as a defence mechanism." Laura had told me that when Tracy found her husband hanging in the shower, her first reaction was "Who's going to help me now?" She hadn't said anything about losing a loving partner. Tracy and her mate were two lost souls who were, in terms of intimacy, total strangers.

Here we were in year three, and Laura had made great strides in the area of boundaries, but we were still talking about basic notions like intimacy. The concept remained anathema to her. After all, her first memory was when she cut her foot and her father said he loved her for being strong. Sharing pain was, in Laura's mind, not strong. Now I was asking her to drop her guard. It went contrary to twenty-some years of learning in her family and her school of hard knocks. No one in the boxing ring ever tells a fighter to drop his left.

Laura cancelled her next appointment, something she'd never done before. She referred to her appointments as her "lifeline." She came in a few weeks later and was deceptively cheerful. I could tell by her face that something was wrong.

I said I felt an undercurrent of danger in the room and added that for her to not show up for an appointment something dire must have happened. She sat for a few minutes looking out the window. Finally, she fired out the following words like bullets: "I tried your *reckless* idea of attempting to get more intimate with my sister. I knew I hadn't opened that intimacy can of worms for a reason." She slammed her fist on the armrest of her chair and looked at me accusingly. I was silent. She continued,

"I went to Tracy's. I was feeding one baby and Tracy was feeding the other in the middle of the night. We were almost in the dark, in matching rocking chairs. I said that we hadn't had it easy as kids, and that I'd learned that in therapy. She was surprised to hear me say that, since she's always been the sniveller and I hadn't allowed it. She said she thought I'd been happy because I 'had everything.'"

Laura revealed to Tracy that not only was she in therapy, she was also beginning to realize that their father hadn't always been a perfect parent. "He may have done all he was capable of, but it wasn't enough. I told her how I'd learned that Ed was just another version of Dad. He was a handsome charmer, but he betrayed me with the herpes."

Laura then looked me in the eye and said, "Yes, Dr. Gildiner, wonders never cease—I told her about the herpes. I went on, saying that Ed was even in the same job as Dad and then, like Dad, got into illegal stuff. I said I kept making excuses for Ed just as I'd done for Dad. When Tracy seemed confused, I went through the whole rigmarole about bonding. *I had all night, right?*"

Laura also confessed that she'd tortured herself about being a bad mother to her and Craig, focused only on survival and not on their emotional well-being. "I told her how sorry I was. Then I paused," said Laura quietly. "I guess I was hoping she would either forgive me or say that I was only a little kid and did the best I could, like you've said to me so often.

"She didn't. She just sat there like a lump. I was starting to feel pissed off, like I'm revealing and she's parked like some rusted, gutted old car. Eventually I prodded her, saying, 'Tracy, do you want to share something with me?' You could hear the creaking as we both rocked on our chairs. Finally, in a perfectly blank tone, she said, 'Dad had sex with me when we were kids lots of times.'"

Now it was time for me to sit blankly. I had not seen that coming. I was as shocked as Laura had been. Laura read my surprise and motioned to me to wait while she finished. "I just sat there with a baby bottle shaking in my hand, waiting for her to go on. She didn't say one more word. I wanted to scream that she was lying. I knew that wasn't the right thing to do, but my heart was pounding in my ears and I couldn't think. I just waited silently for a really long time until my insides weren't churning." Eventually Tracy spoke. "'Once our real mother opened the door and caught us. She just looked for a few seconds and then closed the door,'" she told Laura.

Laura asked how she couldn't have known this, since the sisters slept in the same room. Tracy said he did it when no one was around, but he took big chances.

"I asked her why she never told me," Laura said, then subsided into silence.

She didn't look hurt, she looked angry—furious, in fact. Finally, I prompted her about Tracy's answer.

"She just shrugged in her usual listless way. Then she said, 'You wouldn't have believed me. You thought he walked on water.' No matter what I asked, she wouldn't say any more," Laura recalled. "Then I thought of what you said about empathy, and instead of grilling her about the logistics, I just said how sorry I was. Then she cried and cried, and her tears fell on the face of the twin she was holding. I had to wipe it with a dry diaper."

"This must have come as a great shock to you," I said. "How do you feel about this revelation?"

Instead of answering, Laura described how she'd taken three days off work to travel up north to talk to her father. He was living with a schoolteacher named Jean, a well-off widow, in Sault Ste. Marie.

"As usual, he looked completely happy to see me. Asked what was up, was thrilled to hear about my promotion, and was sorry to hear I was no longer with Ed. He thought he was a real 'live wire,'" said Laura. "He was wearing an almost kind of middle-class outfit—one step under collegiate. And he was drinking a diet Coke *in a glass*, which I assume wasn't spiked. I have no idea how he landed on his feet. It probably won't last long."

Laura explained to Jean that she wanted to discuss some family matters, so Jean left to visit her sister. As soon as she was gone Laura quietly asked her father, "Did you sexually abuse Tracy? She says you did."

Her father exploded. "*Christ, NO!* I have no trouble getting women. I would never turn to my children. That's sick. Tracy is always the victim, no matter what happens. She's just pissed off that Jean and I wouldn't go hole up with her and help her with the kids. She made her bed, she can lie in it." Laura's father kept talking, saying he didn't want to drag Jean "all over hell's half acre to help someone who's always a sad sack no matter what you do for her." Then, Laura said, he slapped his hand on the table so hard she thought the glass might break. "He said, 'I knew she'd retaliate, and this fits. That husband of hers got sick of her being the victim and hung himself, probably just to show "Who's the victim now, Tracy?"'"

"He thundered around the room hollering, 'If Tracy wants to frame me for this, let her. Go right ahead. I just hope you know exactly what Tracy is like and always has been. Both she and her mother were always the wronged party. Ask Craig, he'll tell you it's crap.'"

"Craig has nothing to do with this," I said.

Laura continued, telling me that she'd collected her purse to go, and as she was leaving she told her father that "the jury's still out."

I waited for Laura to say more. She just looked at me and shook her head. In an angry tone, she said, "I know you think I'm defending him but, honest to God, Tracy was never alone with him and she *does* always play the victim." Then she did an imitation of Tracy's whiny voice: "'Why did my husband do this to *me?*' and 'Why did *my* kid get encephalitis?'"

I asked Laura how she could know for certain that Tracy had never been alone with their father. Laura had had lots of friends, and had gone out to parties and play dates while Tracy languished at home.

She made a face, begrudgingly acknowledging that what I said was true.

"The important question to ask is: *Is Tracy a liar?*" I went on. "Has she lied about being a victim? No, she has not. In fact, her husband *did* commit suicide, and her child *was* felled by a terrible disease."

Laura shook her head in disgust and said, "Whenever she wasn't asked out while we were at Grandma's, she said it was because we lived with loonies in a trailer. Well, I was asked out plenty. When we were little, she said she wasn't invited to birthday parties because our mother never talked to the other mothers. Yet I was invited. She always had an excuse, and it was never her fault."

"That is not lying," I clarified.

"She was always jealous of my relationship with Dad. This could be Tracy's pathetic way of competing with me, saying, 'Look, I was close to him as well.' Dr. Gildiner, you don't know her. She wanted to give up the twins to Children's Aid for God's sake. I had to tell her she *could* be a good parent to them. I told her we don't want to be the family with generations of abandoned children."

"That is certainly inadequate, as you say, but it's not lying."

"Honest to God, I believe him. I know your next question. No, he never did anything like that to me, ever—not even close. When people said I was pretty, he never even commented."

"Except at prison, when you felt he used your beauty."

"God, you've got a mind like a steel trap. Am I in the witness box or in therapy?"

She was right. I had to dial it back and focus on seeking *psychological* truth, not the *literal* truth.

We really had no way of knowing the truth. Certainly, Tracy was inadequate and needy—just the type of person a predator would choose for abuse. He knew Laura would never have tolerated it; she'd have gone after him with a kitchen knife. In the final analysis, if I suggested that Laura was defending against believing Tracy in order to protect her father, I'd be taking sides. Saying any more about whether the incest actually happened would be stepping out of my role as a psychologist. The job of the psychologist is to point out patterns in behaviour, and I did remind Laura that she had a pattern of defending against her father's faults and not seeing him realistically. I gave her the tools, and now it was up to Laura to decide on the truth.

One of the details about the incest that stood out for me was Tracy's description of how her mother opened the door and then simply closed it quietly and never mentioned what she'd seen. I pictured that poor mother with nowhere to go, yet knowing her child was being sexually abused. She may have been profoundly depressed, or simply didn't have the personal strength or power in the relationship to defend her daughter. I wondered again if she'd committed suicide. There had been no investigation, and no criminal activity was suggested. I'd wondered, too, once I'd heard about the second wife's death, if Laura's mother had also died by her husband's hand. I'd never gotten to the bottom of why Laura had only one memory of her mother.

I had to be very careful at this juncture. I didn't want to put ideas in Laura's head. I'd been a therapist for three years but hadn't yet encountered a case of incest. I also had to remember that therapy wasn't about truth; as Jack Nicholson famously shouted in *A Few Good Men*, sometimes people "can't handle the truth." Rather, it's a matter of getting your unconscious to stop controlling your conscious mind. Effective therapy is about lowering your defences so that you can deal with the issues that arise in your life.

There was a long therapeutic silence. The shocking revelation had made both of us unusually pensive for the last half of the session. Finally, after about ten minutes, with all the anger drained from her voice, Laura said, "We'll never know the truth, will we?"

I shook my head in agreement.

I switched back to that evening with Tracy. "One thing that did happen was that Tracy tried to be as intimate with you as you were with her. Clearly, she needs help. Whether she was a victim of abuse or not, she thinks she was and needs to see a therapist."

I went about finding a psychiatrist in a hospital near Tracy's home, someone who would see her at no cost. Sadly, Tracy showed up for only a few sessions. Then I found a support group for her, but she went only once. Then I contacted a support group for mothers of twins and arranged for someone to pick her up and take her home. But at the last moment, Tracy refused to attend.

I realized that I was putting too much psychic energy into Tracy, who wasn't even my client and who was resistant to therapy or help of any kind. I also had to remind myself that it was my own need to uncover every rock and to bring everything to light. It wasn't the need of my patients. I had to look at two factors. First, Laura had worked hard in therapy and wasn't afraid of working on herself. Second, she was right: we would never really know the truth. It was a tragic note on which to end our third year of therapy, but it was up to Tracy and her father to sort it out.

5

OUT OF A JOB

I FELT WE WERE in the home stretch. Laura had first come into therapy to address her frequent herpes outbreaks, and now they were down to one or two a year—evidence that she'd learned how to handle her anxiety. She had set boundaries at work and in personal relationships. She no longer allowed people to enrage her while she remained powerless. She was working on establishing intimacy and empathy with others. She had come to realize that she'd had a dysfunctional childhood and was focused on becoming a balanced person.

Still, there were setbacks and relapses. One week, Laura stomped in for her appointment and I could tell by her stride that she was out for bear. When something threatened her, she could still shift into anger overdrive in order to protect her fragile ego. I'd learned long before not to get between Laura and her unconscious fears. She could fight both mentally and physically. Once she was alone on a subway platform at night and a man tried to steal her purse. She kicked him in the groin, knocked him *onto the tracks*, then pressed the intercom and said, "Asshole on the tracks." Then she took a cab home.

When I asked her why she was so mad, she referred to her week as "embarrassing." She began by telling me that Kathy, the daughter of her foster parents, Ron and Glenda, was now an elementary school teacher in Toronto. Her boyfriend was completing a graduate degree in computer science.

Laura had the couple over for dinner and Kathy's boyfriend brought a friend named Steve, who'd just finished the same computer degree. Laura told me it was humiliating because, clearly, Kathy had invited him to meet Laura. "It was so wrong and so embarrassing on so many levels I don't even know where to begin," she said.

Laura wasn't usually melodramatic. She had described her mother's and stepmother's deaths in one quiet sentence.

"Level one?" I prompted.

"First of all, *I* was prom queen. I don't need Kathy, who played the tuba in the band, to take care of my dating needs. I'm not the pathetic orphan."

"Level two?"

"This guy was not my type. He looked like he grew up on *The Waltons*." (A TV show about a poor but close and loving American family of high moral fibre who lived through the Depression. The star of the show was the eldest son, named John-Boy.) "He tried to be Mr. Nice Guy, and while Kathy's boyfriend fixed my TV and Kathy borrowed my sewing machine, he cleared the table. I told him to just leave the dishes, and he said, 'Let's just get them done. We all have work in the morning.' Then," she said indignantly, "he kept carrying out the dishes after I said I'd do it."

"Are we getting to the bad part?" I asked.

"Come on. No one acts like that."

"Would Colonel Potter help his wife if he saw that she'd made a three-course meal and it was getting late and she had work in the morning?"

Laura sat for a few seconds. "Yeah, he might, but I like Colonel Potter as a father, not a sexual partner."

"So, let me get this straight," I said. "A man who comes into your life who has a master's in a competitive field and helps you with the dishes because he knows what it's like to be tired in the morning, and has the good sense to thank you for dinner by cleaning up, is what? A loser? Help me out here."

"I mean, he isn't exciting. He's not a risk taker," she said.

"How do you know that? I'm not pushing this guy Steve, but I need to know why you're using examples of his kindness to place him off limits."

She sat silently, and I couldn't resist adding, "Besides, what do you know about his risk taking?"

"I know Ed had many failings. But he always had wild ideas and knew how to shake things up."

"Like giving you herpes, and getting fired from every job. Your dad was what you call 'exciting' as well, yet his wildness and excitement didn't include taking care of his children, obeying the law, or making a living. It takes guts and brains to compete in computer science." I realized as I said this that I'd gone over the top. I was exasperated by Laura's clinging to her father as a role model and had become shrill. I apologized for hectoring instead of interpreting.

Her eyes sparked with anger. "You're on a roll now, so spill it out. For once, give me my money's worth."

"Laura, you always push me away when I get too close to your pain. You can protect that pain for the rest of your life, but that won't help you get better."

"Sorry. What were you going to say?"

"I think you're bonded to behaviour like your dad's. You had to put up with him. You had no mother. What were you going to do? Where were you going to go? You did an amazing job carving a trail through the wilderness. You were parentless when no one should be without parents. Who was your role model? You had none. You were so resourceful and so tenacious that you discovered

Colonel Potter and were smart enough to use him as your role model. Not many people could have been that resourceful and *created* a parent when they needed one."

"Too bad you're not in charge of Purple Hearts," she said sarcastically.

Laura had improved on many fronts. Yet she had one stubborn symptom to overcome: her relationship to males. She was still attracted to the bad-boy type, whom she termed "exciting" instead of "psychopathic." Here she was again, emotionally rejecting a man because he helped her with the dishes. He wasn't allowing her to assume her customary role of saviour.

I was frustrated by this recalcitrance, so I decided to confront her with my interpretation of her behaviour toward her guest. "I think Steve holds no interest for you because you have no idea what your role would be in the relationship. You might not have to rescue him." Then I paused and said with vehemence, "*You'd be out of a job.*"

Laura leaned back in her chair as though she'd been hit in the chest. I pushed on. "Why were you your dad's favourite?"

"I took care of him. My family was like those old cars in Cuba. I just kept patching it to keep it running with any spare part I could find—no matter if it was chewing gum."

As our session closed, I asked her to think about what she would do with a man who didn't need her but just loved her.

During the next few months, Laura began to see Steve regularly. She bought her first set of hiking boots, and on weekends they cooked elaborate meals and entertained. She was learning how a normal relationship functioned. Steve had a busy life, but if he was going to be late, he'd call to let her know. At first she ridiculed this behaviour, as though it were compulsive and finicky. I pointed out that it was what adults did to be considerate to one another—he was valuing her time as much as his own. Since she had no base-line, I was her window onto what was normal in a relationship.

It was hard for Laura to be emotionally intimate with anyone, but she tried with Steve by sharing some of her past. He seemed to accept most things. He never pushed sex, although they'd done everything but penetration. Laura said she was running out of excuses; she was going to have to tell him about the herpes. She actually contemplated breaking up with him so she wouldn't suffer the humiliation of him breaking up with her. Instead, she forged ahead and revealed her herpes condition. Steve sat silently. She could tell he was shaken. He left soon after, saying he had to think about things. She didn't hear from him for a week, then two, and finally three.

During the fourth week of Steve's loud silence, Laura said, "Looks like John-Boy's taken a powder and is heading back to the Waltons." She made fun of the show, but she still watched it. She studied the kindness and ethical behaviour of the Walton family as a primatologist might analyze a *National Geographic* show on a monkey troop.

I asked her how she felt about Steve's departure, and without a second's hesitation she said, "Relieved." When I asked why, she said, "Now I don't have to try to be normal. It was so much work. Plus, he was cheap. Listen to this: he made popcorn once when we were going to the movies. I said there was no way I'd ever walk into a theatre with my own bag of popcorn. Jesus Christ."

"Well, he has his first job and owns a home that he rents out to students, and he owns a cottage that he and his father fix up every weekend of the summer. That's a lot to own for someone in his first year of work."

"Yeah, well, he pinches every penny. When we go to the cottage, we work from dawn till dusk on it. He won't even turn on the heat if it's over sixty degrees." She rested her head on the back of her chair, lifted her legs as though she were in a recliner, and let out a long breath. "So long, sailor!"

"Laura, what's under the relief and the bravado?"

She sat for a while and then, looking at her watch, said, "Isn't our time up?"

I shook my head no.

After more than three years of therapy, Laura had learned how to dig into her unconscious. I was hoping she could do that now, although this was a fresh wound. I reminded her that when wounds aren't left open, they can fester.

Finally, she let out another deep breath and said, "I'm hurt and ashamed. It's like the first week I ever came in here. My trashy family tarnishes me and he wants out. His mother is an elementary school teacher; his dad taught industrial arts and was the coach for his hockey team. They had a backyard rink, which he flooded with his dad every night, and they've always lived in the same house. His parents are kind and *real* Colonel Potters. I could never have introduced them to my fucked-up brood."

"Anyone would be hurt," I said, and my heart went out to her. "The good part is that you've acknowledged how you really feel."

"I thought, I guess I hoped, that he cared for me. We really liked working on the cottage together. He loved my ideas for decor. I'm really good at that. We're both worker bees by temperament."

"He may have cared, but the herpes was too much of an obstacle. Or, have you ever thought that maybe he's still weighing his options?"

"*Come on!*"

"Not everyone is impetuous. You're used to what you call spontaneity, but if you flip that term and reframe it, it could mean reckless. Some people weigh important decisions carefully over time." Then I asked, "Would your dad or Ed tell someone if they had herpes?"

"Ed didn't, and my dad wouldn't."

"Well, you did; that makes you different from your dad and Ed. Remember, you can always only control your own behaviour."

"Yeah, I've only had one outbreak this year, which isn't bad. It amazes me how those outbreaks are always related to stress."

"Did Steve know everything about your family?"

"Yup, every rotten thing. I didn't tell about the incest with Tracy because I don't believe it. Nor do I think my dad killed my mother, and the jury is out on Linda."

I felt for Laura. She'd been open, and had been rejected. She'd spent so much time beating on normalcy's door that she had to be getting tired.

The following week, Laura arrived, sat down with an infinitesimal smile on her face, and said, "Heeeeeeee's back!" She explained that Steve had had to wait to get an appointment with his doctor, who gave him a lot of information on how to have safe sex. "He had to think about making a commitment, and it took him time."

The relationship went smoothly for several months, until Valentine's Day, when Steve gave Laura only one rose. She was outraged. He said that in his family they saved money for lasting items and bought only token gifts. He felt his family's biggest gift to him was four years of university and graduate school.

Laura had learned long-term goals for herself—she plugged away at a university degree for years—but she wasn't used to it in a *man*. She thought lavish spending was, in some way, manly. She viewed that kind of generosity as a sign of romantic love. Steve, however, viewed it as extravagance.

True to form, Steve didn't apologize. He said that that was his style, and that if they married at any point, the two houses and cottage he now owned would be hers as well.

Laura said to me, "That is such bullshit. He's just cheap. My father spent his last dime buying Linda a designer purse she wanted."

"Before or after he possibly killed her?" I couldn't resist saying.

"That was an accident—mostly. You know, you can be queen of the cheap shot."

She had that one right.

Laura and Steve weathered the Valentine-rose storm and now it was the following Christmas. Laura visited Steve's family home in Parry Sound, a small town north of Toronto. His mother had knitted her a sweater, which Laura described as something people wore on *Little House on the Prairie*.

"How bad can it be?" I said, knowing that Laura was extremely fashionable.

"I was hoping you'd ask." Then she opened her coat for effect. She was wearing a bright red Christmas sweater depicting carollers, all in different hats that had been appliquéd in felt, velvet, and some shag fabric. The carollers held songbooks in white felt and were singing under a lamppost. I couldn't help but laugh. "Can I make fun of this with Steve?" Laura asked hopefully.

"Did he meet your family?"

"Yeah, all except for Craig."

"Did he say anything negative?"

"Not a word."

I waited.

She sat and thought for a minute. "I'm chained to this sweater. It's my fashion statement for every December we're together."

Slowly, Laura was learning how to adapt to middle-class life. She began to appreciate dependability, long-range goals, and their growing savings. Steve appreciated her work ethic, and he loved her lively, spontaneous humour.

She was bothered that he never told her she was pretty, something she was used to hearing. I explained the need to communicate, that sometimes people in normal relationships have to tell their partners what they want. When she replied that she didn't want to grovel for compliments, I told her that wanting to feel loved is perfectly normal.

When she did tell him, he said he often thought how beautiful she was, but he was from a family that didn't "fawn." She said it wasn't fawning if he meant it. Steve was a quick learner, and now told Laura frequently how much he loved her and how beautiful she was. "The wacky part is, he really seems to mean it," she said. They'd been living together for almost a year by then.

One day Laura appeared pale and without her usual effervescence. She sat down on the edge of her chair and said that Steve had left her. She'd had no idea he was at the end of his tether. "When he complained, he did it without raising his voice, so I assumed he wasn't *that* pissed off."

When I asked if there was a precipitating incident, Laura explained that she'd been about to make dinner when she saw a Tupperware container of leftover pasta sauce in the fridge. So she boiled water for pasta, but when she opened the container she saw that Steve had packed away only a tablespoon of sauce. She screamed at him and threw the sauce against the wall. Steve quietly told her that he was leaving for a week, and that she could decide whether she was going to continue handling her anger in a way that was intolerable to him. If so, they had a very serious problem.

I asked how often she blew up. "Once or twice a week, which isn't that much. I mean, really, who saves a dollop of sauce?" Laura looked at me, genuinely confused. "Come on, Dr. Gildiner, if your husband did that, you'd do the same thing. Everyone would."

I had no idea that Laura had been behaving that way. One of the pitfalls of therapy is that all information is filtered through the patient, who can be an unreliable narrator. If the patient reports that things are going well, that's only one perspective. In this case, another perspective was that her temper was out of control. Everything in Laura's family had been handled through shouting and confrontation and then quickly dismissed. Oddly, her father had never punished her when she smashed his liquor bottles and poured the contents down the drain, or when she went to bars where he drank and yelled at him in front of the other patrons. He'd seemed relieved that someone was in control. So now that Laura was in control of dinner, she had no idea why Steve wasn't falling into line and happy to have food on his plate.

I suggested we use Colonel Potter as the test for normal behaviour. Whenever she brought him to mind she could perfectly imagine what he would say, and thus reflect normalcy. I had her role-play him, and she said, in her Colonel Potter voice, "Steve, please don't leave tiny amounts of food in the fridge because it's easy to mistake the container for an entire meal. I understand you didn't want to be wasteful, but it confuses me."

The problem was that the little speech sounded to Laura like a sappy TV show—that it had no bearing on how couples actually interacted. So I told her to do two things. First, to fake it till she made it. I reminded her that she was from a dysfunctional home and that normal behaviour felt awkward and stilted. But if she just kept doing it, with time it would feel more normal. Second, I told her that every time she felt angry she should remember that anger is a defence, not a feeling, and to analyze what feeling the anger was covering.

Laura told Steve that if he came home she would do her utmost to control her temper and even wear her Christmas sweater. He returned home with the stipulation that she had to make some changes in how she handled frustration.

Another unrelated issue soon arose when Steve, who worked for a big technology firm, wanted to start his own company with other computer analysts. Laura was afraid of the risk. Change had always meant disruption and loss to her. Whenever new things had come into her childhood life—eight high schools, foster care, isolation up north, mean grandparents, constant moving—it meant distress. Furthermore, her father's hare-brained business ideas had all failed owing to bad planning. And yet now Steve wanted her blessing before he left his dependable job.

Finally, Laura reluctantly gave in. In our sessions, she wondered what had happened to the solid Steve who plugged away at a steady job. I pointed out that he didn't take unnecessary risks, that this was a *calculated* risk. He wasn't impetuous, yet he was self-confident enough to try to launch his own company. In other words, he was acting in a well-balanced way. If you're from a functional family, your parents role-model behaviour for you and you grow up internalizing the normal way to conduct yourself. However, I assured Laura that she was a quick learner, and encouraged her to look at all she had mastered since the day of her first session five years earlier.

Laura had finally graduated into "normalcy," as she called it. Work was going well, and Steve had proposed; they'd be getting married at Christmas. Now Laura had to introduce her family to Steve's family, a prospect that caused her only outbreak of herpes for the year. She invited the two families for Thanksgiving dinner at their place—and prayed that her father wouldn't be drunk, Craig wouldn't be stoned, and Tracy wouldn't be whiny. Since Laura,

Steve, and Steve's family were paying for the wedding, Laura's father insisted on bringing the turkey (that seemed like a fair deal to him). Laura told me that he arrived late, fifteen minutes before they were to eat, and plunked a frozen turkey on the table.

"Oh no!" I said, imagining her embarrassment.

"I may be more normal," Laura said, "but I'm not stupid. I had a stuffed cooked turkey in the oven, ready to go. I thanked him, shoved the turkey in the freezer, and the show went on."

I waited until after Laura's wedding to suggest that our work was done. Her eyes filled with tears, but she nodded in agreement. Laura was my first client, and the one I'd treated the longest. At times I'd been both mother and father to her, and together we shared a lot of laughs and growing pains as we each grew into our roles.

On Laura's last day she was rather businesslike, as was I, and she smiled and shook hands before she left. An hour later, I walked into the waiting room and there she was, sobbing, with a huge pile of Kleenex strewn around her. She hugged me, and held me for a long time before she ventured out. I too had tears in my eyes.

No psychologist ever forgets her first patient. It's like giving birth to your first child—no one and no amount of learning can ever prepare you for it. You're in uncharted waters. Having once been two separate people in the universe, we were now joined as doctor and patient: each of us had a new role. When you see that first patient sitting opposite you, looking expectant and hopeful, you're struck by the responsibility of the task you've undertaken. You've been handed a life, and it is your job to enhance that life.

Laura was the first but not the last hero I would encounter in my practice. At nine years old she'd managed to live in a forest for six months with two younger children. She had no role model, not one adult she could emulate to give her guidance. However, she did not give up. She reached into the television set and plucked out *M*A*S*H.*'s Colonel Potter, studied him, and then imitated his behaviour. That took a rare combination of ingenuity and imagination. Interestingly, Laura chose a husband, Steve, who was eerily similar to Colonel Potter in his quiet, calm, assured manner.

Laura's tenacity, combined with her innate strength and the bravery to not falter no matter what mayhem she had to navigate, made her a true survivor. She also had natural gifts, among them beauty, brains, and a fighting temperament. Birth order, too, was on her side: as the eldest she had to be the mother, and it was up to her to be "the responsible one." She was shrewd about her father's faults and had realized how to get what little love he had to give. She took that meagre material and worked with it.

Once she'd left therapy, Laura would write to me occasionally. Then, six years after our final session, I received an envelope in the mail. Enclosed was a newspaper article about Colonel Potter:

> LOS ANGELES—A criminal wife-beating charge against actor Harry Morgan was dismissed Wednesday by a West Los Angeles Municipal Court judge who had promised to drop the case if the "MASH" star completed a violence counseling program. Harry Morgan completed a six-month counseling program for domestic violence and anger management.

Laura had attached a Post-it note that read, "I sure can pick 'em."

A few years after that I got a picture in the mail of a huge fishing boat. On the back was scrawled,

I was listening to the Tragically Hip song "Bobcaygeon" on the radio yesterday and remembered when Ron, my foster father, used to take us

fishing at dawn and we'd see the constellations and the stars reveal-ing themselves, like the song said. Thought you'd like this boat I was able to buy for Ron. Dreams do come true!

The last time I saw Laura it was to let her know that I was featuring her in a book about psychological heroes. We arranged to meet at a restaurant, and when she walked in I recognized her right away. She looked the same as she had decades earlier—perfectly coiffed and attired. All these years later she was still stunning, could still turn heads in the restaurant. We both had tears in our eyes as she sat down.

When we were catching up on her family, she told me she was still happily married to Steve, who'd become remarkably success-ful in the computer business. They had two sons. One had gradu-ated from an Ivy League school in engineering and started his own firm in the States. The other was a litigating lawyer in Toronto. (I said I knew where his ability to argue had come from.)

Laura's father had died of cancer about four years earlier. She cried as she told me this. She stayed at the hospital in Sault Ste. Marie for weeks on end, and in the last month he recognized only her. She said between sobs that when he died, she felt that a part of her went with him. Then Laura looked up at me and, probably reading my expression, said, "I know you think I'm crazy to have been so attached to him. I know he had huge faults, but I chose to overlook them and just take what he could give." She paused and added with the steeliness I knew so well, "I'm a born fighter and I fought to keep him in my life."

When I asked why she'd always been so close to him despite what he'd done, she recalled again the childhood hospital scene when he gave her the message that he loved her for being strong and not complaining about her injured foot. "I said to myself, no matter what, I can do that, and I've always had his love in return.

Has he always been the best dad? *No.* Did he always love me or give me all the love he had? *Yes.*"

Laura thought that if it hadn't been for therapy she would have married someone unreliable like her father. She wouldn't have married Steve and experienced his unconditional love. "Steve is my rock, the one who always tells me I don't have to be perfect and rake up every leaf. He tells me he loves me for who I am, and that the hard worker is part of what he loves about me."

When I asked Laura if she had any regrets, she said she wished she hadn't grown up too quickly and not been such a slave to grim self-discipline. Trying to be perfect is exhausting, and Laura knows she missed the carefree childhood her sons had. Yet if she had her life to live over, she said, she probably wouldn't have wanted it to be any different.

"Really?" I was incredulous.

She held up her hand in protest. "Just listen to what I've been up to for the last few decades and you'll know what I mean. Let me start with my brother, Craig." She said that he died as he'd lived, alone, silently in his sleep from unknown causes at the age of forty-six. "He had a sad life."

Tracy—a single mother of three children, one of whom was slightly mentally handicapped—became an alcoholic on social assistance who weighed less than ninety pounds. After the children's father committed suicide, she stayed in that house in the country.

One day when Tracy was gathering wood for fuel, she cut her leg on a nail. She ignored the cut and the infection that followed and eventually developed flesh-eating disease. She lost both legs, and a few years later she too died in her sleep. "The doctors said she had an enlarged heart from drinking and smoking," Laura said. "I think essentially she gave up. Of the whole family, I'm the only one still alive."

Laura and Steve took in Tracy's three children while they were still in school and gave them all the help they could. They each had "special needs" in one way or another, and Laura devoted a lot of time to getting those needs met. "I started a foundation and worked fundraising for the brain-injured," Laura said. "You know I'm like a dog with a bone when I get on a roll. I have all kinds of awards for the work I've done in the field. Steve insists on hanging them in our den, which is totally embarrassing.

"So you see, in some ways I'm glad I lived a life where I needed to work and make things happen. I learned young that no one's going to do it for you. I have corporate sponsors that it took me years to establish. I never, ever gave up, so they finally got on board!" (I found myself wishing that those of my patients who complained about insignificant childhood events could hear this.)

As we waited for the check I elaborated on why I saw her as a hero. But Laura interrupted me, saying, "You know, I think this whole hero thing has had an impact on me." Then she told me a story. At a company dinner, one of her husband's colleagues remarked that she was lucky to have "married up." "That really bugged me," she said in her characteristically spunky tone. "There was a time when I would have felt like he'd found me out, and I would have felt shame. No way I feel that now." That man, she said, had wealthy, supportive parents who'd put him through private schools, funded trips to Europe, and paid for him to attend a great university. To no one's surprise, he became a CEO. "You know, life is a jungle and he drove through it in the Popemobile. I walked, using a hatchet to carve my way through the heart of darkness into swamps with leeches and crocodiles," she said. "I know a hell of a lot more about that jungle than he'll ever know. I had to go it alone and make every wrong turn until I knew it backwards and forwards and, finally, I got out alive. I'd like to see *him* do that. Perhaps not the work of a hero, but it is an accomplishment. So never say I married up, buddy!"

I asked, "Why do you think you made it out and your sister and brother didn't?"

She thought for a long time. "I think I was born with certain bossy traits and my dad honed them and gave me what he had, and I guess it was enough. Don't forget that when he was drunk and I saved the day, he praised me. *Any* praise goes a long way. I was the eldest; I had my ear to the ground and picked up what I needed. Five years of your help made the difference. Before therapy, I had no idea what was driving me." Then her eyes filled with tears. "Honestly, you were the mother I never had. Craig and Tracy just didn't get what they needed. They would have been far better off if they'd stayed at Ron and Glenda's, our foster parents."

We walked out into the cool autumn air with the fall leaves glittering through the now setting sun. Laura said, "Oh, I almost forgot to tell you this strange event that occurred last year. I thought of you the second it happened. Steve's company was sponsoring an event at a big theatre in Toronto. A limo had taken the executives and their partners from the restaurant to the theatre. As the limo door opened there were hundreds of theatre-goers in line and panhandlers begging for spare change. One of them who had disheveled, greasy hair looked familiar." She paused and looked into my eyes. "It was Ed. I just walked straight ahead and avoided eye contact so as not to embarrass him. Then a photographer gathered the sponsors for media pictures, and when the photos were finished I snuck a glance his way, but he was gone."

Laura was silent for a few seconds. "On the one hand, it was too close for comfort. On the other, it was another lifetime."

PETER

Who hears music, feels his solitude
Peopled at once

ROBERT BROWNING,
The Complete Poetical Works of Browning

LOCKED AWAY

IN MANY WAYS, psychology is like archaeology. As you dig down to uncover each layer and carefully dust off the artifacts that emerge, you eventually find a whole buried world that seems stranger than fiction.

In 1986 I got a call from a urologist who specialized in sexual dysfunction. He told me he had an unusual case. He was referring a thirty-four-year-old Chinese man named Peter Chang who suffered from impotence. Although Peter was normal physically, and able to masturbate and experience orgasm, he'd never managed to have any form of an erection in the presence of a woman. And when the urologist had given him a potent drug to inject in his penis one hour before trying intercourse, he was shocked by the result: "In all my years of practice I've never seen this drug fail unless there are major circulatory issues." Peter had no such issues. The drug even had a possible complication whereby sometimes it did the opposite of failing: someone could be left with an erection for three days. Yet this fail-safe drug had absolutely no effect on Peter Chang. The doctor concluded, "Whatever's going on in his head must have been mighty powerful to block this bulletproof shot."

When I asked if he could possibly be a homosexual, the doctor said that Peter claimed a heterosexual orientation and was longing to have sex with women. He'd told Peter that after exhaustive testing the urology team had deduced that he didn't have a physical sexual performance problem but rather a psychological one, and that he was turning him over to a psychologist. The doctor said he would send a written referral and suggested that we do grand rounds together if I ever got to the bottom of this case, for it had left the department stumped. In signing off he said, "This is one for the books. Just when you think you know it all, someone proves you don't know diddly-squat about the human condition."

Although the referral came before Viagra was invented, in recent years I've also had patients who used Viagra to no effect, no matter the dosage. (I've been assured by urologists that Viagra is light compared to those old-fashioned injectables.) Erectile dysfunction drugs work only if there's a *physical* problem. All the increased blood flow in the world won't solve an emotional problem. In any sexual response, the mind has to work in conjunction with the body.

Eager for an appointment, Peter took the first slot I had available. I walked into the waiting room to find an average-looking, soft-spoken Chinese man dressed nondescriptly in jeans, runners, and a black T-shirt with *Yamaha* printed across it. When he came into my office, he presented his history in a thorough style without making eye contact. He recounted some disturbing details as though he were delivering an academic paper instead of talking about himself.

Peter worked as a keyboard player in a band he'd been with for fifteen years. He supplemented that income with a day job as a piano tuner. He lived alone in an apartment and had no significant other. When I asked in what way I could help him, he said, "Mostly, I'm lonely. I want to have a relationship with a woman, but can't seem to do it."

I asked if he was talking about a sexual relationship. "Yes," he said quietly, looking down at the floor. "I can't have sexual intercourse, but I also want an emotional relationship. I want someone to talk to and share things with."

When I asked whether he'd tried to have a relationship before, he said that he had, but only in a very limited way. Then he added with a slightly embarrassed smile, "Mostly in my own mind."

I told him that no matter what the problem was, psychologists always collect information about the patient's family history, since those relationships form the building blocks for all others. Peter's Chinese parents arrived in Canada from Vietnam in 1943, and by 1952 the couple had two children. His sister, four years older than Peter, was now married with a child of her own. Peter was careful to point out that his sister's husband was non-Chinese.

Peter's father died when he was nine years old. When I asked about the details, he grimaced, searched for words, and finally described it as "sort of a suicide. My dad was a diabetic who refused to look after his diet. Every day, my mother made sweets for him and told him that it was time for him to die. He became very overweight and couldn't use his swollen feet anymore. He sat, or sort of stewed, silently for years in what I guess was a depression, and finally one day he had a heart attack and died."

When I sympathized with him, saying that nine was young to lose his father, he said, "I was sad, but my mother said it was best for the family."

Peter described his mother's longing for the father's death, then feeding him sweets when he was a diabetic to hasten the process, and finally expressing relief when he did die, as though this were normal. I was taken aback by the mother's malevolent behaviour, but I didn't want to exhibit my concern on our first visit. I needed to build up a rapport with Peter and collect a history. Instead, with a clear flair for understatement, I indicated that his mother had been a bit harsh. But Peter defended her: "My mother wanted what was best for us and worked three full-time jobs." When I pointed out that there weren't that many hours in a day, he said she did two at once and then had another. They owned the only Chinese-Canadian restaurant in a small town in Ontario called Port Hope—an ironic name, as it turned out.

At one point, Peter told me, his father had cooked in the restaurant while his mother was the waitress and did everything else to keep the business going. And when she had extra time, she did elaborate beadwork that she sold to an expensive department store in Toronto. She also grew much of their food (Chinese vegetables) in big gardens in the summer and ran a wholesale business for Chinese food suppliers. Peter paused for a second and said, "I can still remember in the middle of the night, as I watched from my window, I would see my mother wearing a miner's light on her head while she picked vegetables and weeded for hours."

"With three jobs, and looking after the children?"

He hesitated, then calmly explained that his sister had a crib in the kitchen and later a high chair in the restaurant. She wasn't allowed to talk or make any noise. "She was always good, but I was very bad. When I was little, under two, I would swivel on the stools while my sister sat quietly in the booth. I remember once making an airplane out of a menu and trying to fly it. My mother simply couldn't have this behaviour in the restaurant. She was run off her feet and it was disturbing the customers. I just wouldn't obey."

I pointed out that boys are often more active than girls, and that he was only behaving normally. He nodded politely and then repeated his refrain: "My mother did what was best for the family." I noticed that he'd internalized his mother's message, believing that he'd been "very bad" for doing what every normal boy that age would have done. When I asked what she did about his behaviour, he said, "From as early as I can remember—minus the one airplane memory—I was locked alone in the attic of the restaurant. My mother dropped off food in the morning for the day. I was asleep when and if she carried me home." When I asked how long this isolation had gone on, he said until he was five. His mother locked him away every day, Peter said, because his parents had to work from six in the morning until midnight.

I sat up in my chair and caught my breath, realizing that I had a rare case before me—a man who'd been locked away for the most crucial part of his childhood. Erik Erikson and Jean Piaget, two pioneers of child psychology, posited that there are crucial stages of child development, with each stage building on the last; if Peter had been isolated from before he was two until he was five, he would have had trouble catching up. He would have missed the first stages: attachment, bonding, and language development, to name only a few. As children, we all have what are called "open windows" for learning specific tasks that are developmentally time-sensitive; gradually, those windows close. If children miss a stage chronologically, they may have great difficulty making it up. For example, children who've been totally isolated often can't make up the language deficit.

After absorbing Peter's shocking information, I looked at him in a new light: I had a patient for whom impotence was the tip of the iceberg. If I alarmed him or made him feel he was unusual, it might frighten him. So I proceeded with caution, asking him to describe what he could remember about that time alone.

"Well, it was cold in the winter and very hot in the summer," he said. "I was left in a crib. I do remember the day I learned to crawl over the bars and get out of the crib. I was happy, but then sad when I found the door was locked."

"What's your most vivid memory of that early time?"

"It's an embarrassing memory, but I want to be honest." Peter went on to describe how he had to use an empty stewed tomato can to defecate. He recalled that it was a commercial-sized can and that it was so sharp he couldn't sit down on it. "I worried a lot about that because if I missed the can my mother would be angry, and if I cut myself, she was also angry."

I said, "A no-win toilet system."

He smiled slightly and agreed. Then his face reverted to his original mask. "I remember being frightened of that can because if I caused my mother any extra work, she would beat me with a bamboo whip that caused welts and bleeding."

When I said that sounded painful, he reiterated his mantra that his mother had no choice since she was trying to make a living. She couldn't waste time with him. He grimaced and said, "I got the worst beating when I peeled the insulation to make a toy with it. I wanted something to hold and play with."

I interjected that if his mother *had* given him a toy, it might have helped. Peter said they were poor, and that all Chinese immigrants had to make the same sacrifices; it was the only way to make it in Canada.

Of course, that wasn't true. Chinese immigrants did not have to lock their children in attics alone for eighteen hours a day, seven days a week, for several years. Like Laura, Peter was normalizing his parents' pathological behaviour. The neglect seemed normal to them and they wanted to protect their parent.

As our sessions progressed, I began to question Peter's interpretation of the Chinese immigrant experience. Eventually, I asked if he really thought that all Chinese males were locked in rooms for the majority of the first five years of their lives. His response shocked me. "Well, it was my fault," he said quietly. "I spun the stools at the counter and ran around. My mother couldn't afford to have someone watch me. My sister learned to sit quietly. I could not learn." It was clear that he wasn't ready to look at what was plainly child neglect and abuse.

In fact, his most powerful childhood memory—the only one he could label as happy—was seeing his mother from the attic window in the summer as she sat on the back steps of the restaurant chopping vegetables. Sometimes she'd walk up to the second floor to get a bag of stored rice. He could hear her footsteps and yearned for her to come to the third-floor attic jail; he remembered his heart leaping in the hope that she was coming for him. She hardly ever was. (She came only after midnight when he was asleep to carry him next door to their home; at dawn, when he was still sleeping, she'd carry him back to work.) She'd return downstairs to the restaurant, and his heart would sink.

"The worst thing was the loneliness," he said, recalling those years. "The beatings and the cold were occasional, but the loneliness was a constant, gnawing feeling that never left." He remembered seeing squirrels in the trees and begging them to come to his window. "I didn't know any words, but I remember learning the word *loneliness* long after I left the attic. I must have been about seven or eight, and I was watching *The Incredible Hulk* on TV. He said he was lonely because he had to be isolated so that no one would find out he was the Hulk. The music at the end of the show, when he had to leave a town, was so sad. I remember being shocked that other people felt loneliness as well as me. Plus, now I had a word, a label called *loneliness*, for that awful feeling."

As our therapy continued, I asked Peter if his mother had ever done anything nice for him. He said she'd once given him a small white toy piano. Many years later, his sister told him that it had been left behind in the restaurant by customers with a small son. The piano and the tomato canister were all he had for years in the dingy attic. He said, "I loved the piano and pretended it was my friend."

When I asked in what way the piano was his friend, he said, "His name was Little Peter. I didn't know any other name, since I'd never met another boy except my father. I wanted Little Peter to talk to me, so I began playing him and pretending the plinking sound was conversation. I could make Little Peter sad and happy." (Whenever I hear George Harrison's song "While My Guitar Gently Weeps," I think of Little Peter.) After he got the piano, Peter's emotional life improved; he had a beloved friend, and he became far less dependent on a mother who was perpetually angry and burdened by him.

Between sessions, I went to the reference library to look Peter up (it was the eighties, long before computers were ubiquitous). I discovered that he was a well-known keyboard player in an established band. One review referred to him as "a man who can make his keyboard talk, whine, cry or leap with joy." Given what Peter had said about the role of his piano, I marvelled at how true that review was.

Little Peter was Peter's closest and only friend—in psychological parlance, his "transitional attachment object." A child's attachment to his mother is a complicated yet crucial psychological business. In normal childhood development, at first the child's whole world is the mother. Then, sometime between the infant and toddler stages, the child realizes that he's separate from his mother and experiences separation anxiety, crying when she isn't in sight. Often, to avoid the anxiety, he adopts an object that represents the security of the mother-child attachment. This becomes the transitional attachment object. It's usually a blanket or a plush toy, and the toddler takes it everywhere, especially to bed. The transitional object helps the child bridge the gap between dependence and independence.

Peter had a disturbed attachment with his mother. She never expressed any affection for him. She'd left him alone from an early age, and if he was rambunctious, joyful, loud, or even talked publicly in the restaurant, he was punished. Only Little Peter allowed him any expression. He channelled everything through him, and as time went on, Peter and Little Peter became firmly attached.

Since Peter had said nothing about his father, I asked how he fit into the picture. "My dad had nothing to do with me or anyone in the family. He wasn't a bad man; he never said unkind things to me or hit me. His job was to cook in the restaurant. He always listened to American jazz music on his radio. In the summer, when the kitchen windows were open, the music would drift up to my attic and I'd try to replicate it on Little Peter. I really enjoyed those summer concerts."

When I asked what had happened to cause such a rift in his parents' marriage, he said, "My mother saved all her money from her three jobs and never spent an unnecessary cent. All our clothes, including my parents', came from cousins in Toronto. She walked through town with heavy bags; she had no car. She never took a bus. My father went to Toronto once a month for supplies. To this day I'm not sure exactly what happened, but on one of his trips he invested in some worthless scheme and lost all their money to a bogus Saigon importing outfit. My mother had saved $31,000, and now it was gone."

In my notes, I remarked on how $31,000 was an amazing amount of money to have saved in the 1950s, especially since his mother didn't speak English and the average house price in

Canada was just over $7,000. I pushed Peter to find out more about what his father had been involved in, but he was too young to remember. He didn't know whether his father had an opium or gambling problem or had just made a bad investment. It was never clear. His already brittle mother was apoplectic; every day she expressed how much she wished her husband dead.

The restaurant had to be sold to pay their debts and the family had to start over. Peter, now age five, was taken out of isolation when they moved to Toronto. His mother worked in a factory and took home piecework, toiling until midnight. She again began some sort of food import business that Peter never understood. After they left the restaurant, his father never worked again. They lived in the poorest area of Chinatown with hostile cousins who didn't want to take them in but felt obligated.

After less than a month in Toronto, Peter started kindergarten. At this point in his narrative he looked pained, more pained than he did when he spoke of his isolation. He whispered, "I failed kindergarten. It is my worst shame. My mother said I was stupid and a humiliation to her in the Chinese community."

It took several sessions to find out what had happened in kindergarten, but it seems that Peter was terrified. He had rarely been around children, except for his sister and cousins for a few weeks before school started. Plus, he could speak neither English nor Chinese. For the first years of his life, he hadn't heard more than a few sentences a day in any language. Neither he nor his sister ever learned to speak Chinese, which was an embarrassment to them, especially at Chinese weddings and formal events.

When I checked with linguistic experts, they said that either the children were so ill-treated that they blocked the language, or they were spoken to so infrequently that they didn't pick it up at the crucial age for language acquisition. (Their father had become an elective mute after he lost the family money.) Neither child grew up to have Chinese friends or spouses; Peter felt mildly anxious when he heard Chinese spoken. He said, "When a woman speaks Chinese I get goosebumps, even today. If she yells, it scares me to death."

So Peter started kindergarten without the ability to communicate verbally. When children spoke to him in Chinese he didn't understand them, nor did he understand English. And when they played games, he was afraid to hold hands in a circle. "Once I had to go to the bathroom, and I was used to the tomato can and getting beaten no matter what I did. So I wet my pants because I didn't know what to do."

Eye contact also frightened him. He likened it to feeling naked in public. He experienced it as too much intimacy and felt like fleeing when anyone looked directly at him. He'd also never learned what was normal in terms of sharing space with others: having always been alone, he thought everyone stood too close to him. When he became overwhelmed, he would hide under the large upright black piano in his classroom and hold on to its wooden slats for comfort. In fact, for Peter, that piano was one of the few positive things about school. He thought of it as a father to Little Peter and longed to hold it, pat it, and cuddle with it. (This was yet a larger attachment object.)

Sadly, before Peter heard the traumatizing news that he'd failed kindergarten, he honestly believed he'd been a success. Besides the piano, the other positive influence was a kind teacher. He was amazed by how gentle she was. At first he was frightened of her and cowered in her presence. But she smiled at him—something he hadn't seen before—and he intuitively realized that it was meant as a sign of acceptance. She also recognized his love for the piano, and when she played "Three Blind Mice," she let him stand next to her. He put his hand on the side of the piano and felt it vibrate and breathe; he held it there as a child would hold his mother's hand. Peter saw the large white keys as teeth, the whole piano grinning broadly and welcoming him. It was the most transcendent moment he'd ever experienced. Hearing the notes that turned into a song brought tears to his eyes. He believed the piano was talking to him. It was the first thing he understood in what had been, for him, the cacophony of kindergarten.

When Peter found out that he'd failed, he was devastated. He'd thought the teacher liked him, and now he thought she hated him. His mother told him that everyone else had passed, and that now he'd have to go to school as a big boy with babies. Peter believed he'd failed in the world, just as his father had. "It was so humiliating to find out I just couldn't cut it."

I tried to explain that success at kindergarten is the accumulation of many learned behaviours, ones that can't be acquired in isolation in an attic. Peter had missed so many steps that there was no way he could have been ready for kindergarten. The teacher recognized that, and held him back. I went on to describe how one develops independence in the world through stages. If those stages are disrupted, as Peter's had been, then development is delayed.

First, a mother's love is essential before someone can venture into the world in a healthy way. Peter always protested when I said this, insisting that his mother *did* love the family. All the work she did was for the family. I explained that she was unable to be loving to him *directly*, and that he couldn't feel her love when he was isolated all day long.

The mother must hold her baby and feel attached to it, and vice versa. Around the age of two, children realize that they're separate from their mothers. In order to try out their muscles as individuals, they begin to disagree with those around them by saying no (hence the "terrible twos"). Toddlers who successfully detach from their mothers are able to say, in effect, "No, I will not eat what you want, put my boots on, or do what you say. I am a separate person." This stage helps children learn the concept of "mine," but it's also part of learning to assert themselves. Yet Peter had had no chance to establish a separate self from his mother. In fact, he said that it would never occur to him now, let alone when he was a child, to request something of her—to differentiate himself in any way.

Peter had also been terrified of other children, having no idea how to play with them. The rules for baseball or any game seemed too complex and arcane to learn. Again I explained that he hadn't been stupid; most children have had four years of group behaviour before they get to kindergarten. Other parents would roll a ball to their kids and then let them hit it, or they'd take them to the park to see other children play. Watching kids having fun on a slide teaches a two- or three-year-old about taking a turn, and the first time the child goes down the slide himself, a parent is there. But Peter had had no idea what "taking a turn" meant. He thought he was supposed to spin in a circle while standing in place. He was unable to play monkey in the middle—too chaotic.

I explained that brains are built piece by piece; they're not wholly formed at birth. In the first four years, a child is supposed to build what's called "executive function." The prefrontal cortex has to set up pathways in the brain in order to establish connections that link all learning together. For example, executive function helps to develop selective attention: learning to ignore sounds that aren't pertinent and to prioritize multiple demands. It's a complex world, and we learn it one tiny step at a time.

After he repeated kindergarten, Peter was much improved. He had another teacher who he felt was incredibly kind to him.

When I asked what he meant by "incredibly kind," he said, "She didn't yell at me or hit me with a bamboo whip." That teacher was young and would often play songs on the piano, including "The Wheels on the Bus," which he loved. He thought he and Big Peter were experiencing a good time together.

That piano brought about a life-changing event for young Peter. His sister usually picked him up at school, but one day she didn't show up. Unbeknownst to him and the teacher, she was getting patched up at the nurse's office after a fall in the playground. The teacher went to investigate and left Peter alone in the classroom with the piano.

He went over and hugged Big Peter. As he embraced it, one of the keys was depressed and sounded a note. Peter began to play. He said that at first he played "The Wheels on the Bus" in the cheery way the teacher did, but then he played in a sad way, as though the bus was tired on its route and had gotten lost. He was uncertain what *happy* or *sad* meant, but could reproduce it through the piano. Peter had no idea how he was able to play the tune other than that he'd watched the teacher carefully. Next he played "Three Blind Mice," improvising the mice running as a sort of jazz riff. His feet were too short to reach the pedals, and he had to slide across the piano bench to reach some notes and then scoot back. He was unaware of how much time had elapsed, but when he looked up several teachers were standing near the door watching him, along with his sister, the school nurse, the principal, and the janitor. The janitor started to clap and all the others joined in.

Peter's life as a performer was born. It was one of the happiest moments he'd ever experienced, and as he walked home he felt like a different person. His friend Big Peter had spoken for him and, miraculously, he'd been understood. He remembered that it was a fall day, and that all the leaves were waving at him. The colors seemed supersaturated: he realized that until that moment he'd been seeing the world in black and white, and with literal tunnel vision. He hadn't taken in the periphery. Even his depth perception improved, he said, and he was no longer as clumsy. It was the first time he'd successfully communicated emotion in his entire life, and it felt glorious.

2

AN ACT OF LOVE

ALMOST FOUR YEARS had passed since the Chang family left the small town of Port Hope for Toronto. Although Peter, now nine, was no longer locked away, his home life remained an ordeal. They'd left their cousins' house and were living in a dingy one-bedroom apartment on Queen Street, in the West End. He and his sister would watch television in their tiny home after school until their mother came home. Peter was improving his English through school, TV, and his sister's conversation. He took his toy piano everywhere, replicating every song he heard. He said, "Little Peter had only eight keys, so I was proud when I played the theme song from *Gilligan's Island* and my sister recognized it and clapped."

By this time Peter's father, who'd thus far figured only slightly in my patient's account, had become an overweight diabetic who was cavalier about his insulin and ate sugar at his wife's sugges-tion. Since they'd left the restaurant in Port Hope, the father's neglected diabetes, excessive weight, and crippling depression had rendered him unemployable. He simply sat in a chair all day and listened to jazz records. Once in a while, when there was a particularly good riff, he would vaguely point to the record—and Peter understood that his father, who'd ceased making eye contact almost immediately after he lost the family money, was trying to share his music with him. Peter had heard from his older cousins that his father had been very musical as a child and could sight-read, but was discouraged from pursuing it as a career because it was thought to be frivolous and part of the corrupt West.

Peter's mother never missed an opportunity to humiliate the father who had "ruined the family's future." She wouldn't give him any money, not even for his beloved records or cigarettes. Peter later learned that his father was from a musical family that was, as his wife said, corrupted by Western music and suspected of involvement with opium in Vietnam. His wife regarded all Western music as part of the dissipated failure the father had become.

One day she came home from work unexpectedly when Peter's sister was busy doing beading piecework while Peter and his father, who hadn't been assigned tasks, sat listening to jazz. The mother was furious. "It was understandable how angry she was at us," Peter said. "After all, she was out working and we were lying around. She said my dad and I were peas in a pod, that we'd both been corrupted by Western thought and music and were no better than the decadent French and other European trash." (During his mother's childhood, Vietnam was a French colony.) His mother worked herself into a frenzy, her voice taking on a familiar dangerous pitch that terrified Peter. "She tore into the living room and broke my father's records one by one over her knee. I stood, frozen, hoping she wouldn't turn on me, but she did," he recalled. "The second she finished smashing the record collection, she looked my way, then tore into my bedroom, grabbed Little Peter, and pitched him out the window." She threw him with such force that the window screen went with it.

Peter was nine and ostensibly being punished for not doing fine beadwork. In reality, he was punished for being like his father. I asked him if he'd been devastated by the loss of Little Peter. He said he was inured to loss, that he experienced only an absence of feeling. "It's hard to explain. I looked out the window and felt sorry for Little Peter, like he was Humpty Dumpty. I didn't feel sad myself—just empty." He hesitated, searching for the words. "It was sort of like I wasn't in my own body."

I pointed out that, of the millions of memories from twenty-five years ago, it was Little Peter's death that he remembered. I said I believed it was because it had been so traumatic. "You were suffering depersonalization, which is when you feel divorced from your own personal self. You don't feel your own bodily sensations or emotions. The world seems hazy, and your connection with yourself breaks down."

"I have that a lot. What causes it?"

"A traumatic childhood, usually in the early stages of differentiation of self, combined with high anxiety levels."

Peter said that he thought he remembered the incident so clearly because of what happened a few days later. It was the summer and there was no school, so his sister was doing her beadwork from dawn to well into the night. Peter's father motioned to Peter to follow him. By now, although only in his late thirties, he struggled to walk, hobbling with a cane. He and Peter made their way slowly to the mall. The father was exhausted; his ankles were swollen and he was sweating profusely. But when they arrived he went to a store's music department, picked up a synthesizer, and walked out into the mall's common area. A security guard stopped them and called the police. The police realized that something was amiss with the father, who said nothing when questioned. They drove Peter and his father home with the synthesizer after Peter assured the police that they had the money at home to pay for it. "Now when I look back on it, I guess the policemen knew we weren't thieves, but that there was something mentally wrong with both of us. They kindly just drove us home in silence as I clutched the synthesizer." Fortunately, Peter's mother wasn't home at the time; his sister went into her savings and paid for the synthesizer. The police looked askance at the huge amount of beadwork piled around the room, as though it were a factory. They asked why the sister was alone, engaged in child labour. Peter heard them saying to each other that it might be just a "Chinese custom." They seemed confused, and didn't press charges. Then the mother arrived; the police explained the situation just before they left.

That's when she went completely crazy. She was a frightening woman at the best of times, Peter told me, but he'd never seen her so terrifying. She tore at the father savagely and started hitting him until he was on the floor. She was screaming in Chinese, so Peter had no idea what she was saying. The father stood up, teetered, then slumped down against a wall, breathed heavily for a few minutes, then had a heart attack and died. Peter told me he'd always felt responsible for his death because if he hadn't bought the synthesizer for him, he would still be alive.

Peter had very few childhood memories, but his father's theft of the synthesizer was one of them. He carefully explained that he'd felt humiliated because it was unacceptable to steal; no one he'd ever met had stolen anything. Still, in another way, he saw it as the only act of love he'd ever received in his short life. His father had no money but sensed he was dying and wanted his son to have a piano to replace the one that was thrown out. So he simply limped into a store and took a synthesizer. He didn't even bother to hide it. Peter recognized it as a desperate act of love from a dying man.

He also acknowledged that his father's death had been a slow suicide. I asked how his mother had responded: "She may have longed for it, but perhaps she felt differently when it happened?"

Peter expelled a deep breath. "No way. She was not that type. She wanted him dead and was relieved when he died, saying she had one less burden. After his death she never referred to him again, other than to tell me I was as lazy and stupid as my father."

"Were you like your father?"

Peter said yes. They both had musical talents; they could sight-read and play by ear. Plus they were both quiet, loved music, and didn't care much about making money or competing. Peter would play his synthesizer only in his room for fear that once his mother realized it was important to him, she would destroy it.

Within a few years of his father's death, Peter's mother bought a small building with four apartments in it and, four years later, another fourplex. Eventually she owned a row of such buildings. She did her own maintenance, repair, and rent collection, and fought the city single-handedly on rent control. When Peter was in his twenties she gave him an apartment in one of the buildings not far from her own. She still made dinner for him every night, running home to prepare the food and then running to her next job. Meanwhile, as soon as his sister could get out of the house, she married a non-Chinese man and became a stay-at-home mom, which Peter's mother called the "lazy Canadian way."

Peter believed his mother saw him as her burden; she called him a "good-for-nothing" and constantly urged him to get a real job. He was in fact becoming well known in the music world, although he neglected his financial interests and didn't make much money touring in the band.

Clearly, Peter's mother had defined him as a bad, lazy, slow child from the time he was a baby well through adulthood. No evidence to the contrary convinced her otherwise. Whether that was caused by her hatred of her husband and Peter's similarity to him, her belief that Western music was evil, or her dislike of men in general, I'll never know. The only thing I do know is that when your mother labels you negatively, you believe her—for who else forms your self-image? And yet as time went on and more fascinating evidence surfaced about the mother's life, the more comprehensible her behaviour became. As Freudians say, "There are no mysteries in Vienna."

We were just finishing our first year of therapy. Over that time Peter's voice had become more modulated, and in the last few months he'd begun to make eye contact. Since Peter had been so emotionally deprived, it had taken a full year for him to trust me. He had to learn that I cared about him, and that together we would work toward a cure.

I was, however, concerned about Peter's prognosis. He'd missed so many developmental steps that I worried about how we'd build an ego. With so little raw material, what would we build upon? It was a bit precarious to construct a self on such a shaky foundation. I felt the same trepidation an architect would feel raising a house on wobbly stilts.

One thing that gave me hope was Peter's great kindness. If someone didn't have money, he'd lend it to him. Once, when a woman was crying in my waiting room, he didn't ask her what was wrong but just went out and bought her a coffee, telling her that things would work out. And his loyalty to his mother, however misplaced, was touching. Kindness and forgiveness can take people a long way.

Yet Peter had episodes of depersonalization and severe anxiety whenever he encountered anger or someone became too physically close. I suspected that these episodes were also the source of his impotence. He was so anxious that he was having out-of-body experiences, and it's hard to be sexually successful when you're not in your body to feel arousal.

The treatment goal was to build his ego so that he could cope and not emotionally leave his body in times of stress. The ego—one's sense of self—is an abstract concept; it's hard to define it concretely. Picture it as a house built brick by brick. It protects you from the stresses of the outside world, providing a metaphorical home to shelter in—a safe place. If Peter's mother had been a healthier woman, she would have told him he was sensitive, kind, intuitive, bright, and musically gifted. Praising those positive attributes would have helped Peter form a stronger foundation. When the wolf came knocking at his door, Peter, like the pig in the children's story, would have been protected in his solid brick house.

Instead, for decades his mother had told him he was lazy, stupid, and unable to cope in life. There were no solid bricks in his foundation; he lived in a house of straw. When Peter was about to engage with others or to have sex, he didn't feel protected in his straw house. His ego wasn't strong enough. He had to leave his body and become depersonalized.

I hoped to accomplish two things in the therapy: first, I wanted Peter to realize that his mother was disturbed and had viewed him through her own skewed perspective; second, I wanted to function as "the good mother" who would help him move out of the straw house and into the brick one. It was my job to help him see his positive attributes so that he could be safe from the wolf. I wanted him to be able to say to the wolf, "I am Peter Chang and this is my safe house, and I don't have to leave it—you do."

As we headed into year two, it was time to focus on Peter's impotence problem, his inability to get an erection when attempting to have sex with a woman. Since he was in a band he had ample opportunity to meet women; in fact, they would frequently come on to him. Peter said this had nothing to do with being attractive;

it was just "what happened to guys in a band." I pointed out that as occupational hazards went, it beat coal lung.

He longed to have sex, but being physically close to women made him deeply uncomfortable. We discussed developing a relationship slowly and establishing a friendship. Then he could move on at a rate he could handle.

I told Peter that in order to address his impotence problem, we needed to look at his entire psychological profile since birth. His maternal deprivation had caused what John Bowlby, a famous British psychiatrist, called an "attachment disorder." Maternal attachment is more important than anything else to a baby—even more important than food. A baby will give up anything to have it. Without it, the child is anxious and unable to explore or deal with the world in any normal way. And attachment disorder doesn't just affect the relationship with the mother; it affects all social, emotional, and cognitive development. If the child doesn't experience attachment, that child can't move forward to step two—trusting and emotionally attaching to others and, eventually, sexually attaching to others. In other words, you can't grow emotionally if you didn't have infant attachment.

Konrad Lorenz, a zoologist, pointed out—and this is part of what won him a Nobel Prize—that attachment can be understood within an evolutionary context in that the mother provides safety for the infant. Attachment is adaptive, enhancing the infant's chance of survival, and is therefore hard-wired into the brain. A baby needs to be held, loved, and cuddled by the mother.

But Peter had trouble connecting his disturbed behaviour in kindergarten, much less his impotence, to his early maternal deprivation. Sometimes a therapist hits a brick wall, and has to shake things up by doing something extreme or unorthodox to get the patient to see a pattern. And so, to help Peter better understand the idea of maternal attachment, I arranged a special screening of the 1950s Harlow monkey films, probably the most famous movies to ever come out of a social psychologist's laboratory. It would be a private screening at the University of Toronto (where I had occasionally taught), and the film projectionist had agreed to pause it whenever I wanted to point something out to Peter. Although these experiments would be considered unethical by today's standards, they offer a unique window into attachment disorder. The films used to be only for psychology students, but now they are available on YouTube for anyone to view.

The Harlow movies became a pivotal point in Peter's therapy. The first began with Professor Harlow explaining the concept of maternal bonding, which he called "love," whereby infants bond with their mother. The experiments involved rearing newborn monkeys in cages with two pretend mothers. "Wire mother" held a bottle of milk; the infant monkey had to jump on that mother to get it. The "cloth mother" was a wire figure as well, except it was covered with a towel; rather than food, it provided a tactile sense, and the monkey could hug and cuddle with it. Harlow and others were shocked to find that cuddling trumped food. The baby monkeys hugged the cloth mother for up to nineteen hours a day; they went to the wire mother only for the few minutes it took to drink the milk. When the cloth mother was taken away, the infant monkey cried and screamed in terror with separation anxiety. When both cloth and wire mothers were removed, the baby monkey rocked back and forth, injuring itself.

Peter, whose voice was still somewhat monotone, began talking excitedly. He recognized himself in that monkey rocking back and forth and biting himself; alone in his crib, he used to bang his head repeatedly against it. But his tiny piano had saved him. He said, "Little Peter was the cloth mother who sang, soothed, and hugged me with her music." He could actually remember or imagine his piano playing comforting sounds to soothe his inner desolation. He said he didn't fully connect that he himself was playing it and making the sound. He saw the piano as an animate object, a living being who comforted him.

When the film resumed, we watched as the infant monkey was taken out of its cage for the first time and locked in another room, away from the cloth mother. The room had many items that monkeys typically enjoy, such as ladders and swings. But the monkey was terrified of it all and retreated to a corner, where it trembled in distress. As soon as the cloth mother was reintroduced into the room, the monkey climbed on it and hugged it. Once it had a few moments of comfort from the cloth mother, the little monkey was then open to exploring its environment.

Peter asked for the film to be paused again. "Oh my God," he said, "there it is: kindergarten. Everyone else had a cloth mother and I had nothing. I was terrified in the corner. I feel *so sorry* for that little monkey. I now remember wondering why the other kids weren't freaked out like I was. They were running around and chasing each other in this big cloth caterpillar tunnel that scared me to death."

The film next depicted a monster figure that looked like a gigantic metal bug with huge teeth and a swivelling head. The monkey, clearly fearful, ran and hugged the cloth mother. When the monkey had enough cuddling and was assured of her attachment, it turned around and began to make threatening noises at the big monster.

Peter indicated that he wanted the film paused once more. "I got bullied, and I had nowhere to go for comfort," he told me. "I just hid, and then it became a cycle of me being more bullied."

We watched several more Harlow films. They revealed that those maternally deprived monkeys grew up to be unable to defend themselves. Most striking was the fact that they didn't want to have sex. And when they were forced to copulate and give birth, they had no idea how to behave like a parent. Both males and females became cruel; they were physically abusive and emotionally withdrawn, and their offspring often had to be removed from the cage for their own safety.

The last film came to an end, the lights were turned on, and Peter just sat there. I gazed at his ashen face. He looked at me in astonishment and said, "*They don't want to have sex. Oh my God!*"

The penny had dropped. "That's right. Sex is the endgame," I said. "First you need love, then cuddling, then proximity, then protection, so you can venture out into the world and take chances. When people are isolated in childhood, they miss all those steps, and as adults, sex looks terrifying."

Peter asked, "Did you see how frightened the baby monkey who only had the wire mother was when she was supposed to mate with a normal monkey? *That's how I feel.*" I saw that he had large sweat stains under his arms and that his blink rate had slowed. He was too upset and disoriented to leave the media room. He'd had a terrifying trip through his early childhood.

Peter had believed his mother's description of him as useless, inadequate, and stupid. My attempts to reframe that image hadn't budged Peter from his mother's view of him. It was only the Harlow films that made him understand that he'd missed crucial steps in his development. Peter later told me that nothing had had a more powerful effect on him than the Harlow monkey studies. The therapy had clicked in, and from then on we called it "pre- and post-Harlow."

Peter began to realize that he wasn't stupid, or a failure, but rather someone who wasn't prepared for life. What confused him, though, was why "other Chinese children whose parents worked didn't suffer the same fate." I had to tread lightly. Peter had always been loyal to his mother; he'd never said one bad word about her. His constant refrain was, "She did all this for us as a family."

Yet I regarded her as someone whose maternal instinct was seriously compromised. But as a therapist, I knew it wouldn't be helpful to say that to Peter. He'd need to come to that realization himself, and at a time when he could accept it. If you point out a "truth," for want of a better word, to patients before they're able to hear or admit it, they lose trust in the therapist; their defences take over, and they improve only superficially. Overinterpreting to the client is the sign of a new or insecure therapist. A therapist can lead patients to the door of understanding, but they shouldn't drag them in. Their patients will enter when they're ready.

Therapy was a slow trip, however meandering, from depersonalization to personalization. Peter hadn't been treated as a person, and so, eventually, he didn't experience himself as one. He looked at himself from outside his body. The therapy guided him on the long journey toward feeling personalized, toward feeling human.

3

A BURNING QUESTION

PETER'S BAND WAS ON a tour of the southern United States when he met a woman who was a server at an Arkansas bar. He was playing there for a week. She brought him drinks and requested the song "Georgia," drawling, "Show me how much you miss Georgia, 'cause that's where I'm from." When Peter played the song the whole room went quiet. Afterward he spoke into the microphone, saying, "That was for Melanie, who misses her Georgia home." The band members turned to look at him, shocked: he'd just spoken on stage for the first time in the now sixteen years they'd been together. Peter said he could see how happy they were for him—although they knew nothing about his therapy, they knew it was some kind of breakthrough.

Melanie was waiting for him after the show, and they had a drink. Peter told me that he tried not to think of sex and just live in the moment. She asked where he was staying, and when he named the hotel, she nodded meaningfully and looked at him. He said he thought of our therapy, and how he might shape things so that he could take it gradually. He told her he was tired after two sets, but asked her to lunch the following day. She accepted.

He told himself that he didn't have to worry about having sex; instead he could develop a friendship first. At lunch, Melanie told Peter that her father collected old blues records, so they talked about music, a relaxing topic for him. They went on to have several dates, but no sex. He never did take her to his hotel room.

When Peter got back to Toronto he wrote to her frequently; he was able to become slightly more effusive and even a bit amorous in his letters. He decided to fly down for a weekend to see her. As the time approached, we rehearsed what he would say. I told him he didn't have to discuss his sexual problem. All he needed to do was be kind and loving; I assured him that this would be easy, since gentleness came naturally to him.

"I think there's a normal, loving, kind person in there who would be a wonderful, sensitive lover," I told him. "You've just had way too much childhood isolation and trauma. Yet you still want to try and connect. Your music is full of emotion, sensuality, and expression—so you have those qualities within you. Remember, you're bruised but not broken."

We discussed what cuddling was, and how to do it without seeming artificial. His sister had a child and hugged him often, or what seemed often to Peter. He'd watched it carefully in order to replicate it. None of it came naturally to him.

He took Melanie out to dinner, and then she said she wanted to go back to his hotel room because she lived with three other girls. They got into bed, but unfortunately, Peter's feelings of depersonalization arose again. He saw himself lying on the bed as if through a camera lens whose aperture was getting smaller and smaller; he didn't feel as though he was in his own body. Finally, they both went to sleep.

The following day they went out. Melanie had to work at the bar that night, from eight until two, and he agreed to meet her there. But when her shift ended, she walked over to the drummer and left with him. The bartender, who knew Peter had been waiting for her, said, "Sorry, but Chinamen don't go over so good down here." Peter knew the bartender had said it to be consoling, and had no idea how insulting it was.

I felt sad for Peter, but I told him to think of it as a test drive. Sex was the tip of the iceberg. Ninety percent of the iceberg is below the water, in the unconscious, and we needed to focus on that.

I tried to get Peter to access his dreams, for they were our best route into his unconscious. I told him to leave a pencil and paper by his bed so that in the morning he could write down his first thoughts. His dreams, it turned out, were relentlessly similar. There was always an event transpiring that was out of his control.

"I was spread-eagled on the roof of a bus and it was careening along the road at breakneck speed and I was trying to find something to hold on to but there were no handles. I was flung from side to side as the bus swung from lane to lane. I tried to scream at the driver, but I had no voice. Finally, I inched to the front of the bus where the roof met the front window. I leaned down and peered through the windshield and saw that there was no driver."

Whenever Peter had this dream, he woke up in terror. We talked about in what ways his life, like the bus, was out of control. When he said he couldn't have a relationship, I pointed out that that wasn't true. He couldn't yet have *sex*. He had a relationship with me, his sister, and with his band members, who appeared to like and respect him. The band members communicated through their music, and Peter had no trouble doing that. In fact, his music was intimate and reached many fans. The one time he didn't experience depersonalization was when he was playing his piano, no matter the size of the crowd.

But Peter countered that he had no real feelings in relation to other people, so how could he have a real relationship? When Melanie had walked off with another man at the bar, he didn't feel sad. It was just what happened. When he was featured in a cover story in a big music magazine, it didn't make him happy. When he showed it to his mother, she said that only opium users and stupid North Americans read music magazines.

In the latter half of our third year of therapy, something happened to shake up Peter and his sister. This incident turned out to be another turning point in the therapy.

Peter's sister had been a quiet child, who sat in a booth at the restaurant and drew with crayons. She was the silent, obedient robot her mother demanded. However, she was far less scarred than Peter: she'd never been locked away and was able to interact with and receive affection from the customers. As an adult she was still quiet and deferential, yet she'd never allow her mother to mistreat her child: she'd risen to those occasions like a mother bear. Peter often visited his three-year-old niece and enjoyed making a connection with her. He was learning normal behaviour by observing his sister's loving interaction with the little girl.

One day Peter's niece pulled a pot of chili off the stove; she burned herself severely and had to be hospitalized. The niece's injuries were traumatic to all. Peter said that he, his mother, and his sister went to the hospital together to visit her on the burn ward. He was horrified at the sight of children writhing in pain.

Then his mother began to behave bizarrely. "As we were walking down the hall, my mother started laughing and saying, 'Look at her! Look at her!' She was pointing to a badly burned child and was cracking up. A nurse looked at her and said, 'Either act like a human being or get out.'" Peter was shocked by how the nurse had spoken to her. "Suddenly everything you said about my mother came flooding into my mind. Believe it or not, she continued to laugh and the nurse said she would call security if she didn't stop. Now other nurses were gathering. My sister just looked on silently. I felt so sorry for this horribly scarred little girl. I blew up at my mother and said, 'What is wrong with you? These are suffering children. Shut up now or get a bus home.' She shut up, and my sister put her hand on my back, sort of for support."

For the first time, Peter was consciously angry at his mother. (I can't imagine how unconsciously angry he must have been.) I pointed out that although Peter couldn't feel anger over what she'd done to him, he now had some available feelings of anger for how she treated the burn victims.

Then, mystified as to why his mother would behave so strangely, I asked Peter about her childhood. He implied that her past was a complete mystery to him. She had no parents or siblings that he knew of. They had cousins in Toronto on his father's side, but she had alienated them all—using them when she needed a place to stay after her husband lost the family money and yet, now that she was wealthy and owned several small apartment buildings, refusing to lend them money to start a business.

Peter said that seeing his mother act so unfeelingly toward those wounded children had unleashed a fury about what she'd done to him. He refused to go to her house for dinner anymore.

His mother seemed confused by Peter's withdrawal and dropped off dinners outside his door. As the days went by she became frantic in her protestations, yelling on the phone that he had to come to dinner. Finally, he agreed to visit her. At my suggestion, he attempted to explore her horrifying display at the burn ward. When Peter brought it up, she started laughing the same sort of maniacal laugh. Furious at her callousness, Peter began unleashing about how painful his childhood had been. His mother shook her head again, laughing, saying he had no idea what a painful childhood was, and adding that she'd protected him from all bad people.

Peter asked about her past. She glossed over it, saying only that what was important was providing for oneself so as never to be dependent on a husband. She also said she would never be "number two wife."

It took several weeks for the mother's story to emerge. Peter's maternal grandmother had been the "second wife" of a Chinese businessman in Vietnam. (The family was Hoa Chinese but had lived in Vietnam for several generations.) A second wife in that instance was something between a mistress and a concubine. A wealthy man would support a woman financially in exchange for sexual interludes; children were not part of the bargain. Peter's grandmother was beautiful, and had been a feather in the rich grandfather's cap. But when he lost his money, he began to treat her badly. His societal status had fallen and he could no longer be associated with anyone who besmirched his reputation. He refused to give his second wife any financial support or to allow the unplanned child (Peter's mother) any legal rights. Peter didn't know what his mother meant by "rights," and with the language barrier, he couldn't sort it out. His grandmother wasn't allowed to work, nor could she get a business licence or proper papers since a second wife wasn't considered legitimate. Eventually, she opened an illegal opium den for foreign "degenerates." It was also a place for "men who liked hot opium"—a quote from his mother, Peter said, and he wasn't sure what it meant. He gathered it was a sort of brothel and opium den where patrons burned people as a sadistic perversion. Peter's grandmother procured the opium, and the girls in her brothel, or den, including Peter's mother, were burned with French cigarettes.

"Peter!" I said, totally shocked. I asked if the clients were French. He assumed they were, since this was in Saigon in the twenties and thirties, when Vietnam was still a colony of France. The ethnic Chinese, who were the largest minority in the country, ran many of the businesses. It was Peter's mother's job to make men happy—to be burned and to do "bad things," whatever that meant. She described it in English as "crooked sex" and "hot opium burning." When she'd seen the burn victims in the hospital in Toronto, it reminded her of her home. Peter asked if his grandmother herself was burned, and his mother replied matter-of-factly, "Not so much. Young girls bring more money." He wanted to know how young his mother and the other young girls had been at the time. She avoided him with "I don't understand your English." (Something she often said if she wanted to obfuscate.)

His mother eventually met her husband at the opium den. He and his brother played in a backroom jazz band down the street and occasionally came in to smoke. When he offered to marry her and take her to Canada, she jumped at the chance. She told Peter that all she ever cared about was making money so she wouldn't be a "number two wife": they had no power or rights and had to run a "crooked business." Finally, Peter asked her an important question: "Did your mother ever lock you away?" Her response was very revealing.

"No, you lucky I lock you away," she said. "I always sang for my supper."

I just shook my head slowly, staring at Peter.

"I know, I know," he said. "I always said she did what she could." Then he added an afterthought, "I think part of the reason she hated my father and cousins is that they knew what she'd been."

"Did she ever have anything to do with men after your father died?"

"Never. She wears hand-me-downs, even to weddings. She cuts her own hair. If anyone pays any attention to her, she says all they want is her money. Her money is what she loves."

"Money is what protects her from being burned," I explained.

"She had a mother who offered up her only child for sadistic pleasure. When your grandmother saw the burns, she laughed along with her clients—just like your mother laughed at the hospital."

Peter's poor mother had no idea how to be a parent, as she'd never had a loving parent herself. After a long silence I said, "I feel sorry for your mother as well. She was deprived of one of the most satisfying feelings in human nature—maternal instinct and enjoying motherhood." Maternal instinct is *not* natural without certain prerequisites. It needs to get triggered by the mother remembering her own attachment and by seeing it role-modelled for her in her family or somewhere in society.

Peter was silent for a long time. Finally I said, "I keep thinking of your mother laughing at the burn victims. She *herself* was a burn victim. The customers must have laughed at her, and she was simply role-modelling them. After all, customers were paying for the so-called privilege of burning people. She had no idea how to attach to you since she wasn't attached to her mother. She had a mother who emotionally abandoned her when she was a baby. In fact her mother offered her up to sadistic men for money. It's no wonder that your mother feels she protected you by always providing for you and locking you away from harm."

"She provided for her mother as well," he said.

"She's been providing for others for her whole life."

"She really had a thing about men. She was all right with my sister."

"Was she? She demanded she be silent and not move."

"The one thing she knew how to do was to provide. It's no wonder that when my father lost the money, she hated him. There was nothing worse." Peter sighed and then added, "Why does she yell at me all the time and tell me I'm a failure?"

"Why do you think?"

"I think she's expressing her fears. The music thing terrifies her. She thinks opium and maybe burning is next."

I nodded in agreement. It was ironic that all this interpretation came from a boy who failed kindergarten.

For years Peter had thought his mother must be right about his inadequacies: why else would she have treated him this way? Now he saw that maybe her behaviour had nothing to do with him and everything to do with her tragic childhood.

He tried to have another conversation with his mother about her early life, but she was never willing to discuss it again. She called it "the dead past." When Peter asked how his grandmother had felt when she left for Canada with his father, she said, "My mother didn't care. She just cared about her next pipe." Peter realized only then that his mother's mother had been an addict.

Now that Peter had gained deeper insight into his mother's problems and was reframing his own view of himself, it was time to introduce a new way to interact with her. I'd given him a book entitled *Toxic Parents* by Susan Forward. It must have struck a chord: Peter told me that when his mother had pointed to a mailman and said, "There is stupid man. Job you need," he felt like he was going to scream. Then, for the first time, he said, "I can't take her failure riff anymore."

This was all good news to me, for he was acting as a normal son would act if his mother continually called him a failure.

I wondered aloud, "How can you get her to stop? She doesn't mind arguing. It's her only way to emotionally connect. She doesn't know how to express worries or concerns or affection. She's never seen it."

"She's really alarmed when my sister holds her new baby daughter so much. She says bizarre things to her like 'She won't learn to

walk if you hold her' or 'She'll cry all the time if you pick her up.'
My sister never fights with her—except if she does anything mean
to her daughters. Then she goes ballistic. My mother has learned
to be hands-off. Now she just shakes her head when my sister hugs
her baby." I pointed out that his mother could learn to change her
behaviour toward him. After all, it worked for his sister.

And yet Peter held the fatalistic view that he could never
change his mother. What he could change, though, was how he
interacted with her. I suggested he tell his mother that he loved
her and appreciated all she'd done for him, but that he would no
longer tolerate being spoken to disrespectfully. He would have to
explain to her what rude meant *to him*. If she was demeaning,
such as saying he was a degenerate musician like his father, he
would walk out and not see her for two weeks. This was hard to
do, since they lived very close to each other. Peter had a kind
nature and didn't like hurting her, but I assured him that over
time she'd get the message about what she could and couldn't say.
As evidence, I reminded him that she'd learned not to interfere
with his sister's parenting style. And although she'd arrived in
Canada without speaking the language and without an educa-
tion, his mother owned more real estate than most Canadians
did. She could get the lay of the land.

Peter was reluctant to try this program; he didn't believe it
would work. He said that if he had to empty all the sand along
the Atlantic Ocean pail by pail, he could do it simply through
perseverance. But when it came to his relationship with his
mother, it felt as though he saw the ocean and the sand but he
had no pail. I could see he was feeling tired and discouraged. I
told him that I was there for him: I would offer him the pail and
together we would dig. He agreed to try.

———

One of the positive steps Peter took was to share his professional success with his sister. When I saw a new article on him and his band in a music magazine, I suggested framing the picture as a Christmas gift for her. His response was typical: he'd never do that; she wouldn't want it. Still, I recommended he take the risk, and he agreed to do it. When he gave the framed reproduction to his sister and her husband, they loved it; they even hung it in their living room. Soon after that, they began to attend some of Peter's gigs.

That picture proved to be a catalyst for change in the dynamic between Peter and his mother. At his brother-in-law's birthday dinner, his mother said she had no idea why Peter's sister had hung up a picture of such a degenerate. Peter told his mother that she was upsetting him. Then he stood and walked out. It was one of the few times Peter had actually expressed his own needs. He told me it was terrifying, and that he'd assumed no one would understand why he left. He was shocked the next day when his sister and brother-in-law each called to say what they'd told Peter's mother: that if she was going to disparage her son's accomplishments, she wouldn't be welcome in their home.

And that wasn't all. His sister told him that she knew he'd been a victim of child abuse. "I was stunned to hear this and defended my mother," Peter said. "But my sister, who's usually meek, said I needed to face what had happened to me. She told me that my mother once took me to the pediatrician when I was about three, and my sister went along as a translator. The doctor didn't like the flat shape of my skull and asked if I was getting out of my crib enough. My mother just smiled and ignored him." His sister wanted to tell the doctor the real situation because she knew it wasn't right. "But," Peter said, "she knew she'd be betraying my mother. Plus, she'd get the hell beaten out of her. She stayed quiet. She says she's felt guilty for years that she didn't speak up."

After the incident at his sister's house, Peter's new policy was that every time his mother said something emasculating, he'd simply get up and leave. He offered no explanation. I approved of this tactic. "Believe me, she'll figure it out," I said. "Mice and rats will eventually respond differently to positive and negative reinforcement."

Slowly, Peter's mother stopped insulting him and telling him to get a different job and to marry a Chinese girl. She never turned into an affectionate mother, but she did learn, through behaviour modification, what she wasn't allowed to do if she wanted to sustain contact with her son. She didn't want to be alone. She wanted to give Peter food and shelter, and if he refused to take it, she was bereft. That was what she thought her job was as a mother.

We'd had an eventful and fruitful year in therapy, learning of Peter's mother's childhood and how damaged she was. He was alternately angry and sorry for her. He was also beginning to realize that her response to him had little to do with him per se. Peter was also bolstered by his sister's support. He'd been shocked when she said he was a victim of child abuse, but it helped him to understand why he'd had so many problems in his life. He'd also doggedly stuck to his rules of engagement with his mother and saw the results in her improved behaviour. What else could he accomplish?

4

GETTING JUMPED

NOT SURPRISINGLY, once Peter began to recognize what abusive behaviour was and had started to set boundaries for his mother, he began to look at how he was treated by people outside his family. Peter had also put up with a lot of entitled behaviour from the band's lead singer, Donnie. He was demanding, and had the delusion that the audience was there only to see him. Peter got more respect from guest gigs in other bands than he did from Donnie. Finally, Peter confronted him, saying that he could no longer demand or quash encores on his own; from now on, they would make that decision together.

Donnie, aged thirty-seven, prided himself on being a party animal, and was probably an alcoholic. He wanted to be a rock 'n' roller and have sex in every city they played in. The only snag in his carefully crafted persona was that he'd been married for nineteen years to Amanda and had a four-year-old son and a six-year-old daughter. Peter, who'd known Donnie and Amanda since high school, was appalled at how often Donnie lied to his wife. He wanted Peter to cover for him by lying to her as well.

Peter, in his new effort to be his own person and express his own needs, told Donnie that he wouldn't lie to Amanda about girls on the road if she asked him. The AIDS crisis was in full swing, and Peter didn't think Donnie was being careful enough.

Donnie said he thought they were pals, and Peter agreed, but said his friendship didn't include lying to Amanda.

When people grow up in abusive families like Peter's, or dysfunctional ones like Laura's, as adults they have trouble setting boundaries. Their parents didn't listen to their needs, so they have no idea that the rest of the world would allow them to set some rules of social engagement. They have to learn that they don't have to perform every task for every person. I was pleased that Peter was drawing a line in the sand with Donnie.

Amanda confided in Peter about how much her husband ignored her and the children. She once appeared in the sound studio at their house while they were practising and asked Donnie to come upstairs to their son's birthday party. Donnie refused, and when she persisted, he lifted his hand to strike her. Peter flew out of his chair and came to fisticuffs with Donnie. He said he was sick of Donnie being "a dick."

This anger connected to something else that had been bothering him for years. He wondered how Donnie could afford a house and a state-of-the-art sound recording studio when Peter barely made a living; after all, they had the same charted CDs. Peter finally demanded to see the books.

It sounded to me as if Donnie had been cheating him and Peter had blocked his feelings about it, just as he'd blocked his feelings about everything else. I congratulated him on responding to his emotions. One thing his mother had been right about, Peter told me, was that Donnie was a thief: he'd been stealing from him for sixteen years. I'd kept up with the media on the band, and pointed out that the press hardly mentioned Donnie— they focused mostly on Peter.

Peter was growing emotionally. And now he made a big decision: to leave the band and form his own group, taking the other accomplished band member with him. Eventually he became so successful financially that he didn't have to work tuning pianos any longer. He could be a full-time musician.

Peter wasn't the only one to summon the courage to leave Donnie. Amanda sued for divorce and custody of the children. She expected, and got, no argument from her husband. When Donnie bought her out of the house, she moved into one of Peter's mother's fourplexes. In fact, she lived upstairs from Peter. She expanded her fledgling business as a bookkeeper. Occasionally, she would ask Peter to watch her kids while she met a client. Peter began to relate to the children, teaching the six-year-old girl the keyboard. Amanda couldn't afford to pay him, so they agreed on a free lesson once a week in return for a home-cooked meal.

Peter began to take the family to musical events like *Disney on Ice* and *The Nutcracker*. He played street hockey with Amanda's son. The kids, who'd been longing for some male attention, responded enthusiastically to Peter's kindness and consistency.

One week, Peter acknowledged to me that he was attracted to Amanda and had been since high school, long before she'd married the charismatic but shallow Donnie.

Peter's mother was apoplectic about this friendship, saying that all Amanda wanted was to inherit her property. Peter should find a Chinese girl. He pointed out that he couldn't speak Chinese, nor did he know any Chinese girls other than his sister.

When the Rolling Stones came to town, Peter asked Amanda to go with him. He assured me that it wasn't a date. Still, he was afraid that this might change their relationship, and that Amanda might think sex would be involved. He acknowledged having sexual fantasies about her but was too frightened of failure to act on them. "She's my neighbour and long-time friend and I like the kids," he said. "It could all go up in embarrassing smoke."

I could understand Peter's caution. A failed sexual encounter could really set him back. Yet this was the problem he'd come to me with four years ago!

I suggested that Peter watch very carefully what his sister, who was a good mother, did with her baby daughter. He reported these kinds of attachment behaviours: holding, close-up cooing, holding hands, lying together, smiling, chatting, and soothing when she cried. I went out on a limb and suggested that if he started a romantic relationship with Amanda, he could do some of the things with her that his sister did with her daughter. I said he needed to take baby steps; that sexual feeling isn't built in a day. He had to learn how to be attached, how to have physical intimacy, and that sex was the culmination of all those previous bonding behaviours.

But some of those behaviours were too much for him, Peter said. For instance, he couldn't look into her eyes. Even thinking about it made him nervous.

So we made a list—a hierarchy of intimacy, from most to least, with sex at the top, down through hand-holding, and then to the easiest one, verbal expressions of affection. I suggested that Peter try some of the attachment behaviours at the bottom of the hierarchy with his baby niece until they felt natural. Regarding the date with Amanda, I assured him that there was no pressure for him to perform. The pressure was more in his head than in hers.

Later, Peter reported that he and Amanda had gone to the concert and enjoyed it. When they got back they sat on the couch, but Amanda's son emerged from his room and wanted to hear all about it. Peter was relieved. He slipped out feeling that he'd had a date and didn't want to risk more.

At his next session, Peter related something that had upset him. He'd just finished a piano lesson with Amanda's daughter, and the two of them were waiting while Amanda made dinner when a male client came to the door to drop off some receipts for bookkeeping. Amanda introduced Peter by saying "This is my landlady's son," and then continued chatting with the customer. I was a bit surprised by how angry Peter was, given how much worse had happened to him in his life. However, I'd seen this sort of thing in my practice before. When someone first opens the emotional floodgates, so much feeling roars out that it can be hard to stop the rush.

Peter was quiet during dinner. Amanda's daughter picked up on his tension, and when she asked him what was wrong, Peter said he didn't like his introduction as "the landlady's son." The daughter responded, "My mommy should have said 'my piano teacher.'"

"Or family friend," Peter said.

Amanda said nothing during all of this. Then the daughter added, "Or 'my friend.'"

Peter was touched to the point of tears by the little girl's emotional connection. "I would have liked that," he replied.

Again, Amanda said nothing. After dinner Peter excused himself, saying he had to practise. Amanda coolly said goodbye.

A few nights later, Amanda knocked at his door at about eleven. She didn't say anything other than she was late because she'd had to get the kids to bed. She sat on the couch with tears in her eyes, but still didn't talk. Peter said it was easy for him to hold her hand and put his arm around her. She laid her head on his shoulder. They sat like that for a long time until she left, saying she had to get home in case the kids woke up.

"Did anyone say anything?" I asked.

"Nope."

I asked Peter how he felt and he said, with his usual lack of expression, "It was the happiest moment of my life."

When Peter returned a week later to give another piano lesson, Amanda told him that the children were staying with Donnie's mother for the week, and that this was her first child-free break since she'd been divorced. Peter helped her put toys away and clean up. They went out to dinner and held hands on the way home.

He remembered the whole evening perfectly, as if it were a movie he'd seen again and again. They'd watched *Saturday Night Live* to see a band they liked. Then Amanda went to the bathroom and never came back. Finally, Peter went into the hall and she said, "Hey, come on in." She was lying on her bed, clothed, and smoking a joint. She said, "Gotta do this while the kids are away." She'd put a CD on, and as they listened she put her head on his chest. She told him that Donnie had said she was frigid, but now that he was gone, she didn't feel frigid. When she read books or saw movies, she had romantic feelings, but two things had happened when she was young. She'd been sexually abused by a family member and then gotten pregnant by Donnie, her first boyfriend, in her last year of high school. She married him and then lost the child in the seventh month.

"I let her know how awful that must have been. She said sex was a bit scary for her. Then I realized that she was apologizing to *me* for not having had sex." Peter decided to tell her a bit about his own troubles, although not enough to frighten her. He said he'd been isolated a lot as a kid and was happy to take things slowly. He noted that Amanda looked relieved. After a long silence, she told him how much she admired his music. "Then she told me her daughter had asked if I had a Chinese girlfriend," he said. When Amanda replied that she didn't know, her daughter said she was going to watch for one in the parking lot. Peter looked at me with a hint of a smile I'd never seen before and said, "I told her she'd be looking a long time because I have a girlfriend right here."

I was so happy for Peter. I told him that some people have sex but no emotional intimacy for their whole lives. Peter and Amanda had been honest with each other and become emotionally intimate.

A few weeks later Peter reported that he and Amanda had had a sexual encounter. They'd been lying on the bed together having a joint when Amanda asked if he'd mind if she took her top off. He said she was wearing a beautiful lace bra. Peter began to get an erection as she unbuttoned his shirt. Then she commented that he didn't have much hair on his chest. "I felt inadequate, and was totally knocked off my game," he recalled. "I was sort of dazed after she said that, but managed to respond that Chinese people don't have much chest hair." Amanda just nodded and said "Hmm." Then he felt himself withering—not just his erection but his whole body was shrinking. "I was quietly leaving my body. I got that feeling I'd had in my attic room when my mother came toward me with the bamboo whip. I was no longer in my body," he said. Instead, he was a lonely boy in the corner looking at an adult version of himself sitting on the bed with Amanda. "When I could catch my breath, I made an excuse to get up and go home."

Once you've had a mother who is critical, or, as Freud would say, "castrating," you remain hyper-alert to criticism. Even a slightly ambiguous utterance like *Hmm* makes you shrivel up like salt on a slug. I told Peter he'd have to learn to talk about his real feelings with Amanda.

For Peter, expressing his emotions was a great risk. But a few days later he did discuss the episode with Amanda. He was so anxious he was dizzy, but he bravely forged ahead. It turned out that Amanda thought he'd left because he didn't like her body. Meanwhile, he thought she was saying he wasn't masculine because he didn't have much chest hair. The incident was a bit like an O. Henry story, replete with misunderstandings. They both laughed at their mutual oversensitivity.

On the first day of April, Amanda came to Peter's door in her long winter coat to say that her car battery had died. When he retrieved some jumper cables, she took them from him, clipped one on his shirt, and then took off her coat. She was stark naked. Then she clipped the other cable onto her nipple and yelled, "April Fools!" They both collapsed on the couch, laughing and hugging and kissing. Neither Peter nor Amanda had had fun as kids, but now they lightened up and enjoyed themselves. He took off his clothes and things progressed until, finally, at the age of thirty-eight, Peter enjoyed sex with a woman.

As the relationship with Amanda developed, Peter didn't always have a great sexual experience. He learned that he had to have ideal circumstances. If they had unresolved issues between them, he couldn't maintain an erection. They had to resolve even small conflicts and have emotional intimacy before they could have sexual intimacy. He was like a rare orchid that blossomed only when conditions were optimal.

Peter's mother continued haranguing him about Amanda. When Peter told her that if she didn't stop, he'd move out of the building, she scoffed. "I warned her, but she never thought I'd be crazy enough to pay rent when I had a free place. She thought she had me over a barrel." Then, when his mother dropped off food for him without even saying hello to Amanda, that was the final straw. Peter and Amanda and her children moved out of his mother's property so that they could all live together in a rental house. "I knew I had to follow through on my threat or she'd ride roughshod over me," he said. Still, he visited his mother every week for a meal. Peter was happy with Amanda and enjoyed being a father to the children, complete with hockey leagues, music lessons, and the PTA.

Peter had been through the worst kind of hell, but now he had dreams in which he was literally driving the bus. Sometimes, though, the road was too narrow and he could barely fit his bus down its confines; he'd have to pull over. In one dream I was there, directing him between houses on a tight driveway, but he pulled through without damaging the bus or getting stuck. I told him that this was a sign to both of us that the therapy was over. He could now drive the bus on his own and not get hurt.

Peter came into therapy believing that his mother wasn't wrong to lock him away in an attic. We had to reframe that experience as abuse and get him to understand that its aftermath caused him to fail kindergarten, to suffer from loneliness and impotency. And once he saw the Harlow films dramatizing the centrality of maternal attachment, he turned a corner: he stopped blaming himself; his episodes of depersonalization decreased. Then, learning of his mother's abuse in Vietnam made her much less frightening in his eyes. I believe that his final steps, exhibited in the chest-hair episode, were to identify his feelings, value them, and express them. Once he was no longer depersonalized and could feel, he could have sex. He'd moved into his own body and into personhood.

Peter's transference in therapy, where I'd become the mother he'd never had, was successful. He was able to relive a lot of his childhood nightmares while I was there to soothe and to empathize. Yet, given his attachment to me, he didn't want to leave therapy. I told him that he could stay as long as he wanted, but that I was only a cloth mother after all. Besides, adults have to leave their mothers and make it in the wide world by themselves. Peter, never one to disagree, braved the world on his own.

People can be heroes in astonishingly different ways. Peter, unlike Laura, wasn't an obvious warrior. His nobility lay in his power to forgive. He reminded me of my first hero from my Catholic school days—Jesus Christ—who'd said on the cross, "Forgive them for they know not what they do." It's easy to assume the role of victim, but Peter forgave people their trespasses. One by one, he removed each thorn from his crown. He was resurrected after therapy as a man who became more successful in the music field, loved his new girlfriend, enjoyed being a parent to her kids, maintained an intimate sex life, and made as much peace with his mother as was possible.

It was Peter's forgiving nature, I believe, that was the greatest help in his recovery. Compared to others who'd been locked away at the same age and for the same duration, Peter made a miraculous recovery. He rolled away the boulder from his grave and was resurrected as a feeling person.

Peter had once said that if he had to empty all the sand along the Atlantic shore pail by pail, he could do it simply through perseverance. That's the same way he fought for his mental equilibrium, slowly and methodically: not with one strike, but with many small ones. He could never convince his mother that she'd harmed him—she was too damaged to see that—but he did manage to train her not to speak abusively to him.

My heart went out to her. It must be painful to realize that, although you have no idea where you went wrong, somehow you've been a "bad" mother. She never offered Peter up to sadists, as her own mother had done; instead, she worked hard her whole life to give her son a roof over his head, which she regarded as shielding him from harm. Once a vulnerable, penniless child with an addict mother, she left Peter a lot of money in her will. Given her extremely limited emotional repertoire, she'd been strong and had protected her children.

Almost all abusive parenting is based on generations of the same; those who are abusive were likely themselves abused. That's why there are no villains in these cases, but rather layers of dysfunction to unravel.

The following Christmas, almost a year after Peter had concluded therapy, I walked into my waiting room to find a gift, beautifully wrapped in shiny Chinese-red paper and a purple ribbon. Inside was a new CD featuring Peter, who'd moved on to a big label. The CD was sitting in a red plastic bucket with a blue plastic shovel. It was a beach pail—the kind a kid uses to shovel sand at the seashore.

Twenty-five years later, Peter and I met for lunch at a Vietnamese restaurant. Looking much taller than I remembered him, and buff from working out, he strolled in with a big smile on his face; he made immediate eye contact and then hugged me. I was pleased by how expressive he'd become.

We chatted easily for two hours, lingering over tea. It turned out that he stayed with Amanda for eight years before she returned to her husband, Donnie, now a reformed alcoholic. It had been a shock for all.

Soon after the separation, Peter had a religious conversion. He said that one day he felt "charged with religious energy." I told him how strange that was since I had described his kindness and forgiveness as Christlike in this book. He was flattered that I'd seen him that way. He'd become active in several Christian movements and had met a woman at church whom he loved more than he thought possible. They'd been living together for four years, and were planning a church wedding.

Peter had tired of bands, bars, and road travel, but he still loved the piano. He gave master classes to people all over the world, often flying off to foreign shores. He also did consulting work with piano companies worldwide, and was known colloquially as "3-P": Perfect Pitch Peter.

His mother died of a stroke at age seventy-eight, but ten years earlier, she'd begun to suffer from dementia. Surprisingly, her personality changed entirely. Peter described her as "giddy," like a young girl out on a first date. She was kind to everyone and no longer obsessed about her money or the future of her children. She seemed grateful whenever Peter visited her in her retirement home.

One of the most surprising things Peter said was that if he had to live his life over again, he wouldn't change one thing. He'd suffered so much that I was taken aback. He said, "What if I'd been raised like every other little boy? What if I hadn't been locked away where no one spoke to me? I wouldn't have had to depend on the piano for comfort and conversation, or as a vehicle for my feelings. I might never have, to use your word, 'attached' to it." His piano playing had given him the greatest joy in his life, he continued, and if he'd had friends and a normal upbringing, he might not have needed it. "I now like who I am, and I think all I went through was for a purpose. I think it was God's plan to make me the person I've become."

DANNY

In the social jungle of human existence,
there is no feeling of being alive without a sense of identity.

ERIK ERIKSON

I

TANISI

DANNY WAS A Cree man who came from the hunter and trapper tradition, in which Indigenous people led nomadic lives in the bush and traded furs yearly with the Hudson's Bay Company. His family were from far up north in Manitoba, cut off from the rest of Canada. To me it was astonishing that someone would walk into my office having actually *lived* a life that was such an important part of North American history. And Danny and I were the same age, meaning that while he and his family had been trapping in the bush, I'd been watching Hollywood versions of "cowboys and Indians" on television.

This was a groundbreaking case for me in many ways. I was forced to realize how culturally laden, to the point of inadequacy, psychotherapy was for Danny. I now know how the famous Swiss psychiatrist Carl Jung felt in 1925 after spending time with an Indigenous man: Jung was made aware, he said, of his "imprisonment in the cultural consciousness of the white man."

Freud, along with all the other European founding fathers of psychotherapy, knew nearly nothing of Indigenous culture, and neither did I. But as my father used to say, "Wisdom is knowing what you don't know." So I reached out to Native healers, who spent a great deal of time translating various Indigenous customs for me. Without this help I would certainly have floundered.

This case, more than any other in the book, is time-sensitive.

It was still the 1980s, a time when many white North Americans still didn't know about the full horrors of residential schools, later attested to by the Truth and Reconciliation Commission. The terminology is also outdated: Danny called himself an "Indian" and "Native," common parlance in the eighties.

Danny came to my office in 1988 through a former patient who owned a large trucking firm and would often refer clients to me through his human resources department. Danny was one of his long-haul drivers. I knew this employee must be special for the owner to have called me personally.

He began by saying that Danny Morrison was his best driver. When I asked what that meant exactly, the owner laid it out for me in his customary short, punchy cadences that sounded like a circus barker's. "Taking expensive cargo from coast to coast is a dangerous job," he said. "You need someone loyal, brave, and strong. Let's say a container of Rolex watches arrives from Switzerland by ship. It's unloaded by dockworkers—and long-shoremen can be tied into rings of thieves. They'll tip them off that a truckload is moving from Halifax to Vancouver. Then bandit trucks will follow my truck across Canada, wait until it's unsupervised, even for a few minutes, then hijack it." And if his company used a relay of drivers, he added, handing the cargo from one to the next, no one could be held responsible for the theft. "Every driver blames the other," said the owner. "So what I do is spend a fortune ensuring that those Rolexes get delivered by *one* man, on time, with the full shipment. That driver is Danny Morrison. He has to sleep in the cab. Can't leave the truck anywhere.

"Let me give you an example of Danny's work," he added. "He was taking a double load of industrial platinum across the country, and when he was at a diner in Medicine Hat, three thieves broke into his cab."

Danny had been watching out the window as he waited for his food. "He tore out and threw the three of them off the truck. They were all hospitalized, one for over a month. Apparently, they were laid out like sardines in the ambulance." Danny suffered only a sprained wrist. He never complained or asked for help, and just continued on to Vancouver. "This is all to say," the owner concluded, "that I owe him big time."

When I asked the nature of the problem, he began by saying that Danny was in his forties, a huge man with broad shoulders, and well over six-four. "He has the biggest hands I've ever seen. The guys on the dock call him Fork, short for Forklift." Danny wasn't a talker—in fact, he was monosyllabic—and he avoided eye contact. But he was smart. "He does all the maps and the mileage costs in his head, and he's never a penny off."

Then there was a silence on the phone. Finally the owner took a deep breath and continued. "About two months ago, we got a call saying that Danny's wife and only child, a four-year-old daughter, had been killed in an accident on the 401 highway."

"How is he coping?" I asked.

"That's the strange thing. He didn't appear to grieve at all. Yet he was a real family man. At *some* level, he must be hurting. I asked him if he wanted to take time off with pay, and he just shook his head. He was back at work a day after the funerals."

The owner offered to pay for Danny to come to therapy, but Danny looked dubious. "So I told him I'd come to see you myself, and that it had helped me enormously," the owner said.

"Was Danny surprised by that?"

"If Danny was ever surprised by anything, you'd never know it."

Weeks later, Danny agreed to try therapy.

———

The man in my waiting room had dark skin and long black hair pulled into two braids. He wore a flannel shirt, leather jacket, blue jeans, and grey, pointed sharkskin boots.

I introduced myself. He nodded without looking at me, and stood inside the door until I asked him to have a seat. His face was a perfect mask. To break the ice, I told him how highly the owner had spoken of him. He just looked down at the floor. When I studied his face, I saw how handsome he was. With his height, breadth, perfect profile, piercing black eyes, and flawless skin, he was undeniably striking.

When I expressed my condolences for his loss, I had the feeling that he wanted more distance between us. So I told him it was best to proceed with an intake history and family tree. I asked him about parents, and whether they'd been helpful to him in this difficult time. He said his mother was dead and that his father and brothers, who lived on a reserve in northwest Manitoba, didn't know what had happened. When I asked if he wanted to share his feelings about his loss, he shook his head. He sat there in silence for the rest of our first session, and for all our sessions during the next three months.

Our quiet didn't have the gluey silence of depression—it felt as though he just wanted to be left alone. Yet he continued to show up every week. There was something compelling about Danny, and I found that I could sit with him in companionable silence. That was new for me.

Still, I knew I needed help with the case; after all, I wasn't being paid to sit in silence. So I searched through library catalogues, without success, for an Indigenous psychiatrist—back in 1988, I was unaware of healing circles and other Indigenous rituals and ceremonies. Then I tried the different First Nations offices and the federal Department of Indian Affairs, as it was called then; no one returned my calls. At the psychiatric unit of the hospital that treated the most Indigenous people in Toronto, the intake worker told me, "Indians don't do well in therapy. Most referrals are alcohol-related, so there are some AA groups I can refer you to. Sometimes they meet, sometimes they don't."

I broadened my search. Finally I came across a reference to Dr. Clare Brant, a Harvard-educated Indigenous psychiatrist. He also happened to be a direct descendant of Joseph Brant, the famous chief who fought during the American Revolution. I wrote him a lengthy letter explaining the case and describing my difficulties communicating with Danny. His response was gratifying: Dr. Brant told me that he understood my feeling like a fish out of water, and so with his letter he was including the academic papers he'd written exploring the Indigenous world view. These papers were fascinating, and should be required reading for all Canadians. I will forever be indebted to this man. We went on to share a long correspondence that I still treasure today.

As Dr. Brant explained it, in small, close-knit communities, particularly in harsh northern environments, conflict between individuals had to be avoided at all costs. In order to live in close proximity while maintaining one's privacy, it was crucial not to interfere with one another. This meant that certain conventions of social behaviour had been established. For example, "interfering" meant asking questions, giving advice, and being too familiar.

I realized that Danny probably experienced therapy as rudeness. I'd been "interfering" with his psyche by prying in an insistent way. The more I'd attempted to engage him, the more he clammed up. Yet when I tried being quiet, I could see that it could have gone on indefinitely; he was way better at that game than I was.

So I decided it would be best to simply explain my frustration. I told Danny that I knew how he must perceive my role, but that I was incapable of altering it significantly—it was my culture, it was the way white therapy worked. I asked him for help. I wanted to know what I could do. It was really important to me to have the therapy work, I said, and I knew I had a lot to learn.

Danny asked his very first question, albeit with no eye contact. "Why is it important to you?"

"It's my job, and I like to do it well."

"I thought you were going to say something untrue, like you cared about me."

"I don't know you well enough to care about you." I went on: "However, for some reason I can't explain, I do feel a connection with you and want to help you with your pain."

"I don't have pain," he said in the monotone he always used.

"Okay, that's the first thing you've told me about yourself," I said. "So it must be important to you that I perceive you as having no pain."

"If you say so."

"I do say so." I'd decided to stick to my guns on that one. "Why is that important to you? Are you saying I can't hurt you because you suffer no pain?"

He sat there for about ten minutes, maybe longer. Then: "Yes." Danny said nothing else for the last twenty minutes of the session.

Finally, after four months, I'd made some progress. Danny had admitted, or I'd interpreted, that he was defending himself against pain. I decided to go slowly. If it meant only one interaction a week, so be it. If I pushed for more, I'd noticed he would shut down.

Week by week, a few things would come out. I tried to simply be a witness. I decided not to ask about his wife or child or his lack of mourning—if he never consciously felt pain, then no wonder he didn't mourn.

At one point, though, I did say this: "People who don't feel pain can't feel joy."

He made eye contact with me for the first time. "I can live without joy."

"Do you think there's no pain in your heart, or are you saying you have it locked away?" I ventured.

He said nothing more. But a week later he came in, sat down, and, as though we were still having the same conversation, said: "It is locked away."

I asked, "What if the pain leaked out bit by bit in therapy, and you could be rid of it? Then joy could enter where the pain had been."

"Joy?" he said derisively, as though I were suggesting some sort of mawkish Pentecostal experience.

Rephrasing, I said, "Well, contentment if not joy."

"I'm okay," he reassured me.

I asked him to tell me about his childhood, explaining that he could leave out pain and joy. The following story took shape slowly, over the course of our first year together. I was very careful not to offer any empathy or consolation; otherwise, he'd freeze up. I was simply a witness.

Danny was from a trapping family who lived at the northwest tip of Manitoba, far above the treeline. Most of the year they survived alone in the bush, but at the end of each season, when the furs were sold to the Hudson's Bay Company, they'd move into a small trading-post settlement.

Danny had a sister named Rose who was three years older. When the children were little they'd help their dad untangle the traplines. Rose also helped their mother tan the hides and Danny fed the dogs.

His earliest memory centred on the trapline. One day their father warned Danny and Rose not to come with him on the line—snowdrifts from a windstorm had altered the terrain, making it dangerous—but they followed him into the bush anyway. The father believed that since he'd urged caution, the children came at their own peril. With the usual markers buried in snow, Danny's sister couldn't locate the traps. She ran ahead and got her foot caught in a large snare that cut her ankle into the bone; she had to be brought back to the closest settlement by dogsled, which took days. The injury didn't heal properly, and ever since then, Danny's sister had dragged one leg. Danny learned that day to be careful while trapping.

It was interesting that, after the children didn't heed their father's warning, he didn't insist or intervene—an example of how child-rearing techniques differ between whites and Natives. According to Dr. Brant, the Indigenous parenting style is to role-model but not to interfere, whereas whites believe in active teaching and moulding. Later, that difference in parenting styles would come back to haunt Danny.

I could tell by Danny's almost imperceptible smile how much he enjoyed reminiscing about his days on the traplines. He began to tell me more details of his life in the bush. Once, he even shook his head and said, "Boy, I haven't thought of that in years." His memories were fascinating to me, and Danny was surprised by how much I enjoyed the specifics about trapping. I would sometimes stop him and inquire why things were done in a certain way. Why, for example, did his father use a dogsled instead of a snowmobile? Danny explained that if a snowmobile broke down in the deep bush, you were dead. But with a dog team, the worst that could happen was that you'd lose one dog or rip a harness that could be mended. Also, the gas for a snowmobile would eat up the already slim profit margin.

Danny told me how it was his job to give the dogs their meal of frozen fish. And at the age of four and five, he was proud to carry the axe for cutting the ice as his father retrieved the beaver from the traps. His father didn't talk much, but Danny said that, even when he was so young, they worked like a well-oiled machine. And he knew better than to complain of the cold: everyone knew the trapping season was short and that their livelihood depended on it.

Danny was elated to be out for months at a time with his dad, who was, by the way, still in his twenties. At the end of the season they'd travel hundreds of kilometres to turn in their pelts at a trading post, where fewer than three hundred people lived. There Danny would see boys playing together and wonder what it would be like to have a playmate other than his sister.

In their home there was no TV, no music, no electricity or flush toilets. But once, when Danny was four, the Hudson's Bay trader, who had an office and a desk that Danny admired, gave him a book. He couldn't yet read, so he just made up stories as he turned the pages. (The main characters were always mischievous beavers.) Danny loved the book; he "read" it every night, and would often "read" it to Rose, who listened in fascination. He told me that he credited his lifelong love of reading to that book—the first thing he ever owned. He still remembered his mother calling it, in the Cree language, by the possessive: *Danny's* book.

2

LEATHER SHOES

ONE DAY THE FAMILY was home in their warm cabin, waiting out the weeks it took between laying the traps and collecting the pelts. Danny and his father were sitting at the table whittling when suddenly he heard his mother crying out "like an animal circled by coyotes." He'd never heard his mother speak above a murmur.

She was arguing at their door with two white men who were clearly not hunters "but were somehow dangerous." Danny remembered their strange leather shoes—bizarre footwear for deep snow. Feet could freeze without mukluks, a high, soft boot traditionally made from sealskin and lined in fur. The men came inside and announced that they had to take Danny and Rose to a residential school more than a thousand kilometres away. It was the law, and if the parents didn't surrender their children immediately, they could be jailed.

The men were speaking English; no one in the family understood what they were saying. Finally they got the gist: the two white men from the government were stealing their children. "I'm not sure my parents knew it was forever," Danny said.

"My mother went to the bedroom and packed up our things and the men called after them that we didn't need anything. Our parents looked as though they'd been struck in their hearts with an arrow but were still standing."

In 1988 I had no idea what a residential school was. I assumed it was a boarding school for Indigenous people who lived too far in the bush to attend school. It was not. It was part of a deliberate policy to eradicate First Nations cultures. John A. Macdonald, Canada's first prime minister, called the First Nations people "savages." Then, in 1920, federal officials made their aim explicit: cultural genocide. That year, in the House of Commons, the deputy superintendent of Indian Affairs announced his objective to continue operating residential schools until there is "not a single Indian in Canada that has not been absorbed in the body politic, and there is no Indian question, and no Indian department."

Danny and his sister were bundled into a car; they sat watching as hundreds of miles of tundra disappeared behind them. Many hours later they were put on a train full of other terrified Native children. No one had any baggage. They rode for days, an eerie silence prevailing. Danny was puzzled by the large fields of cattle: he'd never seen animals grazing that he didn't have to hunt, and had no idea what a ranch or farm was. The cottonwood trees and the jagged mountains surprised him and Rose. He felt he was heading into an alarming universe that was ablaze with garish color. Finally they were picked up in a small town and driven out into the country. Then, "in the middle of a flat nowhere," they stopped at a big red-brick building with bars on the windows.

The first thing that happened was that Danny was separated from his sister. He saw her dragged by two priests in cassocks, "who looked like black bears," to another building as she screamed his name.

The second thing was that, shockingly, his long hair was shorn. To this day, many Indigenous people regard their hair as a physical extension of their spiritual being. In many tribes, people cut their hair when there is a death in the family. Others believe that hair is

connected to the nervous system and is needed to process information from society, similar to a cat's whiskers. Danny's tribe believed
that cutting your hair is a way of humiliating yourself for a wrong
you've perpetrated, or a public humiliation for a presumed wrong.
Danny had no idea what crime he'd committed.

All the children were given uniforms and numbers. Danny
was referred to as "number 78" until he was eighteen years old. No
one believed he was five or six—he was tall for his age—so he was
placed with eight- and nine-year-olds. Thinking his parents
would be coming to pick him up in a few days, he kept furtively
looking out the window. "I actually believed I saw my dad with
his pipe a number of times," he said, "but I guess I imagined it."

On the first day of school they were told that to be an "Indian"
or a "savage" (the terms were used interchangeably) was bad, and
that once they left the school, they would no longer be Indians.
They would be Canadians who spoke English. Danny spoke no
English, but he got the point that "Natives were bad." He missed
the part about never speaking Cree again.

The second week of school, while he was out at recess playing
a kickball game run by the priest, Danny gazed across a long field
and saw his sister behind a fence. Danny expressed his first emotion in therapy when he said, "I was so happy I was shaking, and
I ran toward her, screaming, *'Tanisi'*—that's Cree for 'hello.' The
priest caught my arm, stopping me, but I struggled. In front of
the other boys, he beat me with a whip that was made of an old
horse bridle with metal connecting parts. He said that I couldn't
speak Indian now or ever again."

Meanwhile, Danny's sister stood helpless at the gate, crying.
"Still, I screamed, *'Nimis,'* which means 'older sister.'" (In the Cree
language, relatives' names are defined by how they relate to you.)
The priest, thinking he'd been publicly defied, gave Danny such a

severe beating that he was bedridden for days in the infirmary. "I felt bad that my sister Rose had to see that bloodbath of a thrashing from the other side of the fence. It made her so sad." He paused. "I never said another word of Cree for the twelve years I was there. Eventually, I forgot it. I could no longer talk to my parents."

I thought of my twin boys, who were then seven years old. I tried to imagine them being taken from me, and then told that English was a savage language, that they were bad people who would abandon their culture and be remade into another ethnicity. What if they tried to say hello to their nine-year-old brother in English and were beaten to a pulp for doing it? It was terrifying and heartbreaking to contemplate.

It took a full year of therapy to get a modicum of trust built up between Danny and me. Looking back on it, I'm surprised, given Danny's history with white people, that it happened at all.

One of the things that helped him survive emotionally was the good parenting he'd received until the age of five. No matter what happened to him after that, at least he had a firm foundation. But he was so traumatized by his abduction and the cruelty that followed—the loss of his parents, his language, and his culture—that he was emotionally frozen. It had been a means of self-preservation, but it was preventing him from grieving properly for his dead wife and child.

During that first year of therapy, the most important thing Danny said to me was that he could "live without joy." It was my job to restore his capacity for joy—even knowing that with joy comes sorrow. And he'd already experienced so much more of the latter that such restoration had to proceed at a rate he could handle. For Danny, therapy would be a slow thawing from a deep freeze.

3

TRIGGER

BY OUR SECOND YEAR of therapy, I'd learned how to interact better with Danny. As one of the memorable Indigenous healers from Manitoulin Island said to me, "Don't nail him to the cross; just talk to him." I found that the best way to conduct therapy with Danny was to ask innocuous questions that he could then take into deeper psychological areas if he wanted to. If I asked direct psychological questions, he would freeze up, sometimes for the whole session. As Danny later remarked, "Indians have their own way and their own time."

At one session, I asked Danny about his school life. He said he'd done school "like a white man," that he'd tried as hard as he could to be white. He accepted the ideology that was taught to him: Indians were bad. As he said, "Why else would nuns, priests, and all the other white people be doing this to us? We were a Catholic family. I believed in the nuns and priests." He added, "Anyone at the school of any importance bought into the idea that Indians were bad."

At five he was one of the youngest kids there, but no one helped or soothed him. "Everyone just had to keep their nose down, and that's what they did. One day I woke up and the kid next to me was dead. I was afraid to report it in case they'd think I killed him. When he didn't show up at breakfast—I can still remember his number was 122—they found him dead. He was gone within the hour. And no one said a word."

When I did some research on residential schools, I discovered a 1907 report in the *Montreal Star* that cited a 24 percent national death rate of Native children in the schools (42 percent when counting the children who died at home shortly after being returned because they were critically ill). These children died of tuberculosis, starvation, or simple neglect. Many just disappeared; their parents were never informed. In 2015, the Truth and Reconciliation Commission reported that between four thousand and six thousand children had died. The number is probably much higher, since many were simply unaccounted for. Over the course of 150 years, more than 150,000 children went to residential schools. Because the death rates were so high, the residential schools stopped counting.

Danny did well in school and never caused a problem. "I felt sorry for boys who couldn't do things the white man's way; their lives were a living hell." He told me that if they didn't know their multiplication tables, they were thrown out in the cold without coats—just in garbage bags with cut-outs for the arms. Danny was singled out for his achievements in several areas, but he found that embarrassing, even humiliating.

Part of the Native ethos is not to compete or flaunt your success: it could make someone less able feel bad. It's fine to be on a hockey team, but it's insensitive to cheer for your own team since it could offend the other team. In his article "Native Ethics and Rules of Behaviour," Dr. Brant wrote, "This non-competitiveness extends even into working life, despite the fact that it is often seen by non-Native employers as a lack of initiative and ambition." Rather than revelling in his academic success, Danny felt he could hardly relate to it. After all, those who were complimenting him on his "achievement" were the same ones who were starving him (at the end of the school year he'd grown taller but had lost half his body weight), who were torturing him, who'd taken him away from his parents and put him in this jail.

At this point in his narrative, Danny said, "Do you understand that it was not an honour?" I was pleased that he was talking to me after over a year together, and that he was engaged enough to care if I understood. And by this time I knew that Danny had an amazing bullshit barometer. I had to be totally honest. So I said, "I do understand it, but I wonder if there was *any* part of their praise that gave you pride?"

He looked disappointed, so I added, "I mean, as the years went by, didn't you slightly believe in the white man's reward system, since that was all you had?"

Danny said he'd never wanted to be at the school. "I knew I was a prisoner and I wanted to keep it that way. I didn't want to join them." He sat silently for about fifteen minutes. Then: "That was not always true. I liked raising the animals and feeding them and crossbreeding them. I was sent with my pig to the 4H tournament, and I was proud when I won a ribbon, especially since it was un-related to the school." Danny had a way with animals, and became the school's head of husbandry when he was still a teenager. "I also liked farming and growing crops. I had some farming secrets."

"Like what?"

"I'd heat water in the sun in garbage cans in the spring, and then pour the warm water on my tomatoes in the greenhouse— and they would always be ready first."

When I asked how he'd learned such tricks, he hesitated. "There was a priest who taught it all to me." Danny was silent for the next thirty minutes. He sat perfectly still, staring out the window. Even his blink rate seemed lowered.

When he returned a week later, he sat down and said, "That priest who'd taught me so much interfered with me."

"Interfered how?"

"Sexual stuff. In the barn, again and again. He said how much he liked me. It made me sick; I mean, not just mentally." Once they were caught by a man who cleaned out the barn, who only shook his head. "I can still feel the burn of that shame," said Danny. "Then I knew I wasn't good at all those farm things; he just wanted to do that with me. It went on for years."

I think he read the shock on my face. The revelations about sexual abuse by priests in the general population were still to come, and the abuses in residential schools were not yet widely known. Danny told me his terrible story three decades before governments made public apologies to Indigenous peoples and set up the Truth and Reconciliation Commission.

By the time Danny was a preteen, another sexually abusive priest, a Christian Brother well-known for his perversions, ran the whole school. Danny said the boys would be playing baseball outside in the spring and the Brother would open the window, call one of their numbers, and have brutal sex with that boy. "It was humiliating because everyone on the team knew what was going to happen. A half-hour later, he'd call someone else's number. Then we'd all have to return to the game as though nothing had happened. But we all knew, because it happened to most of us," he said.

After a pause, Danny added, "That happened to me from the time I was eight or nine until I fought them off as a teenager. When I was twelve, I was in the infirmary because I had a high fever and the doctor, or whatever he was, interfered with me. I woke up delirious, with him on top of me. What I couldn't understand was why this kept happening to me."

He looked at me for an answer. I said, "Those men were sick. That was probably why they were sent up there to begin with. I suspect the Catholic Church knew something was wrong with them and, instead of defrocking them, they sent them up past the treeline, where they thought no one would ever report what they did."

"But why me? It didn't happen to everyone all those different times." (At the time, we had no idea of the huge percentage of sexually abused children in residential schools.)

"I suspect it was because you're tall and handsome. I doubt they cared that you were smart. They had to choose someone, so why not the best-looking one? After all, they're predators."

Then something shocking happened. Danny got up and left in the middle of a session. I had no idea why. He didn't show up for his next appointment, or the one after. It began to dawn on me that he'd left therapy. I didn't want to "interfere" by calling him, so I didn't. Usually, on the rare occasion when a patient abruptly leaves therapy, I write a note or call, saying that I'd appreciate an exit interview so that we could discuss their termination; I explain that it's important to resolve conflicts. However, no one had ever left in the middle of a session before.

Clearly, I'd failed in some major way. I assumed that I'd made some kind of mistake that only white people can make and have no idea what it is. I had a feeling Danny was gone forever. It was at this time that I realized how important the therapy had become to me. I was fascinated by the cultural differences, the government involvement in a tragic attempt to eradicate a culture. Most importantly, there was something compelling and honourable about Danny as a person. I realized how much I admired him; he'd endured more than most people could.

There's nothing like failure for opening your mind. I was spurred to call on more healers and medicine men in the Indigenous community. I listened harder and travelled around the province to attend smudging ceremonies. I'm sure that smudging was as strange to me as psychotherapy had been for Danny. But during that time I began to understand that the Indigenous world view and psychological priorities were truly different from those of Eurocentric white society.

Most white people enter therapy in order to gain better control of their lives, or as one healer put it, "to stickhandle through life." Indigenous healing is instead about connecting with the spirit world in a meaningful way and achieving harmony. Whereas traditional psychotherapy is based on a man-against-nature paradigm, Indigenous healing focuses on man harmonizing with nature.

After several weeks, Danny returned. When he began to talk as if nothing had happened, I interrupted him, saying I felt strongly that we had to examine why he'd walked out in the middle of a session. "Indians don't argue" was all he said.

I finally broke the silence that followed. "Danny, you walked out on me and I want to know why. It may violate a Native tradition, but I'm a white therapist and I have to work within some of my traditions as well." Nothing. Then I said something out of my own anger. "Danny, did it ever occur to you that not all Native traditions are good, just as not all white traditions are bad? Perhaps we can each learn from the other. I'm willing to stretch if you are."

"You knew what you were doin'," he mumbled.

I was bewildered. He got up and patrolled the room like a tiger pacing in a cage. Finally, he thumped his huge body against the door and said, "You were like the priest—buttering me up, telling me I was handsome. I know the next step."

Now I was stunned. I just looked at him and said, "I appreciate your letting me know that I crossed a boundary and that it made you uncomfortable. I'm sorry for that." I explained that by saying he was tall and handsome and stood out from the other students, I was trying to say that a fox would choose the largest and best chicken from a hen coop. "It was my way of telling you that there was nothing you did to deliberately entice those priests. It was just the way you looked, which you had no control over." I said I understood now how he'd misconstrued what I was saying, since his abusive encounters had started with smarmy compliments. "I actually didn't mean the word *handsome* as a compliment; I meant it as a description. Perhaps to your mind that appeared as flirtation. I assure you it wasn't."

Danny made his first accusation. "I would never have called you pretty." I started laughing—I couldn't help it. I told him he could join the legion of other males who haven't called me pretty. Even he smiled at that.

Calling Danny handsome was a trigger for him. My other clients who'd endured repeated sexual abuse also had strong triggers. I told him that most sexual abuse victims suffer from triggers, and that I'd set one off.

He said quietly, "Sexual abuse victim?" He'd never heard that term before, or else he'd never thought it applied to him. At that time discussions of sexual abuse weren't common; people lived with a private shame that they felt they had to hide from society. I told Danny that sexual abuse victims suffer from a number of symptoms, including emotional numbing. Then I suggested he'd experienced that with the death of his wife and child.

He nodded, as though he'd just now understood something. One of the things I'd noticed about Danny's pattern of absorbing material was that he would acknowledge something, and then confront it or talk about it only later, in his own time. Months afterward, he would circle back to a topic as though we'd discussed it in our last session. In this case, he said he would talk about the abuse when he was ready. That was hard for me; I wanted to strike while the iron was hot, to approach things in a linear fashion. But that was not Danny's way. And I felt I had to respect it.

4

COW MEDALS

SINCE DANNY WASN'T READY to confront his abuse at the residential school directly, I asked him about the relatives he'd left behind. Once, when he was describing something his father had taught him about tracking, I pointed out that it was odd he never mentioned his father in later years. "You've given me a detailed description of an ideal home until the authorities took you away. Then there's a void. I know your mother is dead and your father is still alive. But that's all I know."

"You got the gist. Father still up north." Danny's periods of silence had become shorter, and after two years, I'd begun to pick up slight emotional nuances in his normally flat tone.

I asked him to tell me what it was like when he went home in the summers. Danny said that the first year he went home his parents were shocked when he spoke in English to Rose. He'd forgotten much of his Cree; it had been beaten out of him. I suspect he was too anxious to remember it. The language itself had become an emotional trigger.

His parents took this to mean that he was ashamed of his heritage. "As I grew apart from them, they grew apart from me," he said. "That was how they survived with everything that was thrown at them. Rose was better than me at getting back her Indianness." Likely that was because she was a few years older when she was taken, and was naturally more talkative and wanted to be included, he said. "I remember she told my parents about the priest beating me as she watched from the fence. My mother, a Catholic, told her to stop saying bad things about the priests. I knew right then I could never open my mouth about anything that happened at residential school."

When I asked how the relationship fared as the years went on, Danny described how his parents had two more sons after him, and how their lives changed drastically as a result of new government policies.

"My parents spent most of their time in the bush. It took time to lay the traps and then more time before going to collect the animals. They did have a place in a small settlement of a few dozen people near a trading post for a short time, when they sold their hides to the Hudson's Bay Company," he said of his early life with them. But he and Rose were in some of the last classes in the residential school system. During the years when Danny was away at school, the government decreed that Indigenous people had to move into a settlement where there was a school. "That meant my parents had to give up trapping, plus the government took much of their hunting land in some kind of phony treaty. The government made small, flimsy houses for the trappers and gave them welfare. They all lived crammed together around the kids' school; they called it a reserve."

"What did your parents do?"

"There was nothing to do. They couldn't set traps anymore because they were too far from the bush. It was too cold to grow anything or have animals," he recalled. "Each year Rose and I came home, the house looked messier. My dad was drinking a lot. I asked Rose if my mother had worn her teeth down from chewing on hides, but Rose said my father had knocked them out." Their parents seemed less and less happy to see Danny and Rose when they got home, and their mother started drinking as well. "Getting beaten up hurts less when you're drunk," Danny said. "When I saw my father hit my mother for the first time because she was telling him to get ready for church, something he used to like to do, I decided then and there that I would never have a drink of liquor in my life. I never wanted my son to feel as I did about my father at that moment."

Then Danny spoke with rare emotion, telling me that his parents had been busy all the time when he was little. Their camp was immaculate; they ran a tight operation. There was never a dirty dish, and all the Christmas presents were works of art made in their spare time. "I never saw either of them rest unless it was bedtime. They were up with the sun." Now, he said, their empty lives were filled with drinking, arguing, and sleeping late.

While Danny was describing this debauched scene, he rubbed his hands together as though he were grinding out bad memories and squinted his eyes as though he were looking straight into the sun. It was as if he was blocking what he saw in his mind.

There was a long silence, then he resumed. "I made a mistake once, confusing white culture for Indian culture. Happened because I'd been in white society too long." When he was about thirteen, he showed his father the medals he'd won at the provincial 4H competition. Danny lowered his voice. "He made fun of them," he said, almost in a whisper. "He drunkenly teased me and made mooing noises like a cow and asked me if all my cornstalks were in a row. My mother was laughing, and Rose just looked confused. That was the last thing I shared with my family."

It's noteworthy that the Indigenous custom of anger suppression is the only practice that Dr. Brant, himself First Nations, openly criticizes. He says Natives don't use anger to instruct their children; instead, they let anger seep out through the use of such non-confrontational tools as teasing, shaming, and ridicule. In an academic article, he wrote, "Shaming and teasing as an alternative to loss of privileges and parental anger can serve to erode self-esteem and give rise to an overwhelming sense of humiliation when encountered later in life." He says that because it's too difficult for a belittled child to know the rules and how to respond to teasing and mocking, the child may withdraw, causing social shyness, shame, or even terror.

I said to Danny, "Here you are, the boy who won the math award, the science award, the best student award, and the province's 4H award for animal husbandry. Yet you were belittled. No wonder you couldn't feel or show any emotion. Why not turn off when you're surrounded by assaults on every front? It's the only adaptive response."

He swept his arm in front of me, indicating that I should continue. I remained silent. Finally he said, "Spit it out." We both smiled. Just as I was learning to detect when he had something on his mind, he was learning to detect when I felt impatient.

I asked him to imagine what his father would have said if he hadn't been drunk and if he hadn't resorted to teasing and shaming—if he could have just said how he really felt. "Just be your father and tell me," I implored him. "I honestly want to know why he responded as he did."

Amazingly, Danny did just that. He spoke lower and more slowly, pretending to be his father. "*Ningozis,* you have been taken from us and told we are savages and 'the only good Indian is a dead Indian'; yet you love their trinkets and, as you say, 'rewards.' The enemy who caused us such pain you hold up as gods? They stole you from us." Danny paused and I nodded. He continued: "Farming, what is that? Keeping animals in barns and vegetables in rows. It is not a skill. It's a trade. Trapping takes a man; you have to use your wits every moment of the day. You must share the mind of those you catch—not lock them up, feed them, and eat them. Yet you show no interest in hunting. You think it's for savages and you think we with our dirt floors and no running water are below you."

I nodded again, finally understanding. Then Danny started to speak with real emotion. "You judge my drinking. I have no job; I can't catch a mouse. Your little brothers don't see a proud trapper who brought in more pelts than any other man in the settlement. They see a drunk who plays cards alone at a table. A man who is reduced to hitting his good wife. The white man took my livelihood, my children, my dignity—and you are proud of their cow medals?"

I blinked away tears. His soliloquy had perfectly portrayed the numbed agony of his father and his family. It was tragic that he hadn't understood it as a child, when his father had stabbed him in the heart with his drunken words.

When Danny left that day, I sensed that our therapy had reached a point of trust. Instead of blocking all feeling, Danny was able to imagine his father's pain, to empathize with it, and to share it with me.

5

GRIEF CRAWLS IN

BY THE THIRD YEAR of our sessions, Danny seemed lighter. He still paced in front of the office for a half-hour, chain smoking, but when I went to the waiting room to get him, his step sounded less burdened.

One week after he'd given that imagined speech by his father, he said casually, "I called my father this week."

I was very surprised. As usual, Danny had done things in his own way and on his own schedule.

"When did you last speak to him?" I asked, still reeling.

"Eighteen years ago, at my mother's funeral."

"What did he say when you called?"

"Told him I lost my wife and daughter. He said, 'Not easy, is it?' Then he asked if I'd heard from Rose."

Danny told me that his sister Rose had been missing from Winnipeg for more than ten years.

This was forty years before reports of large numbers of missing and murdered Indigenous women hit the newspapers. Now we are all aware of the lack of police investigations into these disappearances. (In 2017, Statistics Canada said Indigenous women were almost three times more likely to be victims of violent crime than other women.)

"What happened to that sweet girl who did so much to care for you and was so relentlessly cheerful?"

"She kept going home trying to get love from two drunks," Danny said, referring to his parents. "She went way past the twelfth round. I gave up on that shit early. They cut her down till she was like them. She and my two little brothers joined in their drunken parties. My mother died, and then Rose was with my dad until she got out and went to Winnipeg. I never saw her after that."

"I guess it was a good thing you got out to Toronto."

"I don't know; at least she was still an Indian."

"Aren't you?" I sat looking at this man in long braids.

"I'm not white. I know that." Then, after a silence: "My wife was white."

Finally, in the third year of our therapy, Danny had mentioned his dead wife. I wanted to pounce on it. I made myself count to one hundred instead.

"She was from Norway."

Norway. *Seriously?* How did that happen, I wondered.

"A nurse in intensive care. I was in there after I got into a fight in a Winnipeg bar. I went to all the bars to try and find my sister. A guy trash-talked Rose, so we got into it. He slashed my belly with a knife," Danny said. "I got bandaged up, came back to Ontario, went back to work the next day, but it got infected and I wound up in intensive care here in Toronto for a while." The nurse, named Berit, was in her mid-thirties, as was Danny, and shared his love of mystery novels. "She said she didn't like talkers, and I said she'd found her man. She got pregnant and she wanted to marry, so I said okay. Then we had Lillian, our daughter."

"Did you love Berit?"

"I don't know." (Fifteen-minute silence.) "She was a good woman. She never lied or cheated and she worked hard." (More silence.) "We grew apart. She wanted things from me I couldn't give."

"Like closeness?"

He nodded. "I never got any closer to her than when I was in the hospital. She said there was a brick wall between us. I knew it was true. I couldn't feel. Then just being in the same room with her started to make me feel uneasy."

"Why?"

"A combination of feeling guilty and pissed off. I knew what she wanted, and she deserved it. I just didn't have it to give, so I started avoiding her."

"What about Lillian?"

"She was more like me. She looked just like me and was quiet and shy. She was one who watched. They were worried about her at daycare, saying she didn't join in with the others, but I thought she was fine. She was happy in her room with her dolls and toys. Sometimes I sat with her on the floor and I thought we were . . ." Danny hesitated. "Sharing comfortable space is the only way I can say it." Again, his face took on an expression that made it look as though he was avoiding bright sun. Finally he said, "Berit wanted me to put Lillian on my lap, but I felt uncomfortable doing that, especially after what happened to me at almost the same age."

"You suffered sexual abuse and never had a lot of parenting, and yet you were expected to know how to do it."

"I was in a forest with no path, but people wanted me to know the way."

"Was Berit a good mother?"

Danny nodded. "In a white way. She was always teaching Lillian something. There was no down time. I wanted to tell her to just leave the kid alone. Stop trying to tell her how to hold her fork. Lillian and I could drive in the car for hours and not talk, and that was my happiest time. When Berit was there she was always saying *cow* or *horse* or *car* or some word so Lillian would know it. To the Indian way, it was meddling."

"You just wanted to imitate or role-model living as your dad and mom did when you were small and let her get it in her own time."

"When she fell down and hurt herself, I just ignored it, figuring she would just get up, but Berit acted like it was the end of the world, and then everyone would start wailing."

I asked whether Berit had any idea of the different way Natives view the world—how they have different ideas about anger management, conflict resolution, and emotional restraint, which translates to minding your own business, even if it is your own child.

"No."

"Why didn't you tell her?"

"I didn't know myself. I didn't let myself get pissed off. I felt like a block of wood. I only feel that now when I tell it."

"Did Berit ever meet your parents?"

He shook his head. When I asked him about friends, he said, "I'm a loner."

Then I asked about Berit's parents. Danny told me they lived in Norway on a farm, beside their son's family farm. Though he'd met them only once, he said, "They're all like her—good, kind, salt-of-the-earth types who work like crazy. The parents hardly spoke English. Or if they did, I couldn't understand them."

When I asked if they'd been surprised when their daughter came home with an Indigenous man in waist-length braids, Danny said, "I think they thought everyone in Canada looked like that." That struck me as hilarious, and we both started laughing. (Second joke in over two years of therapy.)

After that we sat for a while. Then he said, "I think if I'd had this therapy and there was no Berit, Lillian and I could have made a go at it. She was like me, quiet and serious. I think Berit thought I was a bad parent. She didn't even want to leave her alone with me. She saw me as neglectful."

"I know you didn't consciously feel anything. But unconsciously you must have been hurt and angry being thought of as a neglectful parent. It's kind of insulting, since really you only had different styles." Danny didn't say anything, so I added, "No wonder you grew apart."

"I was just relieved to be on the road for weeks on end in my truck with no one wanting from me what I couldn't give."

"Did you ever argue with your wife?"

"No. I just left and came home when her anger, or maybe it was just frustration, had blown over."

"Did she know about the residential school?"

"Yes, but I just said it was a government boarding school."

"So she had no idea what you'd been through?"

"None. But I didn't know either."

"Do you know now?"

"I'm starting to thaw out a little. Sometimes I feel sad about Lillian and don't want to even see her picture. She has my sad eyes."

"Do you ever see the sad boy you were behind those eyes?"

"The alone boy."

"The abandoned boy," I added.

"My parents didn't want to abandon me."

I said that that didn't matter to his unconscious mind—the feeling of abandonment would have still been there. "The unconscious doesn't assign reasons. It just knows you're a five-year-old alone. You were Lillian's age."

"I never pictured myself as that young when it happened," Danny said. "I was crazy to go back and voluntarily finish high school there from sixteen to eighteen. At the time I thought, 'Better the devil you know.'"

He hadn't considered university, he said, because he had no money. "Plus, it was for white people. I'd had enough of the white world."

Danny hadn't returned to the reservation either, given that relationships with his family were strained. He also refused to drink, and some people there found that strange.

"Interesting you stuck by that," I ventured.

"I'm stubborn," he responded. "I remember my mother saying that about me when I was little."

I pointed out that the word *stubborn* has a slightly negative connotation. "Why wouldn't you say, 'Yes, I have strength and tenacity and have weathered so much, but I'm still standing'? Have you ever felt that?"

"No."

"You're not feeling anything. Rather than having hot lava pulsing through your brain, you just plugged the volcano. It was that or go mad or become an alcoholic so you could let your rage out in alcoholic binges, like your dad. After all that's happened to you, and to most Natives in the residential-school genocide, you had to find a way to cope. You chose one of the least destructive paths because you have an enormous amount of personal strength. You turned off the feeling tap."

"Yeah, but now it's starting to drip. Leaky washer, I guess."

When I asked him to expand, he described how he'd look at Lillian's picture at night. "I feel something, I don't know what exactly, but it makes my heart sag in my chest. I just want to sit next to her on the couch."

We spent a lot of time discussing how Danny's sadness over the loss of his daughter was normal, that the loss of a child was the worst kind of grief. Then one day, he said, "Sad isn't the only feeling that's poached my brain. Other feelings are lurking in the bush." He sat up in his chair, leaning forward with his hands on his knees. I could tell by his body language that anger was also starting to seep into his brain. Again his eyes narrowed. "I'm just gonna dump this out. There's a guy at work—the manager of the loading dock—who calls me Tonto. And I don't like it."

He said he didn't mind being called Fork since a lot of guys had work nicknames, but Tonto was "an Indian putdown."

"I agree, it is insulting," I said. "Have you ever thought of telling him you don't like it?"

"No. He's just some white guy who thinks he's funny."

"You know, anger has a bad rap," I ventured. "Anger is the fuel you use to drive up feelings of hurt and pain from your unconscious. It's how people tell others that they're displeased with their behaviour. The man calling you Tonto is disrespecting you, and may not even know it. What would happen if the next time he called you Tonto, you simply said, 'Please don't call me that.' You don't owe him any more explanation than that."

"What if he asks why?"

"Say, 'I don't like it.'" Danny looked at me as though he'd never heard anything so absurd. So I clarified: "Most people in the world would care if you don't like something."

"Seriously?" He looked dubious.

"You were brought up in a place where your feelings had to be ignored, even extinguished. It was a cultural genocide. The government and the priests and nuns were trying to make Natives into white people. They couldn't accomplish that aim and listen to your feelings at the same time. Their job was to stomp on your feelings."

He nodded.

"Danny, we've been together for over three years now, and I'd like to work not only on the past but to make things work better for you in the present."

"Oh God. I feel something bad is comin'," he said, smiling slightly. "I wish I'd never opened my mouth."

He was great at reading my mind. "It's very small. I want you to tell the manager of the loading dock that you don't want him to call you Tonto. Say it nicely, and if you need to, add only the slightest annoyance."

He looked askance at me. I suggested we try it out, and before he had a chance to object, I said, with a bit of insolence in my tone, "Hi, Tonto."

He snapped back, "Don't call me that, man."

"Perfect."

"What if he asks why?" Danny was fixated on this part of the interaction, assuming he had no emotional rights.

"Just say 'I don't like it.' You don't owe him a treatise on Native–white relations."

"What if he does it again?" he countered.

"I don't think he will. You're six and a half feet tall and have broad shoulders. You're so strong you're called Fork. You're no longer five years old without any power. If I'm wrong, we can cross that bridge later."

Danny gave me a report the following week. "I walked into the warehouse and, sure enough, the manager said over his microphone, 'Hi, Tonto.' And then he looked back at his clipboard in his little glassed-in hut on the loading dock. I went up to the window and said, 'Don't call me that name again.' He looked up, kinda surprised, took a drag on his cigarette, and said, 'Okay, sorry, man. You're in truck 31.' It was over. He didn't do it again all week. I have hated that greeting every day for years."

I was so happy for him. It was the first time he'd tried to directly affect his environment since he was five—when he said hello (*tanisi*) in Cree and was beaten for it. I felt like shouting, "Watch out world, Danny Morrison is coming through!"

6

THAWING

SOMETIMES THERAPY SPEEDS up once patients begin to understand how the unconscious works and when they realize they have a right to personal boundaries. With this in mind, I asked Danny to replay an incident from our first year of therapy. He looked dubious. I said I needed his permission. He reluctantly agreed, muttering, "Jesus, I hate coming here." I said I wanted to re-enact a moment in time and I wanted him, the new Danny, the man who had the right to control his universe, to respond. He said, with an infinitesimal smile, "Uh-oh. Now I know what this is going to be."

It was a risk, but I pushed ahead. "Danny, I think the reason you were so often chosen for sexual abuse was that you're tall and handsome." I held my breath.

He sat on the edge of his chair, small beads of sweat forming on his hairline. "Dr. Gildiner, please don't call me handsome. I don't think it's your job, and it makes me uncomfortable."

"Danny, I'm sorry I said that. That is not how I want you to feel in therapy. I'll never say it again."

He smiled and said, "Man, that could have been a one-liner. I can't believe I was willing to leave the therapy over it. Now I see that it was the abuse in the past that gave me the shivers." (That was the first time Danny had used the word *abuse* and owned it.)

"No matter what it was or is," I said, "you have the right to make a request. You don't have to endure, as you say, 'the shivers.'"

When I referred to this re-enactment as the "handsome détente," he shook his head in feigned disbelief and said, "You got words for every little thing that happens."

Danny had only alluded to his sexual abuse, but after we'd resolved the Tonto and the handsome issues, he seemed stronger. He'd begun to define his feelings and to realize what was his fault and what wasn't. He was now ready to discuss the specifics of his sexual abuse history.

Later, once Danny had dumped out the gruesome details of his prolonged abuse, it didn't seem to plague him as much. The most painful aspect of it was that it occurred with a priest who really had helped and liked him. This priest had taken him to the 4H club and been a father figure. He'd spoken loving words to Danny. He told him he was handsome and cuddled him on his lap, which felt wonderful to a lonely seven-year-old. But then he had sexually abused him without physically hurting him (which is why laps were a trigger with Lillian and the word *handsome* was a trigger with me).

Danny was less scarred by the violent sexual abuse from the Christian Brother than he was by the abuse from the kind priest. When you're brutally sexually abused, you know you have a predator who is your enemy. There is no confusion. However, it was emotionally confusing to Danny to have someone who was loving and kind to him also be sexually abusive. As a lonely little boy he had enjoyed the closeness and affection of the priest, but later, when he realized what was going on, he felt guilty about his participation. Not only had he lost his innocence; he'd also been betrayed by a close friend. In emotional terms, it's easier to know who your enemies are.

After talking about the abuse, Danny said he now thought that, if his daughter was still alive, he could hold her on his lap because he'd sorted out some of his feelings. For him, being cuddled and cradled had been associated with unwanted sexual advances. He was so confused by it all that he'd just avoided touching his daughter.

He wasn't as traumatized by sexuality as he once was. After his wife died, he would have an occasional one-night stand. But he was frightened of real intimacy.

We discussed what his marriage might have been like if he could have shared his feelings with his wife. He couldn't even casually put his arm around her without feeling awkward. Sometimes that feeling escalated to a point where he felt smothered and had trouble breathing. What he liked most as a family man was driving. He had to have his hands on the wheel while his wife and daughter were near him. He felt that was just the right amount of distance. He also said that no matter where he was on the road, he called home every night. He cherished those calls. Again, it was the right distance to feel comfortable.

The next week Danny came to his session and reported that he'd visited the graves of his wife and daughter. He'd tried to say things that he wished he'd said in the past. "I was too weak to say those things when they were alive," he said.

I attempted to dispel that myth by telling him he was very strong. He'd made a vow to himself to never drink and he kept it. He made one "mistake" at residential school by saying hello to his sister in Cree, got a beating at the age of five, and then never made another "mistake" in school. Danny was, in my eyes, a hero. Even at residential school he'd tried to change his environment. He took care of his animals and his tomatoes. He was a hard worker and a striver; the owner of the trucking company saw that in him. Despite all that had happened to him, he still wanted not only to live, but also to be the best he could be. No one could beat that out of him.

As the months went by, Danny began to see himself more objectively. He was no longer mystified when he got a whopping Christmas bonus. As he said, "Well, I gave a lot to the company. Still, I appreciate it."

When I asked Danny whether the other people had received similar bonuses, he said he'd never asked, nor did he ever tell anyone what he'd received. He said, "It's not my style."

Kidding him, I said, "So now you have a style?" (Third joke in three years.)

Danny was content at his job. He compared it to riding the plains: he was all alone, which he liked; he read his maps; he saw most of North America. He was like a modern nomad who was his own boss and was free to think whatever he wanted and to read a book at all his meals. (He always had a battered paperback in his leather jacket pocket.) Also, he was excellent at tracking his environment: no robber had ever gotten the jump on his multi-million-dollar loads. It wasn't only his innate abilities and his early experience that helped make him an excellent tracker; it was also his PTSD. People who have PTSD are hyper-alert. Their immune system never rests—it's seen so much danger that it's scanning the environment constantly. That's part of what makes PTSD so hard to live with.

We were nearing the end of our third year and Danny had made great emotional strides. He allowed himself to feel the loneliness and regrets that haunted him. He was in touch with his feelings for his wife and especially for his daughter. He'd learned how to affect his environment and was building a sense of his self-worth.

―――

Now that Danny had "thawed out," as he put it, we had to begin a new phase of treatment. We'd spent three years engaged in what could only be described as white man's therapy. We'd worked on Danny recognizing his own feelings, learning how to express those feelings to others, and, finally, establishing boundaries. Danny described the latter as putting "an electric fence around what you want to keep sacred." We had met our goals.

Yet I didn't want to measure his success in white people's psychological terms and consider him cured. I knew he had more work to do, and I knew I needed more advice in order to help him.

One of the Indigenous healers I consulted in the first year of the case had said to me, "An Indian has to be an Indian, or he's hollow." Thirty years later, in 2018, the Indigenous American writer Tommy Orange wrote in his novel *There There*, "It's important that he dress like an Indian, dance like an Indian, even if it is an act, even if he feels like a fraud the whole time, because the only way to be Indian in this world is to look and act like an Indian."

I felt that Danny needed to reconnect with his culture and to experience the kind of spiritual healing that's never been a part of Freudian-based psychotherapy. (I've often wondered how widely Freud's theories would have been adopted if he hadn't been an intellectualized Jew from Vienna with mostly Jewish patients. How different would the psychoanalytic process have been if Freud had encountered Indigenous peoples in his consulting room?)

During the course of more than four years of therapy with Danny, I made many trips up north to meet with Indigenous healers and psychiatrists to help me get Danny on board. These healers were extraordinarily generous with their time and I learned a tremendous amount from them. Their willingness to help me, given all that white society had done to try to destroy Indigenous culture, was amazing. I knew I couldn't have treated Danny successfully without a combined approach.

There was one reason why I was cautiously optimistic about succeeding on the last leg of our journey together. Despite hundreds of years spent trying to extinguish Indigenous culture, those efforts hadn't succeeded. Danny was the embodiment of that. He'd kept his long braids, a visible, public statement of his Indigenous identity. And after years in white schools and jobs, he still had an Indigenous dream life in which animals spoke to him. In that spiritual universe Danny was aided by wolves, and a white albino loon once presented him with a giant egg in the forest. (Over the next twenty years, other Indigenous patients of mine had similar animal spirit dreams—markedly different from the dreams of white people.)

It seemed clear that Danny should consider reconnecting with what he called his "Indianness." But as a self-described loner, and understandably cautious about reopening old wounds, it would be hard for him. The path wasn't a straightforward one.

7

ABOVE THE FROST LINE

ONE WAY THAT Danny might connect with his heritage was through his own family members, I thought, and they could help him make other linkages to the wider culture. An opportunity to discuss that arose when Danny was talking about how much overtime he was planning on doing. I asked why he wanted the extra work when he'd already accumulated so much money in overtime and bonuses. "Not much else to do," he said, "and I don't mind it."

"Don't you ever go out with friends?"

"Once in a blue moon I go out with the other drivers. But they just sit in a bar and drink."

"Are any of them Natives?"

"No."

"Do you have anything to do with Natives?"

"If I'm in Winnipeg, I always go to some of the bars in search of my sister, but honestly, it's not for me."

"What? Being Native?"

Reading my mind, he said quietly, "I guess residential school worked. Do you know, when we used to go to confession at school and I was short of sins, I would confess that I was an Indian."

One day near Christmas, Danny said he was driving a load across the Rockies for double-time pay.

"Did you ever think of stopping in at your reserve when you're out there?" I asked.

"Stopping in?" He looked at me scornfully. "You can't drive there. You fly up north. Then you have to fly in by bush plane, and get picked up by an ATV. It's another half day's ride across the ice."

"I'm sure that if you asked the owner of your company, he'd pay for it."

"I can pay for it. I just don't want to go."

Then I asked him for details about his father and siblings. His father would be in his sixties, Danny estimated, but he barely knew his two younger brothers since they'd been born while he was at school.

"What about Rose?"

"I still ask about her in Winnipeg. She'd be forty-five now. She's probably dead—murdered. I've been to the police three times."

"Did the police care?" I asked.

"No one on this earth cares."

"Except you."

He nodded. For the first time, I saw his eyes well up. We sat for a long time.

Shortly before the Christmas break I again brought up the idea of visiting his relatives. But Danny still resisted. "I feel like I'm just getting better and don't want to risk losing myself again and freezing up," he said. "There's a reason it's cold up there." He was right—he was on precarious ground, and maybe he needed to be more solid before going back to the reservation. He knew more about it than I did.

In the first week of January, Danny walked into my office, sat down, and said, "Well, I went to see the old man and my younger brothers."

The timing was typical of Danny. He had opposed my idea but then followed it through in his own time. He described flying in by helicopter and getting a lift with a local constable who was picking up medicine for a clinic. "He was an Indian, so was asking me who my family was on the reservation. When I named my father and brothers, he didn't say anything like 'Oh yeah, he's one of the old trappers, now an elder, kept the language'—nothing like that." He paused. "Bad sign." As the kilometres clicked by, forty-two-year-old Danny reflected on how he hadn't seen his father in almost twenty years, ever since he'd attended his mother's funeral. "I remember him as a man in his twenties who could trap all day, and now he's an old man."

The settlement was barren, Danny said, just flimsy clapboard houses circled around a modern brick school. The constable drove right to his house, which had chipped paint and no door-knob; newspaper had been stuffed in the hole to keep out the cold. "I wasn't sure if I should knock or just go in like a son would," he recalled.

He knocked, but hesitated, fearful that this visit was a bad idea. When Danny entered, he saw his father lying on a beat-up couch. "He looked old, older than his years; his face looked puffy and yellow and for some reason marked with acne scars. I'd never seen him have anything wrong with his skin before," Danny said. "He used to be a big strapping guy, lean, looked a lot like me, but now he looked like he'd shrunk in height, and he had a big gut. It was like he was a hide stretched widthwise." Danny's father didn't rec-ognize him at first, then did a double take and said, "Who sent you? I must be sicker than I thought."

Danny told him he'd been in Winnipeg and had decided to fly up. "He just looked at me quizzically and said, 'Never thought you'd keep your braids.' I ignored that, because I knew he was really

saying I was an 'apple'—red on the outside and white on the inside."
It seemed unfair—Danny's father had to know how hard it would
have been to have long braids and fit into white society at that time.
After a long silence, during which Danny noticed the messiness of
the house and the whisky bottles on the floor, his father said,
"Heard you were in Winnipeg lookin' for Rose."

"That was years ago. Never found her."

"No one did."

His father's English was limited, but they managed. When
Danny asked about his younger brothers, his father waved his hand
around the room, indicating the surrounding beer cases. "There's
nothing for them to do here," he said. "If you're not on the band
council with some pull to get a janitor's job at the school, there's
nothing to do. Still, they stayed with me." Danny felt his dad was
implying that his brothers had been loyal but Danny hadn't. When
his father saw Danny noticing the household disarray, he said,
"Needs your mother's touch." Then he turned on the TV.

"We sat there for about an hour," Danny recalled. "I could tell he
wanted me to go so he could drink, but I had nowhere to go. I didn't
know anyone there. Finally, I went to buy smokes and could tell
when I got back that he'd been drinking." Then Danny's brothers
returned, and they'd been drinking too. "I think their job was collecting empties around the reserve on their snowmobiles and returning
them—even though it was supposed to be a dry reserve."

"How did your brothers respond to you? Did they look like
you?" I asked.

"They had shaved heads and had my mother's eyes. They looked
a bit Inuit but with Cree size. Rose and I looked like my dad.
They shook hands and started drinking beer and watching TV.
They didn't act surprised to see me at all, and they didn't show
much curiosity either."

"Really? A full brother they'd hardly met?"

"That didn't bother me, because it's the Native way not to make a big deal or poke their noses into my business."

Danny got up and paced a bit, which was unusual for him. Finally he said, "I felt anger in the room, and as they drank, it got worse. Once they were loaded and their friends had come over, they started trash-talking me to their friends. They'd call it 'taking the piss,' saying I was a lone wolf who never got laid—that kind of thing. They said I only came home to see my dad die, but, like white people, I was too early. They were all laughing at that joke."

"Is your dad dying?"

"Yeah, the constable who drove me from the bush plane told me the basics. My dad has pancreatitis, cirrhosis, liver cancer or something like that. Basically he's drinking himself to death, and it's only a matter of time."

"So no one in the family talked about it?"

"Just the joke about me being too early."

It was not lost on me that this disastrous trip had been my suggestion.

"My dad just drank on the couch and laughed when they teased me. I could see my brothers wanted the old man's approval, so they stepped it up. I smelled trouble," Danny said grimly. When he finally decided to leave, he called the local police, who gave him a lift to the tiny airport where he spent the night.

"I knew they were thinking I was white for leaving. I wouldn't stay and fight them with broken beer bottles, which would have made me a real Indian in their eyes. I also think they run some kind of drug business, because guys kept dropping by and then suddenly leaving after talking in the bedroom with my brothers. The sad thing is . . ." Danny paused. "Well, I guess there are a lot of sad things." After a long silence he added, "My younger brothers think this is what being an Indian is. Getting drunk and fighting. I noticed that their shaved heads are speckled with scars. They looked like bull elephant seals that are all marked up."

"It's sadder that your dad knows differently. He knows that isn't what being Native is. What do you think he thought about the visit? I mean, underneath all the alcohol and pain?"

"Did he remember me and Rose and my mom out in the bush, bein' happy? I don't know. The place he lives in now is a filthy mess, and I can tell you, my dad never had one thing out of order at our camps. Every knife was sharpened and lined up according to size. There were stations for skinning, for stretching hides, for dog food and harnesses, for every little thing. He worked day and night. He drank once or twice a year when he sold his pelts at the settlement, but it was a one-night thing."

"Was he humiliated for you to see him now?" I asked.

"He's too far gone to know how he feels." He hesitated. "Well, maybe deep down. He just doesn't want me there 'judging him.' He thinks he had it tough"—Danny paused and looked out the window—"and he did. He lost his land, his livelihood, his wife, two of his kids who never came back, and his dignity that never returned. He sees it as too late now to change. I think he's too gone from drink to think clearly."

Danny dragged himself to my office door, walking stiff-legged as though he had huge weights in his boots. With his hand on the doorknob, he said, "They wanted to make him white and that didn't work. But they took away his Indianness. He's just a fat yellow shell with a wet brain. They broke him." I heard Danny's boots scraping on the steps as he slowly went down the stairs. He sounded like an old man.

What Danny was describing is called intergenerational trauma— a term that would become familiar decades later as residential school survivors began to tell their stories. Nowhere was this clearer than in the Morrison family: Danny and Rose were removed from their family and culture and taken to residential school, where they were traumatized by psychological, physical, and sexual abuse. The older generation, the parents, were so devastated by the kidnapping of their children that they could no longer successfully parent and turned to alcohol. Danny's younger brothers were then brought up by abusive alcoholics who had lost both their land and their livelihood. Those young brothers, already alcoholics, will have no idea how to successfully parent their own future children.

At his next session, Danny expressed depression for the first time. "We worked so long so I could have feelings that I almost forgot why I got rid of them," he said. "It was too painful to feel, and now this past week I've been dive-bombed by memories." He cried small tears that he brushed away with his forklift hands. "I am a man without a country or an identity. I'm not Indian and I'm not white. I'm not a father or a husband. At least my brothers have each other and my dad, or the shell of him. They know they're Native. Sometimes I feel it's not worth living." This was a dramatic statement, a cry for help from the usually non-demonstrative Danny Morrison. I was worried that he was having suicidal thoughts.

When Danny was my patient, the suicide rate among Indigenous people was six times the national average, according to The Canadian Encyclopedia. (It has now risen to twenty-five times the national average in certain areas of the north. For Inuit youth, it is forty times the national average.) I knew it was not an idle threat.

One of the big risks in treating depersonalization—the condition where one loses all sense of identity—is what happens when that person regains a sense of self. Authentic feelings may return, but that person may feel trapped anew in the same unbearable circumstances that originally caused the extreme distress. For Danny, feeling "frozen" had been a successful defence mechanism. It's true that he couldn't feel sad or happy, but he functioned well. He hadn't been felled by the loss of his wife and child. He never missed a day of work in his decades with the trucking company, was a star performer, saved money, had no addictions, suffered no conscious depression. Should I have let sleeping dogs lie?

I've made many mistakes as a therapist, but I didn't think that suggesting Danny go home, however sad it turned out to be, had been one of them. Danny had to confront what had happened to his family, just as he had to confront his own issues. He'd avoided his father, and avoidance never helps anyone get well. This way Danny had a history, however tragic.

He did have a rocky path ahead. Eventually, he was too depressed to get out of bed and didn't even call in sick. He missed an appointment with me. His boss called me to say that his attendance had become erratic, and that the always-meticulous Danny looked dishevelled. And when he'd asked Danny if he was getting help from me, Danny had laughed darkly. I was worried about him. I called his GP and asked him to prescribe antidepressants. (Psychologists are Ph.D.'s, not medical doctors, so they can't prescribe medication.) The owner of the trucking company went to Danny's place and suggested he take the medication in his presence. Two weeks later, alarmed, I urged Danny's boss to bring him in himself if he needed to.

Danny showed up under his own steam. The antidepressants had begun to help, and now he was at least mobile. He slouched in his chair and said only one thing: "I've never confronted anything."

"*Really?*" I said. "You have a complex post-traumatic stress disorder." I showed him a book titled *Trauma and Recovery* by Judith Herman and held up my fingers as I outlined each feature it listed:

1. *Growing up in an environment of neglect and deprivation.*
   "You were brought up in a residential school where no one loved you or took care of you. You were hungry, cold, and children died around you regularly."

2. *Having a sense of powerlessness and helplessness.*
   "There was no one to help you, no one to turn to. When you went home, your mother said that the priests, your sexual abusers, were good."

3. *Experiencing social, psychological, and legal subordination.*
   "You were taken away by law, separated from your parents, and locked into an institution for most of your childhood years. When you turned to your parents, they said you'd sided with the enemy."

4. *Being a target of racism.*
   "You were beaten for using a Cree word when you said *tanisi* to your sister. You still have physical and mental scars from that beating. You were told that Natives were bad. You were given a number and not a name. You were so depersonalized that you confessed to being a Native in the confessional."

5. *Living with homelessness and extreme poverty.*
   "You had to work at the school and were given barely enough food to live on. When you went home, your parents were on welfare with not enough money for the extremely expensive food up north. Yet they found money for their alcohol."

6. *Living with a sense of repeated interpersonal victimization, including childhood abuse and other physical violence.*

"The one man who took you under his wing sexually molested you for most of your childhood years. And others, less kind, violently sexually abused you as well. Then your alcoholic father and mother told you that you were a sellout to the whites and made fun of your 4H medals."

I threw the book on my desk. "That list doesn't even include the death of your wife and daughter. *You say you've never confronted anything?* You heroically confronted your demons and won. Granted, you turned off some feelings and we've chipped away at that iceberg and thawed out your psyche, but let's look at what you didn't do. Alcohol is the drug of choice for this disorder. It kills the pain and then disinhibits you enough to let out some of the smouldering anger that accompanies lifelong mistreatment and abuse. However, you never had a drink."

I kept on. "You said you never wanted your child to feel as you felt when you saw your father drunk. Sadly, many residential school victims who were sexually abused have repeated the pattern of sexual abuse and violence. It's all they knew. That was your 'parenting' in the institution. Yet you never did any of those things. You were so concerned about doing the wrong thing you never let your daughter sit on your lap."

Then I brought up his sister. "You never gave up on finding her, as everyone else did. The only fight you ever had, other than with the truck robbers, was with a man who maligned her.

"You had a job, and became the top driver for your company. You saved money. You married a good woman and tried to make it work. You never beat her or did anything to her that had been done to you. You refused to be the conduit for another generation of horror. You lived through an attempted cultural genocide. You are tough, brave, and you held on no matter what was thrown at you.

"Combat war heroes have endured less. They can get a medal of honour for one brave act on one day. Meanwhile, you waged a war on all fronts for most of your life and won! So don't ever say '*I never confronted anything*'!"

I know I have a bad temper, often attributed to my Irish Catholic heritage. It was only once I finished this diatribe that I realized I'd raised my voice and, not noticing the time, did something I'd never done before: talked into the next session. But I'd felt such overpowering indignation that Danny was a psychological hero and *didn't even know it*.

He looked surprised. "Okay, then," he said simply, backing out of my office and quietly closing the door.

Why did I have this inappropriate outburst? Was I afraid he was suicidal? I wasn't quite sure. I hoped Danny had read my concern for him as caring. I was frustrated by a challenge I hadn't encountered before: how do you make a man re-identify with a culture after he's been programmed during his most impressionable years to believe that culture is savage and wrong? Even the Cree language had become a trigger for Danny.

Danny and I were well past the midpoint in what would eventually be our five-year sojourn. We'd logged a lot of time together. Danny acknowledged that he'd talked to me more than he'd ever talked to anyone in his life.

I think I was helping him, but I know for certain that he was helping me with a very particular problem.

In the first chapter, on Laura, I described my countertransference: the therapist's feelings about the patient. And initially, Danny's appearance, with his Indigenous face and braids, had actually been a trigger for me—because I'd once been hospitalized after a Cree patient with braids physically assaulted me when

I worked in a psychiatric hospital. After that, whenever I encountered someone who looked like my attacker, I would feel afraid, experiencing a racing pulse and shortness of breath.

One dark, sleeting winter night, four years into my therapy with Danny, I was coming home from work when I turned up the walkway of my downtown Toronto house. An Indigenous man in braids was sitting on my dimly lit porch steps. (We lived a few blocks from the Native Canadian Centre.) He asked to borrow our snow shovel. "I want to earn some money shovelling snow, but I don't have a shovel," he said. "I saw this one on your porch, but no one was home when I rang the bell. I'll return it in the morning." I agreed and didn't think any more of it, and the shovel was indeed returned to our porch in the morning.

When I got inside the house, I realized that I'd experienced no physiological or psychological reaction of fear. An Indigenous man with braids was no longer a trigger for me. My growing positive transference for Danny had ended any PTSD I'd had.

8

A HUNTER RETURNS

DANNY WEATHERED HIS serious depression, brought on by delayed mourning for his child, his wife, his sister, his parents, and his own lost childhood. It had fallen upon him all at once. Now that he could experience real feelings, he realized that the worst part of his childhood wasn't the sexual abuse, the physical abuse, the hunger, or the cold; it was, by far, the desperate loneliness.

He took his antidepressants for two more years to make sure he didn't relapse. One week I told him to get a lot of rest and take his medication, because in our next session we were going to embark on a new path. "Great," he said, in his usual deadpan tone, which I was beginning to understand he meant as humorous.

Expression and tone are different in every culture. When I first met Danny his voice sounded flat, but having spent almost two hundred hours talking with him, I realized that his way of speaking contained particular emphases and tonal inflections for humour, pain, frustration, and other feelings. Now that I knew him better, I understood how much I'd missed in his subtle tonal modulations during our first years together.

Just as I found him quiet, he found me loud and emphatic. (To be fair, so did most white people.) Danny came in once and said he'd heard me talking on CBC Radio and liked it. He'd never paid me a compliment before, so I asked what he'd liked about it. He said, "I could turn it down."

———

In the next session, Danny tried a pre-emptive move against the "new direction" I'd mentioned earlier. "I know what you're going to say and I'm not ready," he declared.

"Oh, I didn't know you're a mind reader as well as a truck driver. How do you have time for it all? Enlighten me."

"You want me to meet a woman."

"Really? I wasn't going to say that, but it's interesting you thought I was heading there. That tells me a lot."

"Oh, no," he said, knowing he'd given himself away, which was very unusual for him. He shook his head, indicating he wasn't going to talk about it. I suspected he'd met someone or wanted to, but decided to leave the matter for another time.

What I wanted to discuss was the idea of Indigenous healing. I told Danny that I'd been educating myself about it over the years and felt he needed it. "One thing I learned for certain is that I can only take you so far," I said. His eyes narrowed slightly, which I knew meant fear, or at least concern. "I'm not saying our therapy is over. I'll be here as long as you need me." Then, I added a touch of wryness: "After all, I've taken you from a state of no feelings into deep depression."

"Yeah, thanks for that," he deadpanned.

"I honestly believe you need Native healing. All your dreams are of animals in traps or animals transmogrifying into half human. Your psyche is begging for it," I implored him. I explained that I thought he needed more of a spiritual dimension to his treatment—that whereas Western European tradition deals with the mind, body, and emotion, the Native perspective has a more holistic world view. From what I'd observed and learned from Indigenous healers, their healing ceremonies focused on spiritual contentment and feeling at one with nature and the universe.

The idea of what makes for a healthy psyche is different in each culture, I added.

Then I asked that Danny hear me out and consider group healing. "Groups. Jesus, no." He looked appalled.

"Danny, this was a *group* trauma and therefore needs *group* healing," I said with feeling. "Only someone who's Native can understand the effects of their people being traumatized over hundreds of years."

It seemed obvious to me. So many Indigenous people had experienced the same traumas—loss of land and livelihood, sexual and physical abuse at residential schools—and felt the same self-loathing just for being Native. And it's a multigenerational trauma: so many of the children taken to residential schools were so ill-treated that they became adults who had no idea how to bring up their own children. "Those generations need to hear each other's pain and heal together in a way that's grounded in their own cultural traditions," I said.

Danny was shaking his head in refusal. I gave it one last shot. "It's a little like Alcoholics Anonymous in that you were all caught in the same web and you show each other how you managed to crawl out of it. You can serve as role models for one another." I told him that I consented to treat alcoholics only if they agreed to go to AA—sixty meetings in sixty days, for a start. "It's hearing other people's testimonies of how they overcame their problems that inspires others."

Danny shook his head again; he wasn't buying it. "I live in the city. How am I supposed to get into that? Beat a drum at the mall? I'm not going back to the reserve."

"I totally understand that," I said, knowing his family situation, and that his reserve was one of the country's most troubled. I reminded him that more Indigenous people than ever were living off reserve, and that many were living in Toronto.

"Hmm" was all he said. Then, after a twenty-minute silence,

Danny asked, with a mixture of derision and trepidation, "What do they do for spiritual healing downtown?"

"There are sweat lodges, drum circles, feather circles, trapping crews—all kinds of things going on. Not all of it happens in Toronto. There's bush in Ontario, you know," I said. "But why not start here, with some Cree lessons?"

"*Namoya*," he said, presumably "no" in Cree.

I can be like a dog with a bone, so I barked on. "It sounds like a fascinating language, particularly the way it reflects the mores of the culture; the language expresses how crucial kinship is to the Cree."

"Cree? Seriously? I'd have to start from the beginning. Even hearing my father speak Cree made my heart pound when I was up north. I had that beaten out of me," he said. Then, challenging me, he added, "Want to use your language? Okay then: Cree is a trigger for me."

I ignored that, telling him he probably remembered more of the language than he thought. "Birth to five years old is long enough to acquire a language, plus you were back for some summers. Let's not allow the nuns and priests to win that battle. They should be in confession, not you."

He tried to wriggle out again by citing the demands of his job. "Stop taking overtime routes for the company and work overtime on yourself," I urged him. "Protect your psyche like you protect your cargo." He got that squinting look again, which meant he was anxious or wanted to bolt. "Is becoming more Native something that scares you? It would me if I'd had it beaten out of me."

"I kept the braids."

"You did. It says a lot. I've never met anyone who looks more Native than you."

"I've never met anyone as white as you."

We laughed over that—I have white hair and really white skin. "I've given 'pale face' a whole new meaning," I said.

I didn't mention the Native healing again. Danny would or would not act on it in his own time. And his time wasn't my time, not by a long shot.

A few months later, just before Christmas, Danny wanted to buy a gift for the secretary at work who'd invited him for Christmas dinner. She had an adopted Native daughter who'd been labelled "troubled." Today she would have been diagnosed with fetal alcohol syndrome. The white secretary was quite open in telling Danny that she'd invited him so that her daughter could meet another Indigenous person. He was going to get a household present, so I suggested he buy a Native artifact.

"Where? I don't want some made-in-China dream catcher."

"Two blocks away at the Native Canadian Centre. They have a store."

When Danny arrived for his appointment the following week, he said, "*Tanisi.*" I remembered it was the word for "hello," so I returned the greeting.

"When you sent me to that Native Centre, did you know they taught Cree twice a week?"

"No, honestly, I swear," I protested. Danny looked at me dubiously. "I knew only about the library next door to the Native Centre. It's my local library—I take my children to the story hour on Saturdays—and I've noticed that it has the most extensive collection of Aboriginal writing and tapes in the city."

Danny said he'd been to the Native Centre to get the gift, and had seen the library sign next door. "It said *Mahsinahhekahnikahmik*, which is Cree for 'the lodge or place of the book,'" he said.

"You remembered that?" I asked him in surprise.

"I guess so. I signed up for Cree lessons."

———

As it turned out, those Cree lessons, as well as connecting with the Native Centre, where urban Indigenous people gathered to keep in touch with their culture, was the best thing for Danny. During our fifth and final year of therapy, he worked at reconnecting with his Indigenous identity.

His first foray was into outdoor life. Danny realized that he'd been simulating hunting for many years—"tracking in his truck"—and now decided to do the real thing. First, he started hiking in the Canadian forests. (I'm also a hiker, so we had a bonding moment and laughed when we met in the waiting room wearing the exact same Mountain Equipment Co-op jacket.) He stayed alone in various forests from Ontario to British Columbia and logged hundreds of miles hiking. Then he began hunting moose on his own in northern Saskatchewan, and loved it.

One week Danny came to his appointment and announced that when he'd been in Manitoba, he'd run into someone from his reserve who told him his father had died eight months earlier. No one in his family had contacted him. He didn't seem upset, saying that for him, his father died when he was five. Danny referred to him as "exterminated." He didn't seem to be interested in connecting with his brothers, whom he referred to as "lost." However, he *was* interested in connecting with other Natives who wanted to explore their roots.

Around the same time, Danny expanded his wardrobe: he still wore black jeans and his leather jacket, but he'd replaced his black T-shirts and flannel shirts with ironed cotton shirts. He'd also developed a routine of coming to see me and then walking over to the Native Centre for his Cree lessons.

Therapists aren't supposed to tease clients, but by now Danny and I knew each other pretty well. I couldn't resist saying, "How come you never dressed up to come to my office until you were suddenly on your way to the Native Centre?"

"You getting at somethin'?" he mumbled.

"Learning Cree doesn't usually mean a trip to the dry cleaners."

"I guess you learned that from all the guys you know who take Cree lessons."

"Just sayin'." That was a catchphrase of Danny's, and I could mimic his low-key delivery fairly well.

He smiled. "Okay, okay. Her name is Sasina. She's Ojibwe. She's in charge of the book exchange at the Native Centre."

"Tell me about her."

"Not much to say."

Why was I not surprised? Finally, Danny told me that she was good-looking, eight years younger, and, like him, interested in connecting with her roots. Her parents had gone to residential school, and later became alcoholics. She and her brother were part of the Sixties Scoop, when many Indigenous children were adopted out to white homes. (The practice was stopped only in the eighties.) The two were adopted by a German-Canadian couple from Waterloo, and were their only children. "She said the parents were good people, but they never mentioned that she or her brother were Native. She married a white guy, got a divorce after a year," Danny revealed. "Then she and her brother started looking into their heritage about ten years ago. She runs all kinds of programs on Indian this an' that."

"Does she work full time at the Centre?"

"No. She's a social worker at SickKids hospital."

"So, have you had dates?" I asked, staring meaningfully at him.

"We've gone to some Indian talks together. And I've gone to some Ojibwe stuff with her. She's close with her brother. They share a house they bought in the east end."

"Did you ask her out?"

"No. She got me interested in stuff at the Centre. I used to just sit in the lounge, get books from the book exchange, and read. She introduced me to her brother and all that."

"What is she like?"

He thought for a few minutes. "I'd say calm. Best part—she likes a quiet man."

"Well, she found him." He nodded and I couldn't help but laugh.

"So you don't feel pressure when you're with her."

"I can just be a Native with no explanations," he said, leaning back in his chair.

"That must be a relief," I offered. "Although your wife was nice and kind, you had to try to put on some sort of white performance all day long. That had to be exhausting."

"Like residential school."

As we talked about Sasina (her name means "nightingale" in Ojibwe), it became clear over the weeks that he cared deeply about her. She, like Danny, felt stranded in a white world, and when she investigated her birth parents on the reserve, she found that they were too dysfunctional to make a meaningful connection. Yet her heritage was important to her. She'd always felt different in white society, and although she had respect and even love for her adoptive parents, she knew she wasn't wired like them. Still, they'd sent her to university; she, like Danny, had a strong work ethic and was good at "white people tasks" (unlike her brother, who didn't do well in school).

Therapists are supposed to ask about their patients' sex lives, but I knew that Danny was a very private person. However, since he'd been a victim of sexual abuse, and I didn't know Sasina's history, I had to ask. "Sex?"

"What about it?" he replied, as if I were a lunatic.

"Well, it's been a childhood issue we've worked on."

"At least I don't have to explain why I don't have hair on my chest," he said obliquely.

I smiled and nodded, knowing it was Danny's roundabout way of saying that he wasn't nervous, that having sex with a Native woman he cared for was comforting.

After a silence, he almost whispered, "Once she sat on my lap at breakfast while I had my coffee." We both knew this was one of his triggers, since the Catholic priest had made him sit on his lap from an early age. Danny looked out the window and said, "I thought of you and what we worked on with the Tonto episode. I said to her, 'I don't like people to sit on my lap.' She stood up right away and looked kind of hurt and embarrassed, so I said, 'It reminds me of really bad stuff at residential school. It has nothing to do with you.' She seemed to understand and not have bad feelings. To be honest, it frightened me to say that. I hated it, but I did it. I had to, or we'd grow apart like I did with my wife. I don't want that."

"Intimacy is a hard language to learn, especially if it's been discouraged. But you've done it."

"I hardly had an accent," he said wryly.

When I asked Danny if he and Sasina were living together, he smiled and said he guessed they were, since she'd come to his place one weekend several months earlier and hadn't returned home.

Another milestone was passed when Danny came in one week and said he'd gone with Sasina's brother to a powwow. He described it as noisy and crowded and "not my thing." I encouraged him again to participate in some Indigenous healing ceremonies.

He did. He went to a sweat lodge in Hamilton, a city close to Toronto, with eight other men. During the ceremony they sat in a circle in a covered dome with heated rocks in the centre. He learned that the rounded teepee represents pregnant Mother

Earth; the rocks are called grandfathers because they're ancient and have seen everything. The rocks are heated up and the participants talk and sweat. Danny said it got unbelievably hot in the tent. There were four rounds of heating up, and in the second round, one by one, the men poured out their feelings as their sweat poured off their bodies. It took an entire day.

Danny told me that being in the darkness felt like being in a hot womb. He heard the same "awful crap" that had haunted him for years pour out of the other men. He felt poisons from childhood releasing from his system; he sweated them out and towelled them away. When he heard men who'd disappointed their families with alcohol abuse, he thought of what his father might have wanted to say if he could have shared his pain.

Over the next six months Danny became involved in all kinds of Native healing, such as the pipe ceremony where he attempted to connect with Mother Earth and express some of his hopes. He went to talking circles where people spoke, as he said, "until they were done talkin', and it could take a long time." His favourite ritual was smudging, a cleansing smoke bath that's used to centre a person and to remove negative energy. He and Sasina smudged almost every day, purifying their home and their souls. Danny liked it because it forced him to think about each day's energy; it would set him on the right path every morning.

He looked at me once toward the end of our therapy and said, "You know, you were right."

"Music to my ears," I replied.

He shook his head. "White people love being right. They'll tell you fifty times if they were right."

"My extremely white hair and skin match how white I am when it comes to loving being right. Let me know what I was right about so I may bask in my success," I said, laughing.

"White therapy has no spirit: it's a doughnut with a hole in the middle of it," he said. "I learned from you that I had pain, how to get at it—all that stuff—but there was nothing spiritual about it, and that's the most healing. I needed the Native part."

In the last few months of our therapy, Danny went on a camping trip far up north in the winter with a hunting party that included Sasina's brother. "We had to lay in wait for a moose," he told me. "They're animals that spook easily, and you have to see them coming from a long way off. They can sense that the hunter is near. But none of the hunting party could wait it out in the minus-forty cold. So I said I'd give it a try."

I couldn't resist almost yelling in triumph, "Those old Ojibwes had nothing on this stealthy Cree."

"You got that right. I was on my stomach for days, but I got him."

I started clapping. I had lost all my objectivity. In most cases, a therapist has to present an unemotional front. But since our therapy was effectively finished, I wanted to be more than a Freudian therapist for Danny. He needed an advocate, someone who was on his side but who asked for nothing back—someone who longed for his well-being. People who've experienced severe trauma are numb until they meet a compassionate witness. When they believe that individual is for real and can be trusted, they can turn into a "real" person and dare to attach.

Danny said that the hunting trip was wonderful. When they set traps he remembered all the little tricks he'd learned as a child about how to bury them in the snow. He also remembered his father's kindness and patience as he'd taught Danny hunting techniques. So much came back to him that he was overjoyed. For the first time since he was five years old, he felt that the spirits were with him. He smiled while telling me this, and it was a smile I'd never seen before. It showed all his straight white teeth.

After I saw that unguarded smile, I knew our work together was over. I was sad, but it had to be said: "Danny, our work here is done. You must feel it." He stood up, and we both knew this had been our last session. He was undemonstrative and so was I. He just turned and walked out.

I watched him through the window, looking at the man who'd once frightened me and who now felt like a brother. He strode out in his leather bomber jacket and snakeskin boots with his braids swinging behind him.

9

REUNITED

DANNY FOUGHT AND WON his life battle when most other humans in those circumstances would have succumbed to mental illness or substance abuse. Why was that? The first reason, I think, lies in Danny's personality traits and basic temperament. His mother, who figured very little in this case, had said something crucial about Danny: he was "always stubborn." In other words, he could not be swayed. He made a decision to never let anyone in to destroy him, and stuck to it. He decided not to drink and then *stubbornly*, as his mother would say, or *resolutely*, as I would say, stuck to that as well. Second, he was always, even as a small child, a loner. He didn't have the same social needs as most others. His sister Rose, for example, stayed with their parents and tried to get their love, even in their decline, and then she herself declined with them. Third, and more important than any innate qualities, Danny had had the love and affection of well-functioning parents from birth to age five, which are a child's most formative years. If Danny's parents had been damaged by attending residential school, as so many Native parents have been, Danny may have had a very different and sadder profile.

Danny used one of the most powerful defences known in psychology: depersonalization. He cut off all his feelings. It was the perfect armour. The only problem with his perfect weapon was that he could barely attach to anyone, or feel life's pleasures. As he said at the beginning of our work together, "I don't need joy." He was right, in a way. Is it better to feel or to maintain your sanity? For many years, he chose the latter.

Although he'd been carefully programmed for thirteen years to renounce his Indigenous identity, he stubbornly refused to do it. There were times in his life when he wavered: he'd confessed to the "sin" of that identity in the confession box as a child, and felt anxious when he heard the Cree language. However, Danny was a fierce warrior. He wore his long hair in braids, proclaiming his heritage. And he came to therapy sessions for five years, working inch by inch to reclaim the identity that had been stolen from him.

For me, Danny's was an unusual case. First, it taught me a lot about multicultural therapy. It illustrated the sad fact that white society's institutions and attitudes had destroyed his family dynamics, with consequences beyond one generation. I had to face the uncomfortable realization that I was a member of the group that had tried to assimilate and extinguish the culture of Indigenous people. It was no wonder that Danny had trust issues with me.

Second, this case taught me the limitations of psychotherapy. It wasn't designed to deal with cultural annihilation, something Dr. Brant had made clear to me early on. I recruited a small army of Indigenous healers to provide what psychotherapy could not: spiritual healing. It was the first time I realized how culturally specific psychotherapy was, and I had to face those limitations head-on.

Several years before Danny became a patient, I'd enrolled in a sweetgrass basket–making course at the Royal Ontario Museum. It took me months to make the tiny basket that sat on the desk in my office; it was so minute, it could only hold about four paperclips. Danny had found this weeny basket funny. As he said, "Why bother?"

A few weeks after my exit interview with Danny, I walked into my waiting room and found a large beautiful sweetgrass basket with unusual visual patterns on it. It was an astounding Native artifact, a collector's item. I knew it was old and that it had been dyed using a potato to make the intricate design.

I was very touched, and it took pride of place in the foyer of my home. Ten years later, while renovating my house, moving men packed up our things and put them in storage. When I unpacked later, only the sweetgrass basket was missing. The insurance company told me it was worth thousands of dollars and was of museum quality. I didn't care about the cost, I just wanted it back. But I never saw it—or Danny—again.

I later found out that Danny had begun mentoring others in their spiritual journey, and that he was involved in healing ceremonies. He was considered to be very good at it. He travelled all over to conferences and used the tools of his trade. The reason I know this is that every so often I'd get an Indigenous client referred to me by Danny. The client would say, "Danny said that before I work with him I need to see you for a tune-up and a retread." Danny loved automobiles and engines of any kind, so I took this as a compliment.

It had been almost thirty years since I first laid eyes on Danny. I wanted to let him know that I was writing about him as a case study. Danny would now be seventy years old.

I tracked down his former employer, who was now in his late eighties. When I asked how Danny was doing, there was a sigh on the phone. Then, "Danny died of throat cancer when he was in his early fifties." I was too shocked to say much. The employer said, "He never complained. He lost weight, coughed all the time, was hoarse but kept working—just like when his wife and daughter died. Once he collapsed, he lasted only a few days. He asked to be buried next to his daughter."

The boss said he went to the funeral and was surprised to see hundreds of people there, mostly Indigenous people in ceremonial dress. A woman, who he presumed was Danny's girlfriend, sang a song in a Native language and the men played large flat drums that they carried.

Just as I was about to hang up, the employer had an afterthought. "Throat cancer is a strange thing to get. He never worked with asbestos or any of the substances that give you throat cancer. I would never have let my workers do that. Wonder what caused it?"

I wanted to say that maybe it had to do with having to swallow all those Cree words throughout his entire childhood. They stayed in the dark and became diseased. His residential school beat the Cree out of him, but that pain literally stuck in his craw, a physical reminder of what he had heroically endured.

Ikosi (goodbye), Danny.

ALANA

Cruelty, like every other vice,
requires no motive outside of itself;
it only requires opportunity.

GEORGE ELIOT

THE TED BUNDY FAN CLUB

PIERRE JANET, a famous French psychologist, said of the human psyche, "Every life is a piece of art put together with all means available." Alana, one of my most rewarding patients, did indeed use every means available, and some of her methods for maintaining her sanity were so ingenious that they rose to the level of art.

Alana's abuse was severe and relentless. But as horrific as it was, that depravity, I would come to realize, was more than matched by the glory of the human spirit. This young woman's strength of character, intelligence, and maternal instinct pulled her through the trauma. Alana, more than anyone I've ever met, shows what the mind is capable of enduring while still remaining intact.

Alana was referred to me by a psychotherapist colleague whose specialty was gender issues. This colleague began by recounting how she'd come to hear of Alana in the first place.

Years before, she'd had a patient named Christopher whom she saw through to becoming Jane. Christopher, a linguistics professor, had divorced his wife when their children entered university; he then began his long, arduous transition from male to female. Transgender psychotherapy clients are more common now, but forty years ago, when Christopher transitioned, they were very rare. Not only was the public less accepting, but sex-transitioning hormones and operations were more primitive than they are today. My colleague helped him during the most painful stage of the process, the removal of his sex organs and the introduction of female hormones, which were hard on the system. Back then, when the field was a tiny new sub-specialty, transitioning took years. Still, given all the perils, Jane, who was a maverick, made a good recovery both physically and mentally.

In October 1996 my colleague got a call from Jane (formerly Christopher), asking whether she would treat her partner, Alana. Jane explained that Alana was a lesbian, and that she herself had long since identified as a lesbian. The couple, having shared an interest in computer languages, had met in the computer section of the university library. They'd been living together happily for eleven years.

Since it's generally not a good idea for a psychologist to see members of the same family in individual therapy—loyalties can become murky—my colleague made the referral to me instead. When I asked about the nature of the problem, she replied that her ex-patient Jane had said only this: "Words couldn't describe it." Coming from a linguist, that was saying a lot.

I agreed to see Alana, who, at thirty-five, was nearly twenty years younger than Jane. There were a lot of firsts for me with this case—and they began right off the top, when I entered the waiting room to meet Alana. Whereas patients are usually sitting down, Alana stood facing me, plastered against the only window like a soldier at attention, looking wide-eyed with fear.

She was pretty in a pixieish way, fine-boned with short, naturally curly strawberry-blond hair, fair skin, and no makeup on her slightly freckled face. She wore a grey T-shirt under an unbuttoned plaid flannel shirt, khaki cargo pants, and black high-top running shoes. (For all the years I saw her, she wore only slight variations on that same outfit.)

Hoping to calm her down, I suggested I bring in some tea. Then I led her into my office, where she sat perched on the edge of a chair, ready to bolt. Once we'd settled in with our tea, I asked what I could do for her. "Probably nothing," she said, not in a hostile way but rather as though she was simply stating a fact. I asked what was troubling her. She looked down, smiled, and scratched her hands, which were bright red, as if she'd dipped them into beet juice. "I guess I'm nervous," she said. By now she was taking short, stabbing breaths that sounded like the Little Engine That Could climbing the mountain. She was so pale that even her freckles were fading. To prevent her from fainting, I urged her to drink her tea.

When I asked about her family life, Alana said she'd been brought up in Prince Rupert, British Columbia. Her mother left when Alana was almost three, having been declared unfit by the Children's Aid Society. After that, her father, an alcoholic drug addict, raised her and her younger sister, Gretchen. Alana went on to explain that her father had framed her mother by planting heroin in her pockets and then calling the police. When the police arrived, Alana's father pointed out that his wife had been a teenage prostitute in Calgary, which, as Alana said, "wasn't a great lineage." Her mother, then only twenty-two, fought in court to keep her children. But Alana's father was deemed the more responsible parent, since he'd been labelled a "genius" and had an impressive job as a programmer at one of the big computer companies. Years later, the company fired him owing to his drug and alcohol abuse and his bizarre behaviour.

I wanted an example of this behaviour. Alana said he'd once killed a cat, named Live Wire, that lived in the company's warehouse. "He electrically shocked it to death for fun, putting a sign around its neck that read *My name now is just Wire.* He found out it wasn't so funny to everyone else when he was fired."

Sadists—people who derive pleasure from inflicting pain or humiliation—often have no idea how repellent their behaviour is to others. Eventually they learn, as Alana's father did, to associate with other sadists, who approve of their aberrant proclivities.

When I asked more questions about her father, Alana told me that it upset her to call him that. (It had also upset him. He demanded that both his daughters refer to him as Art, his first name.) She asked that I never again use *father* in speech or in writing, but instead call him Art.

At the end of the first session, I tried to understand why Alana was so upset about being in my office. "I'm afraid that if you knew what was inside my head, you'd have me locked up," she confessed.

This is always a difficult fear for a therapist to deal with, given that if Alana *were* a danger to herself or others, she would indeed have to be hospitalized. Since her mother had been framed as an immoral, incompetent drug addict, Alana may have feared a similar intervention. I didn't want to frighten her, so I chose not to address the issue directly, asking her instead if she could describe just one of her symptoms. "Tell me one that isn't life-threatening, and we can explore it next week," I suggested.

"I gag at certain things and have dry heaves. If I don't get out right away, I have uncontrollable projectile vomiting."

It was apparent that collecting an entire history from this patient might be more than she could handle. Her physical responses—pooling blood in her hands, hyperventilation, and pupil dilation—were outward signs of her extreme inner turmoil. We would move ahead cautiously.

At our next session, Alana brought a list of triggers that caused her to gag, dry-heave, or vomit. I asked how those symptoms affected her work. She'd been at a law firm for a few years now, she told me, and whenever she was ill, she just left the room for as long as she needed to; no one would question her.

When I asked about her law credentials, Alana said she'd gone to university for less than a year. In her early twenties she'd gotten a job in the firm's IT department and worked her way up; now, she mostly prepared briefs for court. She was, it transpired, performing important legal tasks in multimillion-dollar cases for one of the best law firms in the city. But since she wasn't a lawyer, she'd never been paid as one. Alana had a near-photographic memory and a high IQ; she could work on several cases at once, keeping all the details straight in her head. And although her favourite area was family law—she'd done research on her own childhood case—the firm valued her most for her knowledge of patent law. They needed Alana. As she put it, "I've saved their bacon hundreds of times. They know I'm weird and they just leave me alone." Alana could come and go at will, "but if they have a big case in court, I can log several all-nighters in a row without blinking." The obvious question was why she wasn't a lawyer herself, with all the advantages that would bring. But I refrained from asking—the last thing she needed at this precarious time was any form of confrontation.

At this point Alana became more businesslike, pulling out the sheet of paper on which she'd written her triggers. "The first thing on my list of causes of projectile vomiting," she began, "is the smell of fish. I can't go through a food court for fear of spewing vomit on random tables." When I asked why, she calmly revealed that Art had raped her from the age of four to fourteen. He'd also told her that if she didn't relish having sex with him, he'd move on to Gretchen in the next room. Young Alana had no idea how to make it look like she was enjoying what in fact hurt and humiliated her. "I always loved math, so I used to count the flowers on my wallpaper and then make up math problems with the flowers while he was raping me," she said. "I finally learned to make sounds and make myself wet for him at the age of eight. I hated myself for doing it and I hated him, but I saved my sister. He made me do it until I smelled, as he said, 'like a fish.' So fish makes me sick."

I did not betray the shock I felt at such astonishing cruelty. I'd learned from other patients who'd endured extreme situations that if I conveyed any sense of these being far out of the norm, they would become frightened and clam up. Alana was unused to sympathy or empathy; over time, I would glean that she found it phony, bizarre, and alienating. She later explained her feelings about empathy this way: "If you went home one day and your father started talking like a saccharine kindergarten teacher, you'd probably be freaked out or, at least, smell a rat. Well, that's how I feel when people are being empathetic."

The second thing on her list of symptoms was light touch: this was how Art had approached her. It would give her dry heaves. The third thing was the sound of chewing, or, as she called it, "smacking." Again, this had to do with the sickening things Art did: he would bite her genitals if she didn't express pleasure.

The fourth thing was bathrooms. She had to hold her breath while in a bathroom of any kind. When I asked her why, she ran out of my office and vomited in the washroom. In all the years Alana was in therapy with me, she never disclosed what her father did to her in the bathroom. She said that if she spoke of it, it would be real; she might not be able to "come back to the world."

I was conflicted about Alana's reluctance on that subject. In therapy that's in any way Freudian, or that's based on a belief in the unconscious, the goal is to bring unconscious material forward into the conscious mind so that patients no longer act on their powerful but unconscious needs. Traumatic events need to be revealed so that they can be relived in the presence of a supportive therapist who can help the patient through feelings of anxiety, shame, or guilt. However, at that point, I'd been in practice long enough to know that there is no orthodoxy about anything and that no two patients are the same. I came to realize, through Alana, that some experiences are too hard to live through twice.

Her entire list of "vomit items," as she called them, was based on her frequent rapes. What made her the sickest, she said, was Art's forcing her apparent complicity in these with fake orgasms. She said, "I could live through the physical torture of rape, and, believe me, a four-year-old has a small vagina. But the worst damage, or the gift that keeps on giving every day of my life, is having flashbacks of me pretending to enjoy an orgasm with Art. That image looms in my psyche, and the shame of recollecting it makes it hard for me to breathe—like my chest is in a vise."

I nodded. In the long run, shame always outlives physical pain. "Anyone who thinks of a shameful memory will experience it at least as vividly as when they had the original experience," I said.

Alana, despite the horror in her life, could be quite amusing, and black comedy was her forte. For example, when she first saw the famous scene in *When Harry Met Sally* where Meg Ryan fakes an orgasm in a diner, she said she'd learned to do that by the age of five. She'd finally figured out what she needed to do to be left alone for the rest of the night. As Alana said, "Art was not only a rapist, he was also an egomaniac. He needed to believe he was a good lover."

He also made Alana have sex with his friends. He told them she was a nymphomaniac with a tight vagina, which in his mind, and in the mind of his drunken, drugged-out, sadistic friends, was perfect; it singled him out as important in his crowd of pederasts. Sometimes, if he were hard up, he'd charge them cash.

Taxi Driver was Art's favourite movie; he was fixated on Jodie Foster as the preteen prostitute. The actress was born the same month and year as Alana, and they looked somewhat alike, particularly at twelve. Art bought the same pink shorts and flowered blouse that Jodie Foster wore in the movie and made Alana wear the outfit while he raped her. He wanted her to speak in the slang that Jodie Foster used in her dialogue with Robert De Niro.

And as if that wasn't bad enough, during their encounters Art made Alana take alcohol and drugs—anything from marijuana to cocaine to hallucinogens. About once a week, from the age of about six to fourteen, she took LSD. Amazingly, she did not have a drug-induced psychosis or any flashbacks. (People who've taken copious quantities of drugs often have flashbacks and suffer hallucinations, persecutory delusions, and confusion, even years later.)

Alana presented herself as a lesbian; she'd been "born that way," she told me, and did not believe her past exploitation had anything to do with "making her" one. Ever since she'd become aware of the concept of sexual orientation, she'd always considered herself gay. She was never attracted to males and always had traditionally male interests, from building computers to competing in karate, judo, and kickboxing to playing violent video games. Alana didn't focus on her homosexuality as an issue, so neither did I.

When I inquired about her present sex life with Jane, she said she had no sexual feelings whatsoever. "I have lots of physical and psychological scarring, as does Jane. Neither of us cares much about sex. To me the term *great sex* sounds like an oxymoron." She and Jane had been through enough and were happy just to live quiet, decent, uneventful lives. As Alana put it, "I have bigger fish to fry, like maintaining my sanity." Since she didn't consider the lack of sexual desire a problem to be dealt with, I decided to focus on her more pressing issues.

When I asked about her father's physical violence, she said there was very little directed toward her. She was usually a few steps ahead of Art—she knew when to disappear and how to appease him. Art did, however, beat Alana's mother regularly when she was still there.

One of the most terrifying events of Alana's childhood occurred when she was about six and Gretchen three. They were riding down a river on their homemade raft with Art, who was high on LSD, when "he suddenly flew into a rage, pushed my sister and me off the raft, and returned to the shore without us," she recalled. He yelled that they were "succubae," and to stop being babies and learn to swim. "Gretchen began to drown and so did I, from trying to buoy her up in the water."

Art's friend Tim, a man who'd been jailed for child pornography and other sexual crimes, had been laughing from the shore at Art's antics. "He finally realized we were actually drowning. Gretchen had already gone under." Tim swam out and saved them. When they got to shore, panting and terrified, Gretchen had to be resuscitated. Tim slugged Art in the mouth, telling him that he'd gone too far. Art said, "I guess you're right. I almost killed the goose that laid the golden egg."

Alana said she remembered that day as though it were a movie in slow motion. Gretchen was never the same, and developed phobias; Alana realized that Art was willing to let them die. "But the most incredible thing, the thing that actually helped to maintain my sanity, was that Tim had called Art 'a sick fuck.' That was the first time in my life that I had some idea there was something wrong with Art. I thought the problem was with my mother and me. Art would frequently yell that I was like my mother, a 'frigid bitch.' I wasn't sure what that was, but I picked up that it was wicked."

"As a child you had no idea you were being raped, only that you were being uncooperative and *frigid*, whatever that meant," I summed up.

Curious, I asked if Tim ever helped them again. She said the only reason he saved them was that he didn't want to be complicit in murder. He, unlike Art, had been in prison and didn't want to go back. He had big fights with Art but remained a lifelong friend. As Alana said, "Where else do you find friends who are sadists *and* into kiddie porn *and* sexual abuse?" I agreed it was a select group.

Art had met Tim through the Ted Bundy Fan Club. Ted Bundy, an infamous American serial killer, was finally executed in 1989 after raping, killing (or sometimes in reverse order), and dismembering thirty women. He escaped from prison twice, each time going on new killing sprees. He, like Art, was highly intelligent. Bundy had been in law school and provided his own defence. Art, imitating Bundy, acted as his own counsel at the trial where he had his wife declared an unfit mother. Bundy was tall, dark, and good-looking. Art was a short, slight, freckled redhead who fantasized that he was as evil and as devastatingly handsome as Ted Bundy. He was right about the former but woefully wrong in the latter. Alana related the following as though she were describing someone whose father was a member of the local Rotary: "Every year on November twenty-fourth he and his sick buddies would sing 'Happy Birthday' and make toasts to him. They'd have regular Ted Bundy Fan Club meetings."

Bundy received thousands of love letters from female fans. Art delighted in discussing Bundy's popularity with the ladies, saying that, deep down, all women really liked killers and rapists. Both

Tim and Art idolized Bundy, and wanted to be adored just as Bundy's fans had "adored" him. It wasn't until she became a teenager that Alana discovered Ted Bundy wasn't actually a hero.

I've left out most of the gruesome details of this case, since they'd be too distressing for many people to process. And when I consulted with a psychiatrist about the possibility of medication for Alana, even she found it hard to listen to her history. With tears in her eyes, she asked how I could be so matter-of-fact about such horror.

I thought about that for some time, and realized that it probably goes back to my childhood. My father mostly raised me. From the age of four to thirteen I worked with him in our drugstore and delivered medication. I saw many dire situations: poverty, prostitution, people dying alone, battered women, forms of mental illness. Yet, as my father pointed out, it wasn't my job to be there for each client on the route; if someone needed help I should instead offer to call the police or an ambulance. My job was to keep moving and make all the deliveries. If I were to dwell on one needy person, if I were to be swayed by emotion, I wouldn't get the job done. The driver and I often didn't finish until well after dark as it was. In short, I learned to compartmentalize at an early age.

Alana, too, learned to compartmentalize, and even to use black humour as a way to deflect her pain. She once told me how her father would neglect to leave them with any food: she and Gretchen would forage through the cupboards for something, anything, to eat, including raw flour and sugar. She called herself "the originator of the raw food movement." You might wonder how anyone could find anything humorous in that situation, but Alana managed it. That was her art.

2

OFF TO GRANDMOTHER'S HOUSE

SOME EVENTS IN Alana's life sounded as if they were right out of "Little Red Riding Hood," except that in Alana's case, the grandmother and the wolf were one and the same.

For a while, Art lived on his severance pay from the computer company. When that was gone, and having been denied welfare, he found work four thousand kilometres away in a mine in Kirkland Lake, Ontario. He lasted only two weeks before being fired, but then he stayed on in the town, selling drugs. Before he'd left he deposited Alana and Gretchen at his parents' home in Kitimat, British Columbia, while his mother and father were at church; they were deeply involved in the Jehovah's Witnesses religion. Art left a note saying he'd be back in six months, but that stretched into two years.

I was relieved to hear that Alana, then seven years old, was out of Art's clutches and into a religious home where there was a mother and a father. Alana disabused me of that notion in short order. The grandmother was as evil as Art, but in a different way.

I use the non-psychological term *evil* to describe Art and his mother because there is no psychological term or diagnosis that adequately covers the breadth of their cruel natures. The term *psychopath* comes closest. Psychopaths lack empathy, have a superficial charm and a grandiose sense of self-worth, and are pathological liars. As well, they are cunning and manipulative, lack remorse, are emotionally shallow, refuse to accept responsibility for their actions, and indulge in a parasitic lifestyle. Certainly Art exhibited all those features, and his mother had several of them. They were indeed psychopaths and sadists, but they had so many more evil features than those two categories encompass. Art and his mother formed a category that is not to be found in any psychological manual.

Art's abuse, although horrific, happened in short spurts. Most of the time he was so narcissistically self-involved that he didn't bother with discipline unless he'd been affected directly: if, say, Alana took food before he did, he'd get angry; if she didn't go to school, he didn't care. Not so with his mother, Alana's grandmother—a disturbed religious fanatic with a lot of energy to wreak havoc on those around her. Art had a sister who'd been in some kind of institution since she was a young teenager. No one knew what was wrong with her, and she was rarely mentioned. But Art, the favourite child, could do no wrong. Alana's grandmother was a smart but uneducated woman. Her son, who won awards all through school, was a verification of her intelligence, his achievements feeding into her grandiosity. Meanwhile, her husband was an obese man in suspenders who sat in a rocking chair all day and said nothing; he had the vegetative signs of depression. His wife had to tell him to bathe.

Gretchen and Alana were administered enemas on the day they were dropped off and every day after that. They were called "dirty brats, filthy inside and out" who had ruined their father's chances for a Nobel Prize. (Their grandmother thought there was a Nobel for programming, which was one of her more benign fantasies.)

In our sessions, Alana was a soft-spoken but gifted raconteur. Her stories would be peppered with droll observations about, say, the grandmother's tacky house decor, including the hoop-skirted

Marie Antoinette toilet paper holder. Inevitably, though, as Alana got deeper into the actual events that occurred at her grand-mother's house, the comic presentation would tip into terror. Her hands would turn into red, itchy appendages. Alana would gag and vomit. I always kept a bucket next to her.

It took several months for the full story of what happened at Granny's house to surface. The grandmother's campaign to "clean the filth from Alana" resulted in mutilation. In her twenties, Alana had to have her vagina and anus reconstructed because the scar tissue impaired many of her bodily functions. No doctor ever asked what had happened. Her surgeon said only that "he would do what he could." She would never be able to have children. Her family doctor verified this damage for me.

Alana had also taken birth-control pills since the age of eight. The first time Art gave them to her he simply said, "Take them," so she took the whole packet at once. Eventually she learned to take one a day. When she went to a Prince Rupert gynecologist at the age of thirteen because of her internal bleeding, he asked how long she'd been on the pill. He never asked why a child of eight was on the pill. As shocking as Alana's sexual abuse was, it was equally shocking that, despite myriad signs of physical and mental abuse, no one from school or from the health services ever inter-vened. It was as though Alana were invisible.

Until she went to live with her grandparents, Alana had no idea of the workings of the outside world. They had no television and no close neighbours in her rural home, and she'd been told not to talk to people at school. "Art and his demented friends in the Bundy Club were my version of what went on in the world," she told me. "It didn't seem like the Yellow Brick Road, but I assumed it was life's quotidian." Her grandmother's home was an eye-opener into another, albeit horrendous and fanatical, reality. Alana said, "There was church, and church breakfasts where people talked and were instructed with fire and brimstone on the general morass of moral decay."

Alana was unsure what sexuality was when she first moved in with her grandparents; she had no idea that what she'd done with Art was considered "sexual." However, through the Jehovah's Witnesses services at Kingdom Hall, she got an inkling that it was something heinous. At the church, prurient elders ranted about the evils of sexuality. Alana understood that her father had violated a taboo and that she, too, had engaged in a loathsome act. Imagine a little girl suddenly realizing that what Art had forced her to do was considered so disgusting that she could be forever locked out of "the Kingdom of God." She said, "I had no idea then who God was, but he sounded a hell of a lot better than Art and Grandma. Then again, who wouldn't? I liked that God accepted everyone in his Kingdom. But then I was broken-hearted when I realized he would never accept me after what I'd done."

It was during that time that she had her first hallucination of body distortion. Her grandmother insisted that she wear ironed cotton dresses every day. Alana began to believe she had huge genitals and that everyone could see them. She said they pulsed with blood, were large and purple, and hung below her dress almost to the floor. During this time she was almost catatonic. (Catatonia is a state of immobility accompanied by mental stupor—much like hibernation in animals.) She sat in a chair all day, and was unwilling to get up for fear that people would see the giant genitals sway when she walked. She refused to go to school, and no one made her.

Hoping to find one kind act in this sea of cruelty, I asked her if she could remember just one good thing during her stay at her grandparents. She thought for a long time. "Once, Grandpa, who never moved from his chair except to go to church, silently, without looking at me, handed me the comics from the Sunday paper." Her eyes clouded with tears and she choked out, "I can still see the front page with the comic strip with Jiggs and Maggie." She closed her eyes, smiled, and then added, "I can still smell the newsprint. And even today I could draw each line of each panel and speech bubble." When I told her that the comic strip was called *Bringing Up Father*, she shook her head and said, "Ironic title, since I've been 'bringing up father' for years"—referring to her ever-present "vomit items."

Her grandmother made her sleep in the attached garage, giving her a sleeping bag during the winter. Even at a young age, Alana preferred to stay alone in the garage and tinker with the tools while her sister cleaned the house. At night, she was so cold she'd use the barbecue cover and the car's floor mats as blankets.

Art never came to visit. However, he was eventually kicked out of Kirkland Lake by the RCMP, escorted to the city limits, and told never to return. After that, he arrived to pick up the girls. The next time he raped Alana he became disgusted by her genitals, which had been mutilated by his own mother. But he said he'd "make the best of it." Alana told me it felt as though a hot iron was entering her, and that she almost passed out.

At that point, Alana decided to kill herself. The next day she dragged herself to the shore of the Skeena River, lay down on a rock, and hoped to die of exposure. She remembered thinking that she simply could not go on, that she was too tired even to lift her arm. She could not endure one more day of torture. Now that she was older—she was eight—she felt not only the confusion, pain, hopelessness, and loneliness she'd always known. Since living at her grandmother's house, she could add guilt and shame to the mix. She spent the entire night on the rock, and when she woke, her legs no longer worked: it was the start of hypothermia. She was relieved—she was beginning to die.

It was helpful for me to pause and reflect on that scene. I believe it was the most important moment of Alana's life. She was deciding whether she would live or die. Many people have arrived at this juncture in life, if not literally then metaphorically. Is it any wonder that Hamlet's speech is the most famous in all of Western literary history?

> *To be, or not to be, that is the question:*
> *Whether 'tis nobler in the mind to suffer*
> *The slings and arrows of outrageous fortune,*
> *Or to take arms against a sea of troubles,*
> *And by opposing end them.*

Anyone who contemplates suicide has to decide to be or not to be. Yet, at some level, don't we all have to make that same decision? There are times when we've had to decide to change or remain the same. Will we be slaves to safe, mundane routines or break out and remake our lives the way we imagine them to be? Real change may entail risk, pain, probably anxiety, and hard work, but it's a way "to be" versus not being. We've all been heroes or cowards in our own narratives, depending on the occasion and the choices we've made. In this scene on the rock, Alana, like Hamlet, had to decide whether she'd do battle with the slings and arrows of outrageous fortune.

In his book *Man's Search for Meaning*, Viktor Frankl writes of confronting the same dilemma when he was in a Nazi concentration camp. Frankl outlines how prisoners experienced three psychological reactions to their dire condition. First was shock, second was apathy, and third was depersonalization and moral deformity. Frankl makes the point that only those who gave their life *meaning* did well. He points out that in every situation, there is always freedom of choice, even in extreme suffering. For Frankl, the highest goal was love. He tried to do kind things for others and to wait in the hope of seeing his wife. The Nazis could not take hope or kindness from him.

Alana was living a life of "outrageous fortune," and the slings and arrows could not be sharper than those she endured. Yet she did have choice. As Frankl said, we must find meaning in suffering; he quotes Nietzsche, who said it another way: "He who has a why to live for can bear almost any how."

Eight-year-old Alana, lying half-frozen on a rock, had never heard of Frankl or Nietzsche—yet her crisis fit their description perfectly. Alana thought of what Gretchen would have to endure if she lost her older sister. Gretchen had already suffered more than Alana had from the drugs Art administered, and she was by nature more compliant. Alana knew she was mother to Gretchen, and the only person between her and Art. Art had chosen Alana as his nighttime sexual partner and sworn daytime enemy; if she were gone, Gretchen would be the next victim. Alana decided that suicide would be a selfish act—that for her sister's sake, she had to live.

She tried to stand up to walk home, but her legs were too numb to support her. Alana waited until noon, when the sun beat down on her. At first she had to crawl—her arms worked before her legs did. No one even asked where she'd been.

When Alana told me about her decision, she cited the myth of Prometheus. She'd read how Zeus, wanting to inflict an eternal punishment on Prometheus, had him chained to a rock on a mountain where every day an eagle would come and devour his liver. Because Prometheus was immortal, his liver was regenerated every night. Alana said she knew exactly how Prometheus felt. When she'd decided to live that day on the Skeena River shore, it meant allowing her body to be figuratively eaten by a predator, over and over again. Most heroic acts occur within a short period of time. But Alana, like Prometheus, opted for daily torture. It was a *truly* heroic act.

The maternal instinct is a selfless one, and it helped Alana rise up from the rock. "That was my low point," she told me. "I feel like such a despicable human being for even thinking of abandoning my sister. Plus, I'd have been so sad without Turing." Turing was her beloved cat, one of the few constants in her life. He and Alana were both named after Alan Turing, the British man hailed as the father of the computer. It is ironic that Turing, Art's idol, was also tortured. Having been charged with "gross indecency"—in England at the time, homosexual acts were deemed a crime—he was forced by the court to choose between jail time and chemical castration. He eventually committed suicide in 1954 at the age of forty-one.

I tried to persuade Alana that she had nothing to be ashamed of—quite the contrary. "You're a hero. You were a prisoner of war during your entire childhood, and yet you got up every morning and maintained your sanity. You did it to save your sister from what you were enduring. You're braver than anyone I've ever encountered." There should be a medal for children like her. I felt so strongly about this that I didn't realize I'd raised my voice to an emotional crescendo.

For only the second time in her therapy, Alana exhibited real emotion. Tears welled up in her eyes as she asked if I really meant it.

"I do. I'd even like to write a book on brave people like you," I replied. "To me, bravery isn't a single act; it's facing impossible odds and getting up every day to repeat the whole ordeal." I'd said this spontaneously because I meant it. However, in psychological terms, it was a therapeutic device called reframing, which I'd also used in Laura's case. Instead of seeing herself as a coward for wanting to die, Alana needed to see herself as brave for enduring her torture while holding on to her sanity. It was this reframing method, I believe, that helped her more than any other technique I used. I knew her past and could reframe incidents and patterns for her.

It was the end of our first year of therapy, and I was slowly realizing that Alana was the most abused patient I'd ever treated. I had mostly listened, but I'd been able to bear witness to her brutal testimony and reframe it as personal strength.

A person's sense of self-esteem or self-importance—the ego—starts to develop early in childhood, usually with the help of parents. The ego mediates between our basic instincts and reality. Alana's ego was fragile at best. She hadn't been allowed to build a self. Every time she tried to shore up some perception of reality, or a sense of herself and how to navigate in the world, her father or grandmother would rip it to shreds. My concern was that sometimes when people have weak egos, they lose their grip on reality. So I wanted to go slowly with Alana—to fortify what sense of self she had and then to build on it.

As we moved into our second year, I noticed how Alana seemed to discount her intelligence. When she was successful at work, she'd say she'd been able to sort out the problem only because people at the firm were "nimrods who had their heads up their asses." I doubted that she was outsmarting morons. She had a remarkable memory, she could write good poetry, and in the evenings she read math and physics books. As well as enjoying kickboxing and karate, she played violent video games so well that she entered national championships. She even sent gaming companies ideas on how to improve their products, with the result that one of them offered her a programming job. But when I complimented her on this, she said, "Only empty-headed geeks play these games, so the owners must have been shocked to find someone with a brain stem."

She also rejected the idea of her intelligence because she didn't want any trait she'd inherited from Art. Not only did she resemble him physically, with the same pale coloring, freckles, strawberry-blond hair, and frailness; she also had his prodigious brain. Father and daughter could accomplish the same feats in programming and do other mental gymnastics, including word play. "Remember, he was one sick fuck," Alana said to me, "so why would I want to be anything like him? It makes me sick that I'm like him." Therefore, just as she ignored her delicate good looks by, say, cutting her hair with a nail scissors, she ignored her sharp brain by denying her intelligence.

Moreover, Alana had bought into Art's image of her as stupid. When you're told something thousands of times, you believe it. Alana said she was good at fooling people (I should have paid more attention to that confession) and that she wasn't smart, just wily. So one day when she walked into my office, I ambushed her with the Wechsler Adult Intelligence Scale, known as the WAIS IQ test. I hadn't given her any warning, since I knew she'd fret. I felt this would help lay to rest her delusion that she wasn't bright.

Alana attained the highest IQ score I'd ever given—she was in the 99.2 percentile of the population. Dismayed, she said, "Oh, no. That's exactly what Grandma said Art's IQ was." I pointed out that although he had a high IQ, he was *also* a sadist and a pervert—three discrete categories. "Ted Bundy was a law student *and* a murderer; it doesn't mean that all lawyers are murderers. Millions of people would love to have an IQ like yours." I said she should be thankful she got *something* good from him. She was both pretty and smart, and while beauty and brains can't guarantee a good life, they can make for a smoother ride. And during her years in therapy, Alana did begin to value her intelligence and to make strides in her sense of self-worth.

One month after the IQ test, at my suggestion, Alana asked the law firm for a raise. Those who've never had any personal rights find it difficult to suddenly assert themselves, and the prospect caused her great anxiety. We rehearsed the meeting many times.

Afterward, Alana told me that when she approached the founding partner of the four-hundred-person law firm, he sneered. He suggested that since she wasn't even a legal clerk, she should be content with her "unprecedented freedoms." Alana felt so belittled that she began to crumble, but then something strange happened. "Gild," she said, using the nickname she'd given me, "I rose like the phoenix. I just pretended to be you. I pulled your mind down over my ears and blasted the partner. I told him to find someone else to expedite their major patent claims and read all the similar patents and find in what way some engineering device was different from another, and then write a thirty-page report on those differences in twenty-four hours. I am the queen of widget differences and he knows it."

People in the patent department, and in other departments, went to bat for Alana. They depended on her abilities. They were making money from—and often taking credit for—her work. Alana's salary was doubled. The next year, she was given a whopping bonus.

Although Alana was moving forward and making strides in her life, which is the point of therapy, this period was very stressful for her. I pushed her slightly to apply to law school or to embark on an advanced math degree. She demurred, saying she wouldn't be able to concentrate. When I asked the reason why, she opened up. After more than a year of therapy, Alana finally began to tell me what really went on in her head.

3

THE TAPES

ALANA HAD ONCE described Art as "the Art-iste who just keeps on giving." His legacy to her was his voice, which she said was preserved on "tapes" that ran on a loop in her head. And the more stressed she got as she moved out of her underachieving comfort zone, the more intrusive the tapes became.

I asked her to explain their content. "Well, yesterday I was reading a document about a well thermometer that I have to prove is different from other well thermometers and defend why this particular one deserves its own patent," she began. "The tape running at that moment was Art saying, '*You* can't do this. You don't even know how to add. You know nothing about engineering.' Then it gets puerile and he calls me a 'ripped-up cunt,' and on it goes for maybe an hour. I have to try to ignore it and think while the screaming reverberates in my head."

I began to think that it was only Alana's high IQ that allowed her to function. Even though she was constantly distracted, she could still perform at a high level.

The tapes were worse in high-pressure situations. "That's why I avoid too much responsibility," she said. "When I achieve something, Art yells 'You fucking phony' so loud that my heart pounds." Alana was getting visibly anxious as she recounted this. When I asked her if Art yelled often in real life, she said, "Rarely. He had other means of control, which he enjoyed. He loved a game of wits." I pointed out that a game of wits with a child who's terrified of and dependent upon the parent isn't exactly a fair game. In fact, it's a coward's game.

She described a situation that illustrated Art's malevolence. "When I was little I used to like to fool around with numbers—I'd play with dice, piling them up in ascending order. But when I went to school I was terrified. I thought the teacher was tricking me." I was puzzled until she told me that Art had deliberately taught her incorrectly. "He said that two plus two was four, but two plus three equals six. He called me stupid for thinking it was five." Alana suffered terrible headaches and nausea trying to cope with the confusion. "Finally, I couldn't add at all. I would hand in blank pages at school. It was better than ridicule." Not a single teacher ever contacted the home.

A bookworm, Alana said that Art would rip up books she'd borrowed from the library. "So the librarians, whom I really admired, took my card away."

At this point in her narrative, Alana sat with her head lowered, looking dejected. When I probed a little, she pointed to my desultory poinsettia, remarking that Christmas was coming—and that Art always did things to make others think he was normal, like having a Christmas tree. But there were often no presents under it. One year when Art asked what she wanted, she said she'd like a desk more than anything in the world. Art got her a doll and Gretchen, who'd asked for a doll, got the desk. "I was nine years old—way too old for dolls, plus I'd never liked them. He would punish me if I ever sat at my sister's desk. I learned never to tell him what I preferred or wanted—he'd take it away or make fun of it. He always tried to set Gretchen and me against each other." But it never worked, she said.

"That was a battle you won," I offered.

Alana then recounted a horrific incident involving their beloved cat, Turing. On one occasion, Alana had been too tired to fake enjoying sex with Art. He told her nonchalantly not to worry because no one likes everything all the time. Alana recalled that his understanding shocked her. Later that night he took Alana and her sister for a ride in the truck, saying he wanted to see the moon from the other side of the mountain. "So Turing, Gretchen, and I all piled into the front seat of his pickup at midnight. Art held Turing out the window and kept driving. He smashed him on the first stop sign as we left town. Turing fell and died instantly and Art kept driving. I knew I'd be next if I acted hurt or upset. We all just looked straight ahead as my sister and I fought back tears."

"So you had to pretend you didn't like what was important to you. And you learned your lesson about not faking a sexual response."

"Exactly. He didn't have to yell or hit."

Art's mind games were reminiscent of the 1944 film *Gaslight*, in which a man tries to drive his wife insane by tricking her into thinking she's going mad. When I brought in the video for her to watch, Alana commented dryly that the husband was an amateur and that Art should have been consulted on the script. She added that she wasn't able to bounce back as fast as Ingrid Bergman, the film wife, had. In fact, she said, "his mind-fucking was why I had to leave university."

For a psychotherapist, the process of treating a patient can be like solving a mystery—and when Alana described her abrupt exit from university, I missed an important clue. Although I was in mid-career by that point, I had yet to learn to not always rely on the patient's description of events. Just as a reader can encounter an unreliable narrator in literature, so can a psychotherapist encounter one in her office.

First, I'd been surprised that Alana had gone to university at all. She told me she'd won a full scholarship from the Rotary Club after submitting an essay called "How to Change the World," the topic the club had chosen for applicants. "Like *I* knew how to change the world? I felt like writing 'Get rid of Art and his friends and the world would perk up mighty quickly.' Probably the reason I won was that hardly anyone in Prince Rupert applied." She also told me that Art thought she got the scholarship because everyone else in town was too dumb. I pointed out that she didn't need Art's "tapes"—she'd internalized his criticism to such a degree that she'd supplied her own matching narrative.

Avoiding any subject area in which Art had excelled, Alana majored in literature with an emphasis on poetry. One of her professors, a respected poet himself, asked students to submit their own poems. In a later class he said that there was one set of poems he really admired, and then he called out Alana's name, asking her to read one aloud. Alana was mortified. "I thought he was pulling an Art-mocking-my-work stunt, so I ran out of the room and never returned to university." After that episode she had a long stretch of what she thought was catatonia; the only thing she was sure of was that she didn't remember anything for an indeterminate stretch of time.

Instead of asking about that lost period, which, in retrospect, I should have done, I focused on Alana's reaction to her professor's praise. "Do you see now that he would never have undermined you in the style of Art?" She looked confused, so I rephrased: "Do you realize in retrospect that he truly admired your poems?"

After a long pause she said, "I do and I don't. Part of me knows my thinking was crazy, but another part just didn't want to fall for it again. I was afraid of going over the edge. At the time, I totally believed he was another Art."

I had to remind myself that Art was all she knew; Alana had had no friends or any other adult to guide her through the world. The professor was the first man who'd been kind to her. "So at the time you believed he was making fun of you, and now your intellectual side knows he wasn't playing you as Art had. But your emotional side is still not sure about that?"

"Right, even though the professor wrote to me for a year asking me to please contact him. Art was so smart and devious. It was like he'd spun a cocoon of crazy thread around me. The threads were gossamer—I could see through them like I was looking through a gauzy film, but I just couldn't get out of the nest."

Confused, I asked for an example of the miasma she felt had enveloped her. "When we played chess, if I was winning, he'd make up rules—like if I made a certain move with a certain piece, I'd have to remove my queen for the next three moves," she recalled. "I found out he was lying only when I started playing chess after I left home. It was amazing to not be at a disadvantage. But then when I won, I felt like I'd been cheating because they weren't the rules I knew—the ones that were stacked against me." She went on to tell me of the byzantine ways Art would alter the rules so that she'd always lose at games. He'd constantly pull the rug out from under her shaky perceptions of reality. It went on day after day, week after week, and year after year.

We talked about how parents are in a unique position to positively or negatively reinforce their children hundreds of times a day. With each glance they cast our way, our parents tell us who we are and where we belong in the world pecking order. In other words, they unconsciously program us. But Alana's programming had been *literal* brainwashing.

She still heard the tapes—and the further away she moved from the pathetic, stupid girl Art told her she was, the louder they became. "That's why the tapes are yelling when you try new things," I explained. "Whenever you try to advance in the world, to move away from Art's programming of you as a dumb failure, the tapes get louder."

Alana corrected me. "Not just a failure, but a stupid liar who's also a slut. After all, in his eyes I begged him for orgasms. He ignores the fact that he made me do it. If I had a job where I actually told people what to do and they had to respect me, the tapes wouldn't let me function." I reminded her that she did fine intellectual work for one of Toronto's finest law firms; that they came to her for arguments to use in court. She explained that when she was alone in her office, everyone knew not to bother her. They sent her the work and she'd write her responses. Sometimes they'd come in to ask a question, and she would answer. Occasionally they'd ask her to come to court but she'd refuse, not wanting to be with other people and never wanting to be in charge of them. "I don't know when my mind is going to go AWOL, or what I call ARTWOL, so I need to be able to get out fast."

I asked her to elaborate on what could "go wrong in her head" other than the tapes, but she found it difficult to respond. She said that sometimes she just went blank, and long periods of time would elapse before she was herself again. She described it as a vegetative state, like catatonia, which she didn't want anyone else to see. Alana couldn't risk having an episode in court; she had to work quietly in a room where she could leave if she lost control of herself.

Alana had now mentioned these episodes, which she vaguely labelled as "catatonia," twice within a few weeks. I should have investigated more carefully, but I was far too preoccupied with understanding her father's mind games than I was with her reaction to them.

After Alana left that day and I was writing up my notes, I realized that although she mostly looked calm and collected, she'd perfected that demeanour so as to defend herself from Art. If she showed any vulnerability he would swoop in, attack her, and take what was precious to her. She was, not surprisingly, far more fragile than she appeared. Given the tragic events that occurred in the latter half of our therapy, I should have seen her composure for the mask that it was.

Sometimes a therapist has to ask herself why she's pushing a patient in a certain direction. I'd wanted Alana to pursue a career commensurate with her talents, but I soon realized that I wanted this more than she did. I could hear my parents' voices saying that I should never underestimate myself and that I needed a career; it was an important goal to them and, ultimately, to me. In other words, I'd been projecting my needs onto Alana. I'd been slightly fooled by her humour, her calm deportment, her frequent élan. I was now learning how wounded she really was. I decided to proceed more slowly.

In a year and a half of therapy, Alana had never mentioned her mother other than to describe her disappearance before she turned three. Finally, during one session close to Mother's Day, I asked what had become of her mother after she lost her children. Alana, speaking in a flat tone, said she'd moved to England—she feared what Art would frame her for next, and knew she was no match for his mind or his menace. She used up what little money she had to sue for visitation rights, and finally, when Alana was nine and Gretchen was six, she got legal permission to visit with her daughters one week a year in England.

Alana's first descriptions of her mother were glowing: she was the best mother in the world; her life was hell without her kids. As a child, Alana must have idealized her and longed to be with her, even though she barely remembered her. Her most vivid memory was hiding in the truck with her while Art rampaged through the house looking for them.

As the weeks went by, Alana acknowledged that she preferred the idealized mother of her dreams to the real mother they redis-covered. The fantasy cracked when the girls made their first annual one-week trip to London. Their mother bought twin dresses and twin dolls; it was as though the real Alana was invisible to her. To be fair to her mother, Alana probably performed a perfect rendition of a well-adjusted, urbane child playing at being a tourist. They visited Buckingham Palace, took buses to old mansions, looked at fusty furniture, and shopped. When I asked about the emotional quality of the relationship, Alana said, "I hardly knew her. I hadn't seen her since I was three years old. Now I was nine or ten, wearing a silly dress and Mary Janes with white ruffle ankle socks for her sake."

"But that still doesn't tell me about the emotional timbre of the time you spent together."

She responded by recounting a telling exchange. When her mother asked why the girls were so painfully thin, Alana explained that Art barely fed them. "My mother cried and said she hoped that wasn't true. 'Alana, that's a lie, isn't it?' she said, with pleading eyes. Of course she knew it was true since she'd lived with Art and knew what a sicko he was. She just couldn't handle hearing it." So Alana relented and said it wasn't true, which confused her sister. "It was hard pretending we were two happy girls in starched dresses, bouncing around London in two straight lines."

I pointed out the contradictory roles she'd had to assume as a ten-year-old. She had to act wantonly so that Art could feel he was a great lover; then she had to play the role of an innocent girl abroad for her mother. There was no room for the real Alana.

She looked at me blankly. Alana still wanted to protect her mother. "I don't blame her," she said. "Art was cunning. She'd lost her battle with him and had to give her tiny daughters up to a pedophile. It must have been excruciating." She described how her mother had fought Art's legal manoeuvres for years until she ran out of money. "But she never forgot about us."

I can't imagine a worse torture than losing your children to a pedophile. However, I hoped to get the real Alana to give me an authentic emotional reaction to her mother. No matter how hard the mother tried to get her daughters back, emotionally Alana remained an abandoned child. "It must have been difficult to deny your pain, especially when you were drugged, starved, and a victim of repeated sexual abuse," I said. "And yet your mother made it clear that she couldn't bear to hear it."

She'd done all she could, Alana countered, and what was the point of hearing about their awful life if she couldn't do anything about it? She went on to explain that her mother had been raised in the foster care system, with many placements. She'd been beaten, had had to run away as a teenager, and had a police record for prostitution at the age of fourteen. She went some distance in explaining how she could have chosen Art: she was used to abuse and found it normal. In a court battle, she was no match for the educated Art, who, when he was still functional, could feign normalcy and had a responsible job.

I suspected that Alana was more unconsciously angry with her mother than she was ready to acknowledge. Psychological feelings of abandonment in a child aren't based on logical reasons. A child can feel angry at being left even when a parent dies. It's not the parent's fault, but it doesn't lessen the feeling.

The next day Alana sent me an account of one of her dreams. Titled "Spiders and Water," it described Alana's life and state of mind after our discussion about her mother:

Alana is back in Prince Rupert and walking along her old road. All the houses are flooded inside; the people in them, mostly babies, have drowned and are floating in the windows. Finally Alana finds her old house, which isn't flooded but just dirty and abandoned. She goes to her old room and finds a girl in her old bed. Alana looks up and sees dozens of hairy spiders that are the size of small poodles. The girl in the bed doesn't seem alarmed, but insists the spiders must be fed. So Alana gets bowls and feeds them. Then she climbs out the window and walks to a trading post whose ceiling is so low that she has to walk doubled over. There's a woman inside, rather crazy looking, wearing clownish clothes—tights and a loose top with huge red polka dots. She's holding a baby that's screaming its head off. The madwoman leaves as soon as she hands the baby over to Alana, who takes the baby from her and tries to walk it, but this is hard to do bent over. The dream ends with Alana trying to soothe the baby.

When Alana arrived for her next appointment, I asked her to free-associate to the dream. The flood, she said, was an Art trick: he'd made it seem as if theirs was the only house with no flood just to lure her in. Spiders too represented Art, since in that house, Art was everywhere and terrifying. He used to pretend he was a spider once he found out she was deathly afraid of them. "He also used to bring them in the house and put them in my bed, and then just crack up and say 'Got ya.' The other girl in the bed was me. I was also the artful dodger, pun intended, who escaped through the window. The girl in the bed, the other me, knew there was a piper to pay and that she couldn't get away. I had to make the food for all the spiders—all the awful hairy Art-spiders that filled the house. That terror is what I felt every morning getting up to make breakfast."

Alana had no idea who the crazy woman was in the polka-dot blouse. But when I asked whether she'd ever known anyone with such a blouse, she raised an eyebrow as though she'd had a private revelation: her mother had gotten one for Christmas.

It seemed clear that her mother was the madwoman who left her with the baby, who was Gretchen. The house was tiny with a very low ceiling (Alana joked that Art believed in low overhead) and Alana had to walk bent over, which made childcare difficult. Still, Alana did it. As she said, "In real life it was me that was tiny, not the house. I had no idea how to take care of a baby; I could hardly lift her. The dream has me doubled over." She sat and thought for a moment. "Talking about my mother last week brought up a lot of resentment I didn't know I had. In real life, she isn't a crazy woman at all. Why the madwoman in the dream?"

I explained that dreams have to present pictures, concrete images of emotional content. Just as mythology explains the human psyche through its images—its universal archetypes—dreams do the same thing on an individual level. They provide the dreamer with pictures of that individual's unconscious mind. In this case, the blouse was the tipoff. It changed in the dream from polka dots to clown dots. Alana's mother was unable to cope with Art, and then was framed to look insane and incompetent (in the dream, clownish). Alana took over her mother's role, but it was hard on her. "The dream was the first time you acknowledged, albeit in a camouflaged form, that being a mother as a preschooler was very hard. You were literally and figuratively doubled over," I said.

As Alana's hands began to redden I assured her that being angry with her mother wasn't disloyal; it was simply how she felt and how anyone would have felt.

Children who are given adult responsibilities when they're too young to handle them are forever after worried about properly fulfilling their responsibilities; they never seem to accept that they were too young to manage the task but instead internalize their failure to accomplish it. Laura, who'd been left in the woods, focused on her supposed failure to parent her siblings and rarely mentioned her own abandonment. Alana was much the same. Instead of congratulating herself on caring for Gretchen from age three, she worried that she'd been neglectful by attending school.

Abused children are often hypervigilant, for they feel themselves to be ceaselessly in peril. And they've learned to sense threats; their life often depends on it. One week Alana told me about an alarming situation that had occurred at her law firm. A disgruntled man had appeared at reception, asking for a specific lawyer. Later it turned out that he was an enraged spouse who'd lost custody of his children in a divorce case and intended to kill his wife's lawyer. At the time, though, no one recognized how deranged he was—except Alana, who'd noticed him in the crowded waiting room. She called security and the police. When the man was approached, he drew a gun, and the entire twenty-one-floor office building had to be evacuated while he was subdued and taken away.

Alana explained that she had a sixth sense for violent loonies. "All abused children are like bloodhounds," she said. "They have to always be scanning the environment looking for what can go wrong. If you don't you're a dead duck. I'd call it the opposite of sheltered."

She was attuned to danger just as Danny, the truck driver, had been able to detect robbers on the road. They'd both lived with predators. Alana said that Art used to flash guns at her and

Gretchen when he was drunk and high on cocaine, telling them that they'd better line up against the wall and sing his praises. "The wall behind us was full of bullet holes. Eventually he'd pass out and we'd throw a blanket over him and put the gun away."

"Did you ever think of taking that gun and shooting him? I mean once you were a teenager?" I asked.

"Sure. I used to fantasize about shooting him whenever I played video games, and I still do. That's why I'm so good at them," she said. "But I decided that he wasn't worth life imprisonment. It would just make me as perverse as he was."

"You were at war and fighting for your sanity," I said, shaking my head. "It sure must have been a temptation."

Much later, Alana told me that that moment was the turning point for her in therapy. She could tell by the look on my face and the way my eyes narrowed that I really meant it. Up till then she'd regarded empathy as phony in general, and in my case as just part of my job. But when I hinted that she'd have been justified in killing Art, she knew with certainty that I was on her side.

Clearly, asking Alana why she hadn't killed her father wasn't my most professional moment. Yet it clinched something in our relationship. It was my way of saying that I understood not only the impotence and entrapment she felt but also the rage—the *rage*—that was never allowed to see the light of day. She saw her rage reflected in my eyes.

4

BEHIND THE FURNACE

ALANA MAY HAVE fantasized about killing Art, but she did escape him without doing him violence. And in keeping with the fairy-tale grotesqueness of her story, it was someone else from Prince Rupert who engineered her rescue. To better understand that rescue, let's look at how the outside world of the town interfaced with Alana and her family.

When Alana reached kindergarten age, Art offered some pedagogical advice: school was a terrible place, so it was best to lie low there or she'd be taken away and never see her sister again. That advice, combined with the confusion from having been taught arithmetic incorrectly and her fear for Gretchen at home alone with Art, made Alana withdrawn at school. While she read prolifically at home, she handed in blank pages in class. As it turned out, Art didn't molest Gretchen; instead he left her in the house, untended, while he spent his day visiting his buddies. When Alana would get home, Gretchen would cling to her. Gretchen rarely cried, but she'd dig her fingers into Alana's hand and not let go.

Shockingly, to Alana's knowledge, no one in *twelve years* ever called Art at home or ordered a psychological assessment of her. No truant officer checked her frequent absences. Not one school official investigated when Alana came to school in the same dirty clothes for years, or when Art habitually refused to sign forms for Alana to go on field trips, or when she never brought a lunch or milk money.

No doctor who saw her at age eight for pills or in her early teens for infections in her damaged vagina ever contacted anyone.

Long after I had Alana as a client, I was once fogged in overnight at the Digby Island airport near Prince Rupert. The only other person waiting to get airlifted out was an important official from the area I'd seen many times on CBC Television. He was talking about how much money had been put into Prince Rupert's social services. I couldn't resist telling him how I'd once had an abused patient who never once during her eighteen years in the town got any help from anyone. He responded that Prince Rupert had high unemployment, that its fishing and forestry industries had been destroyed and its canneries burned to the ground, and that 40 percent of the population was Indigenous, with all the social problems this entailed. So if one white girl who went to school, had a parent, and had a home to live in slipped through the cracks, he wasn't in the least surprised.

When I asked Alana why she never asked for help from anyone or called Children's Aid, she said it was too dangerous. They might have believed her as a teenager, but she didn't want to risk being separated from Gretchen. Besides, they had nowhere to go, except foster homes. This was almost a quarter of a century ago, when incest and family abuse issues were rarely discussed. If the authorities didn't believe her and trusted Art instead, as had happened with her mother, she'd be forced to stay with him *after* accusing him. She knew he would kill her or Gretchen or torture them both in some unimaginable way. It was too big a gamble.

But when she was fourteen, Alana got out of Art's clutches. One day she was walking down her semi-rural road and passed a home where Rachael, a classmate, was sitting on the front porch with her mother. The mother invited Alana to visit with them. Alana winced as she gingerly sat on the edge of a chair; she was in pain from Art's attentions. The mother noticed, and asked about it—and Alana's terror at being questioned alerted her that something was terribly wrong. She'd heard rumours. Her own husband sometimes frequented Art's wild parties, which she hated. She called the police and reported Art.

Less than a week later, the police arrived while Art was "entertaining." The police recognized several local child molesters. They also found large quantities of drugs—enough to book Art on possession—and his huge collection of child pornography. There were unregistered firearms, and bullet holes in the wall. There was no food. The house was filthy. No one had used sheets in years. The police removed Alana and Gretchen immediately. Neither of them ever saw Art again.

Gretchen was placed with a German family who owned a bakery. She liked it there, and took to the baking. In fact, it became her profession; she eventually taught baking and pastry arts at a college in Toronto.

Social services had more trouble placing Alana, given that she was a teenager. She wanted to be placed near her sister in a group home, not a foster home: she didn't want to run the risk of having another lunatic control her life. "If there was a loony working at the group home," she explained, "it would only be for an eight-hour shift. The worst I'd suffer would be neglect, and that sounded like heaven to me." For the next three years Alana did stay in a group home near Gretchen—until she "aged out of the system," as it's known. Later, after she crashed and burned at university, she stayed near her sister until Gretchen turned eighteen, and the two moved together to Toronto.

Although Alana was geographically removed from Art, she never really freed herself emotionally from him. His tentacles had hooked into her brain, where her self-hating tapes played on.

Art's cruel manipulation made her doubt her own perceptions. She was so damaged that she continually struggled to distinguish reality from Art's demonic world. In university those struggles came to a head and, tragically, she had to leave the program.

We'd finished our second year of therapy and I'd begun to see how fragile Alana really was. She'd been quick to tell me what had happened to her, but I was only now realizing the toll it had taken. On the other hand, as I pointed out to Alana, she'd taken some concrete steps forward. She had asserted herself at work by demanding and getting a wage increase. She'd also begun to talk realistically about her mother, and about how difficult it had been to act as a parent to Gretchen.

Alana was poised to make her "great leap forward," a phrase we borrowed from Mao Zedong. But just as in his grand scheme, along with the gains came unforeseen ramifications, ones that resulted in catastrophe.

Alana's recovery took the form of progressing, as every child does, through the stages of psychological development. Most of the stages are remarkably consistent, with the child spending a certain number of years in one before advancing to the next. Amazingly, these stages have occurred across the human spectrum, from primitive times to modern. (And you can find rebellious adolescents everywhere in the world. Nelson Mandela, for example, describes in his autobiography how all thirteen-year-old boys from his African tribe were taken to live in a separate teenage house so that peace could reign at home.)

Trauma can retard emotional development. As long as a child is trying only to cope, she has no energy to emotionally grow. As Alana began to improve in therapy, and to mature emotionally, she began to cycle rapidly through the stages—from infancy to late adolescence to the edge of adulthood—in a remarkably short time. It was a bit unnerving for me, since I was never sure which stage of development I'd see each week.

At the beginning of our third year we began talking about Alana's self-described "babyish temper tantrums" that had only recently emerged with her partner, Jane. For example, Alana felt slightly embarrassed that she was arguing about what food to eat; she was sometimes even throwing meals in the garbage. (Jane, twenty years older than Alana, would just shake her head and leave the room.)

Around the same time, Alana insisted on buying all new clothes. It took her weeks to replace her wardrobe, even though to my untrained eye the new items were nearly identical to her old plaid flannel shirts and cargo pants. She, however, thought her duds were a walk on the wild side, and each week would parade her new outfits from Mark's Work Wearhouse. Still, her own behaviour was confusing to her. "I'm like my two-year-old nephew," she once remarked, "who flips if he can't wear his Superman suit outside in the winter without a coat." I pointed out that throughout her childhood with Art she'd never been allowed to have a single thing she ever wanted, and that exercising choice is an important part of developing an identity. Alana was going through the classic developmental stage called the "terrible twos." When she'd been chronologically two her father was trying to get rid of her mother while Alana was locked in a room; she'd had no psychological opportunity to act out and differentiate herself. The family couldn't take one more spoiled baby—Art was enough. Now she was finally learning what the word *mine* meant. Although she was undergoing the terrible twos late in life, I was pleased to witness her climbing the developmental ladder.

Alana spoke with a kind of surprised wonder at her new changes. "Plus, I've been making jokes at work and imitating the head of the litigation department. He has strange intonations and an ostentatious vocabulary. Instead of just having a conversation, he says things like 'If I may interject at this juncture.' Also, instead of 'Hello' when he sees you in the hall, he says 'Felicitations.' I can imitate him exactly, and I'm suddenly finding that I'm amusing. *It is so new.* I never wanted people to pay attention to me, and now I quite like it." She was now heading into a social stage and wanted to interact with others; instead of hiding herself away, she wanted to differentiate herself.

It was the latter half of our third year of therapy. Alana continued to send me accounts of her wild dreams that tapped into her unconscious and often preceded her conscious feelings. One of them involved a beached whale, and she'd typed it up.

Jane and I are in the park near the shore of a large lake. There's a woman with us who resembles the Gild. She's exploring ahead of us. Jane and I find a beached blue whale. We call to the Gild, who rushes back, inspects the whale, and determines that it's alive. We have to get the whale back into the water. Gild produces a bag of some chemical that will make the lake salt water and dumps it in. We make an elaborate pulley system and drag the whale into the water. Then the whale is swimming very energetically around the pool, making jumps, etc.

I head back to the car to find Jane, who has suddenly disappeared. She's in the stairwell, spray-painting graffiti.

We climb into the VW with the Gild driving, and head for home. On the way, Jane is reciting poetry to me she wrote when she was young. It's very painful, depressing poetry. In the end, we're sitting in the driveway of our home talking. I'm disturbed by Jane's poetry and feeling frightened for her. She seems suicidal.

Alana said that she was the whale and I, the Gild, was the female explorer who had the chemical to make the salt water. When the whale was in danger, Jane and I tried to keep her alive, going through all kinds of contortions to get her into the necessary salt water. We were on her side, trying to make her well.

I questioned Alana about the last part of the dream, where Jane separates herself from the final stage of the rescue, uncharacteristically draws graffiti (she was law-abiding in real life), and is sad once the whale has been saved. Why would she suddenly become suicidal when Alana, the whale, is saved? Perhaps there was some threat to their relationship now that Alana was learning to express her own needs? She denied this (while I filed it away for future consideration).

About a month later, Alana bounced into her session and said, "Well, you won't believe this, but I'm in love—or at least in lust?"

"Love?" I said, confused.

"Yup. I fucked the new articling student in the lunch hour. Our firm has a hospitality suite at the Four Seasons, so she got the key and we went there. She is so gorgeous you wouldn't believe it."

"*Sex?*" I seemed to be capable of only one-word responses. Up to this point Alana had been asexual, marooned in latency, much like a preteen. Of course, it made sense: now that she was growing up, she wanted to have a first love. But what about Jane? They hadn't had much of a sex life, but otherwise it was a happy partnership.

As I sat quietly, Alana said, "I thought you'd be happy for me." I pointed out that being happy or sad wasn't my job. I was just trying to understand it. "I had an orgasm and screamed and so did she. She has a normal body—great knockers—that responds normally. I didn't compartmentalize, as in, I wasn't frigid. I just let myself rock on for once. We were three hours late getting back. She got in a lot of shit, but no one said a word to me. I don't think they knew we were together, since she works on a different floor."

She chatted on about the day and what an orgasm was like. She said she now understood why Hollywood made so many movies about attraction and romance. I was taken aback by the suddenness of the changes in her and the forthright way she discussed them. It was as though Alana had receded and someone resembling Madonna had emerged.

The next week I heard rapid footsteps on my stairs and Alana entered, flopping down in her chair, looking tired and slightly dishevelled. "You know why I married Jane?" she began. "I needed her. I needed a mom and dad and she filled both roles. In many ways, it was an inspired choice. But now I want a real woman. Jane still has to shave, she has to have electrolysis. She's never happy with her female self because it's never right." Alana reiterated that she still loved Jane for her kindness but that she wasn't attracted to her. "I now want to have fun, to have wild sex and dance. She's not that type."

I felt sad for the loyal, stalwart Jane, and my conflicted feelings must have been written on my face. "I know, I know," Alana said. "Jane is intelligent, a great professor, she cares about people, she's normal in her head. She's just trapped in the wrong body. Her sex change really never worked well. It was fine from a distance."

"Have you told her?" I asked.

She didn't answer.

"Are you serious about the articling student?"

"She doesn't matter. I want to experience life: to party, to travel." Alana pointed out that Jane had health problems that made travel difficult, and besides, she was twenty years older. We sat in silence. Alana's face fell suddenly into despondency and she finally asked, "Gild, do you think I used Jane and now want to throw her away like a used Kleenex?"

I explained that when people grow, their needs change. Alana didn't need a loving parent as she once did; now she needed a lover. Emotionally, she was heading into her adolescent stage, where sex and fun were paramount. "And I'm happy that, after all you've been through, sex has been a pleasure for the first time. Everyone deserves that."

"Like, *who knew?*" Alana threw her hands gleefully in the air as she left my office. Her demeanour and vocabulary had been peculiar, more raucously adolescent than her usual reserved self. However, since I had three teenagers at home, not much could shock me in that department.

I should have paid more attention to those personality changes in Alana. I was too focused on how fast she was growing up and not enough on how erratic her behaviour had become. That changed when Jane called me at home that weekend. Alana was in the intensive care unit at the hospital. She'd taken a large dose of Tylenol, combined with copious amounts of alcohol, and then hidden in the basement behind the furnace and passed out. Their cat, Font, was making strange sounds by the basement door when Jane, who'd returned early from an out-of-town conference, found Alana. She was almost dead.

The news struck me like a bolt of lightning. The last time I saw Alana she'd behaved like a giggly adolescent. Yet she had reported that, in her dream, Jane was suicidal. In real life, it was Alana who was suicidal. As I drove to the hospital, hoping Alana would make it, all I could think was that she'd felt terrified of leaving Jane, whom she loved. Yet she needed to get away from her in order to grow up. She felt suffocated and panicked. By the time I was slamming the car into park at the hospital, I was thinking of my role in this. I ought to have recognized Alana's guilt and self-loathing when she asked whether I thought she was "throwing Jane away like a used Kleenex."

I was beginning to learn—and I would encounter this several times in future cases—that when a deprived person begins to improve, the stress of making life choices can be remarkably intense. Alana had been like a tiger in a small cage. It was hell in there, but she knew every square inch of her space. When the tiger was set free, she was terrified of the jungle, having no idea how to manoeuvre within it. My hypothesis was that she'd been speeding through developmental stages at too fast a rate for her psyche to absorb what she needed to learn.

Outside the hospital entrance I met Jane, who was smoking. The first thing I noticed about her was that she was attractive, but much older than Alana. She wore expensive shoes, a silk blouse, and a matching scarf and trousers. Her shoulder-length dark blond hair was perfectly coiffed and highlighted with lighter blond streaks; her makeup was flawlessly applied, as though she'd just left a Chanel counter. She approached me, saying that Alana was still in intensive care and had had a seizure. She might have liver damage, but would probably pull through. As we walked down the hall to the unit, Jane told me that during the week "Alana had been ranting about leaving the marriage, insisting she didn't love me and never had." She said Alana wasn't herself, screaming such cruel things she couldn't repeat them. Alana had also referred to terrible things she'd done in the past.

Jane had assured Alana that she loved her and always would, that no matter what she'd done they could work things out. The whole episode was out of character, Jane told me, as Alana was rarely dramatic and never yelled. We both knew her for her self-control and inscrutable face. Jane also told me that whenever they needed to have an emotional conversation, Alana would get drunk, which happened about once a month. She never drank at other times. Jane had since instituted a system wherein Alana could write out her feelings in an email and Jane would answer it. This tactic worked quite well, since it seemed to prevent the drunken episodes that took so much out of them. Alana couldn't stand the intimacy of a one-on-one conversation but could express things beautifully in writing.

I had no idea Alana drank. I was beginning to realize that, after three years of therapy, there was a lot I didn't know. Had I been treating a fictional character Alana had created for me, just as she'd presented a false self to Art? I knew two things: the case had gotten away from me, and we both had a lot of work to do, if and when she recovered.

I walked into the hospital room and saw what looked like a baby blue whale, much like the one Alana had described in her dream. Her skin was pale grey and her lips had a dusty blue cast. She was still groggy, almost unconscious. Every orifice had tubes protruding. When Jane held her hand, Alana pulled it away. I could see the pain on Jane's face.

Jane was understandably perplexed about why this had happened now, just when Alana seemed to be getting better. "Getting better is a lot of work," I offered. "And God knows she's been working hard in therapy. She's had to scrape away defences that weren't helping her in the long run, but change made her vulnerable. Jane, I don't feel I can say any more than that."

Jane squeezed my hand, saying she understood completely. In the brief time I knew her, she struck me as a kind, well-adjusted person who cared deeply for Alana and gave her unconditional love. They'd had over a decade of good years together.

Alana was in intensive care for a week and then on the ward until her liver was mostly repaired. Jane told me that Alana had been enraged at her for "bothering" me at home. Alana also left strict instructions that I wasn't to visit her again, that she'd pay for her missed sessions, and that she'd get in touch when she could return to therapy. It was very hard for Alana to accept help or any signs of caring, even after a suicide attempt. I respected her boundaries and didn't return to the hospital.

5

CHLOÉ

AFTER NINE DAYS AS an in-patient, Alana was discharged from hospital. Then she disappeared for three days. Jane, who was frantic, called to let me know.

About two days after her call, I walked by my waiting room to find the missing Alana slouched in a chair. She had a scowl on her face. I said, "Well, hello stranger." (Only later did I learn how ironic that greeting had been.)

She shrugged her shoulders as though I were a flea or a telemarketer. Then she walked beside me down the hall but strangely bypassed my office; I had to tell her to turn around. She came in, collapsed into a chair, and said, "So?" When I inquired about the suicide attempt, she bellowed, "How the fuck else was I supposed to get out of that stultifying relationship? You make the big bucks, so you tell me!"

I was taken aback by her uncharacteristic rudeness. When I mentioned meeting Jane at the hospital, she said, "What were *you* doing at my hospital? Intensive care is for relatives. You're not my mother." I sat silently, wondering if her brain had been damaged from her overdose or if she'd been drinking. This new strident voice sounded totally different in tone, intonation, and accent.

Finally I asked, "Where have you been?"

"I honestly don't know. I just found myself on the steps of Hart House," she said, naming the university's recreational facility about a block away. "So I wandered over here for a cup of tea, which I notice I'm not even being offered." I made her one, and while she was drinking it I brought up Jane's concern for her. "Every fucking thing is about Jane," she said angrily. "She refuses to give up the stranglehold. She's as mangled physically as I am emotionally. I'm in my thirties, and I don't want to be with some half-man, half-woman fuck-up. I want a young woman with big knockers, for fuck sake."

I was floored. This was *not* Alana. The sharp tone, the anger, the vulgarity—it was all wrong. She began pacing, something she'd never done before, and then whirled around to address me: "Why is it all about Jane, Jane, Jane? I tell her we're finished and she wants to die, she says she can't go on, she'd rather be dead. You want dead, Jane, *I'll show you fucking dead.* Then I swallowed the pills. Was that enough? *No.* She was smothering me. No wonder I needed an oxygen mask. I am *so* sick of her and her kindness and her sanctimony. I *have to break out.*" Alana was speaking in the exasperated tone of an adolescent. "She wouldn't even come home from her conference when she was supposed to. She had to get home early and find me. The doctor said a few more hours and I'd have been gone."

"She wouldn't even let you die. How selfish," I deadpanned.

"Yeah, that's pretty fucking controlling. Sartre says whether to live or die is the only real choice in life."

I decided to ignore philosophical issues—we'd lose the psychological thread—and asked if anyone else missed her. Her employers had called, she said. "I told them to fuck themselves and the shyster ambulance chasers they came in on." I didn't bother mentioning that I'd noticed the firm had sent a huge flower arrangement to her hospital room.

Alana's indiscriminate rage now turned to my woeful inadequacies. "And speaking of rooms, I've wanted to tell you something about the magazines in your waiting room. Don't you think it's rude to have *The New Yorker*, *The Atlantic*, and *Harper's* when the articles are long and you can't finish them while you're waiting? You just have them there so you can look smart to your patients. Well, it's not working." (I later found that an article had been roughly ripped out of *The Atlantic*.)

"Pretty angry today?"

"*No.*"

She was clearly now a teenager. Only they can repudiate their anger with such primitive denial. I didn't respond, and finally she said, "Well, how useless is this?" and stormed out.

Before I left for home that night I wrote the following note for her file.

I know I wasn't speaking to Alana today. She didn't walk the same way, talk with the same voice, or have the same personality. She was aggressive and impolite. It was another Alana. Another personality. She didn't seem to know where my office was when she walked down the hall and she didn't pay me when she left. She always leaves a check and walks out quietly so as not to disturb the other clients. This person stomped out and slammed the door. It was strange how she just showed up with no appointment. I should have said all these things to Alana and asked her name and told her that I didn't believe I was speaking to the Alana I knew.

For the first time, I began to think that I might have a multiple personality on my hands. I decided to review the whole case carefully. The problem with Alana was that she'd been trained as a child to never show what she was really feeling. She often exhibited *la belle indifférence*, a French term for patients whose lackadaisical attitude doesn't match their dire circumstances. This cover-up presented a challenge for me. If Alana had ever alluded to having a multiple personality, it had been so opaque that I'd missed it. Now that this new enraged personality had emerged—someone who talked and walked differently from Alana and who didn't remember where my office was—I needed to consider a multiple personality diagnosis.

I set myself three priorities. First, I would learn everything possible about multiple personality disorder. Second, I would carefully comb through three years of notes to try to decipher what Alana had been trying to tell me between the lines. Third, when I was sufficiently prepared, I would confront Alana and ask her who had been in my office that day.

I read everything I could and consulted with specialists in England and Texas. I told them that Alana had experienced more than a decade of sexual trauma and emotional and physical abuse by family members. They agreed that this was enough to indicate a multiple personality disorder. One expert asked me whether she was also smart, strong, and creative. When I said yes, he said that in his practice he'd found those personality characteristics to be essential in the development of the disorder.

Multiple personality disorder was redefined in 1994, when the name was changed to dissociative identity disorder (DID) so as to reflect a better understanding of the condition. Whereas the term *multiple personality* means that the person has developed several different personalities, *dissociative identity* means that a fragmentation of the main personality has occurred. And since that main personality remains lacking in certain life skills—for example, the ability to express anger, sexuality, or assertiveness—new personalities splinter off that are personifications of these missing traits.

In the films *The Three Faces of Eve* and *Sybil*, Hollywood sensationalized multiple personality disorder while simultaneously simplifying it. I think the diagnosis is so unfathomable, and seemingly so fantastical, that we find it hard to take in.

It's a complicated disorder. After reading the literature, viewing tapes, and consulting with experts, I concluded that several phenomena have to happen simultaneously for it to arise. The patient has to have a *complex* PTSD, such as what Danny suffered—meaning that they've experienced severe emotional, sexual, and sometimes physical abuse over a prolonged period. That same patient must exhibit great natural tenacity and resilience, thus refusing to go completely insane. It also correlates with a good memory, creativity, and a relatively high IQ. This unusual combination of variables doesn't come along that often, which is one of the reasons why the disorder is so rare. It's a sophisticated way to make the unbearable bearable— a way to protect your mind and keep a piece of yourself, the largest piece, safe.

Research done, I reread all my session notes to see what I'd missed. I felt like a Dickensian scribe as night after night I bent over my desk into the wee hours, surrounded by papers from a file almost two feet deep. Finally, I found a letter that Alana had once sent me: a six-page, single-spaced epistle ostensibly intended to explain how her mind was like a computer. Alana titled all her missives, and this one was called "Let's Keep Them in the Cage." It had been written in a jaunty voice, but now, as I deconstructed it, I realized that it was darkly foreshadowing her psychological condition. It had been a warning to me, one that I hadn't understood at the time.

She buried the lead by mentioning casually at the end that she'd seen *Sybil*, a serialized TV movie based on an actual psychiatric case. Sybil, who'd been physically, emotionally, and sexually abused by her mother, developed a multiple personality disorder. Alana was mesmerized by the film, quickly bought the book, and read it in a day. She wrote how surprised she was that Sybil had multiple personalities when, in Alana's opinion, "so little had happened to her." (In reality, the film was so horrific that many couldn't watch it.) Buried in the text and camouflaged by technical jargon was Alana's fear of Sybil's disorder. What frightened her most was that Sybil wasn't in charge of her personalities. They controlled her. Alana acknowledged that she too used different personalities, but that they stayed in her head and she controlled them. She compared her mind to a computer's central operating system that could run several programs at once, except the programs were different personalities. (She called them her minions.) For example, if she didn't want to appear in court to represent her firm, she'd send out a different personality, an assertive minion who would confront the lawyers and refuse to go. She contended that no one ever noticed it wasn't the real Alana. She said it sounded as though Sybil's programs "had gone rogue." Alana acknowledged, in an oblique way, her worry that lately she'd been experiencing some "slippage." Only when I reread that passage did I realize what Alana meant: she, like Sybil, was no longer in charge of all her personalities.

Now that I had the evidence I needed, it was time to confront Alana with the diagnosis. I called her at work and she greeted me warmly. "Oh hi, Gild. I was going to call you. It's been ages. Are we on for our regular Tuesday appointment?" It was her usual Alana voice, soft-spoken and polite.

I had to think carefully about how to handle this upcoming session. Was Alana truly a multiple personality, or more precisely a DID? On the yes side, I had to acknowledge that when she appeared unexpectedly in my office, she'd had a different voice and personality; she'd even walked differently, with a bow-legged gait like a chaps-wearing cowboy in an old western movie. Yet there were a couple of reasons to discount the diagnosis. First, the different personality had emerged only once in three years. That in itself was strange. Labelling someone with any disorder that has manifested only once in a therapist's presence is dicey at best. Second, it all seemed so far-fetched. I'd been in practice for twenty-five years and had never seen anything like this. I had to be cautious—there'd been a great debate in the literature not only about the legitimacy of the diagnosis but also about the possibility that some therapists may, consciously or unconsciously, plant the idea of different personalities in the mind of the patient.

When Alana came in for her Tuesday session, I could tell just from her facial expression that she was back to her old self. She reported that her employer was concerned about her thirteen-day absence, and that she'd told them she had a chronic problem with her liver and had had a flare-up. "I didn't want to lie, and at least that was true."

In order not to say anything leading, I simply asked, "What were you doing for the four days after you were out of the hospital?"

"I don't seem to remember." After a long silence, she changed the subject. "I left Jane. I now live in a new apartment just a few blocks from here. I don't really know how that all happened. I'm missing so much stuff that I'll have to call Jane—which I'm dreading." When I asked how Jane was doing, she said she was broken-hearted and couldn't even go to work. I acknowledged that it must have been hard leaving their home.

"Honestly, I have no idea how I did it. I really don't like hurting anyone, unless it's Art, and even with him I'd rather just ignore him. I guess I can be cruel because Jane told me I was."

"It doesn't sound like you."

"I *had* to get out of there."

"I get it. You had to move on. Jane was a parent. She was an ingenious choice, because being transgender meant she could play the role of both mother and father. But as you got better, you no longer needed to be her child. You wanted to be a teenager and then a young adult and have relationships with girls your own age." Alana looked confused. So I said, "You're starting to emotionally grow up. Wanting to date and get away from your parents is the most important development of a teenager."

I asked why she had so much trouble telling Jane she wanted to leave.

"It's cruel, and I refuse to be cruel. I decided when I was a kid to leave that to Art," she replied. "Jane did nothing to deserve my heartlessness, especially since I promised I would always love her. In a way, I do love her and always will. She's a wonderful person. But I'm not *in* love with her."

In an effort to get her to understand that she had emotional rights and it wasn't cruel to exert them, I asked Alana, "Is the near 50 percent of the population who gets a divorce as cruel as Art?" (At the time the divorce rate was just over 45 percent; it has since declined.) "That 50 percent once loved each other, but then one or both of them changed, and it didn't work out. It happens. Everyone has broken up with someone, unless we marry the first person we ever date. Ever heard the song 'Breaking Up Is Hard to Do'?"

"Thanks, Neil Sedaka," she said. "I guess I get it. Everyone breaks up at some point in her life."

I pointed out that therapy helps people grow, and that sometimes the collateral damage involves having to change partners and friends and leaving others behind. Alana had faced a dilemma: she desperately needed to get out of the relationship yet had no idea how to assert herself to make that happen. Therefore, she was trapped.

"I tried suicide but lived. *That sucked.* Then I was really painted into a corner."

"What came out when you were in that corner?"

"I don't remember a thing."

"Well, I can tell you that the girl who popped in here last week without an appointment was not Alana."

She looked bewildered. "I wasn't here last week." When I assured her that she was, she said, "Oh no." She walked over to her coat, reached into her pocket, and pulled out a crumpled magazine page from *The Atlantic.* When I reminded her of her angry magazine outburst, she put her elbows on her knees and held her head in her hands. She was ashen and breathing like a locomotive, but it was time to push her.

"Who was here last week? It was *not* you."

Finally, she sat up and said, "Unfortunately, that sounds like Chloé, with an accent on the *e.* She gets really pissed off if you mispronounce it."

Alana sat for a few minutes and then looked directly into my eyes, a rare occurrence. The Art tapes ran all day long in her head, she said, and she'd had to take measures. "It can get tiring dealing with Art. I needed help. Years ago, I invented other people to try to deal with the tapes so that I could function." (Alana later told me that she assumed everyone had other personalities in their head that they didn't discuss publicly: how else would they handle the world?)

"Alternate personalities?" I asked.

"I guess so, if you want to use that lingo. I call them programs." When I asked her to elaborate, she described Chloé: "She's nasty, like a mean polecat. She yells and screams at Art and tells him to fuck off."

When I ventured further and asked whether Chloé was the only person who emerged to do battle with Art, Alana divulged the existence of another alternate, a sulky teenage boy named Roger. "He gives Art withering glances, like he's an unsightly wart," she said. "Art always hated it if you didn't engage with him, and Roger has his number on that." Again I pressed her, asking if there were any others. She smiled, and described someone called Amos. "He's a redneck hick, sort of a well-intentioned hillbilly. When Art yells at me and calls me filthy things, Amos just makes fun of him."

Then, for the first time in the course of three years of therapy, Alana laughed a real belly laugh and began addressing Art in a slow, country drawl. "Hey, you slimy little tree toad. Stop your croakin'." I didn't find Amos as hilarious as she did, but Alana said he was the best thing that ever happened to her: his laughter could take away Art's power and reveal him as the "weaselly coward" he was.

I wanted to know when these people came out. Alana insisted that they never emerged, that she was in complete charge of them. "Chloé, Roger, and Amos are just programs I run when *I* choose to," she said.

"Why then did Chloé leave your control?" I asked, in reference to her last visit.

I felt that Alana was on dangerous ground, that she might attempt suicide again. I no longer believed in her false air of calm; we had to move quickly and decisively. "Think about it," I said, slowly and deliberately.

About five minutes later, she began to recap and link recent events. The breakup with Jane, however necessary it was, had been agonizing for both. "She kept saying we were happy and we could work it out," Alana recalled. "I tried taking all the blame and saying I was too bad or too screwed up to love, but she wouldn't let go. Trapped, I guess I then had to let Chloé out. I let her be incredibly cruel to Jane, and I got too drunk to even hear her.

Well, actually, I could sort of hear her—as though I was at the bottom of a deep well and there were voices up at the top."

She addressed the suicide attempt by summing up her state of mind at the time. "I just decided that no one needed me anymore. Art was a thousand miles away and my sister had a husband and two great kids. She was fine without me. Now I was being cruel to the only person who gave her life to helping and loving me. I thought, 'Art was right. I really am evil.' Then I took the pills."

Alana couldn't remember coming to my office the previous week, let alone renting her new apartment. She'd wound up back at work that day, but was unsure how. Chloé, it seemed, had done it all.

"Are you sure that was the first time she ever came out?"

"It was the first time that I know of," she admitted. "After I ran out of class when I thought that poetry professor was making fun of me, I had a missing week. I thought I'd had catatonia. I'd had it before. *I think.*"

I was now wondering whether Alana's alternate personalities had emerged when she'd left university. I also thought it possible that I'd been talking to Chloé when she described her "nooner" with the law student. I'd noted that she spoke with uncharacteristic brashness and vulgarity on that occasion as well.

Psychologists might argue whether Alana was suffering from multiple personality disorder or dissociative identity disorder, where, again, the alternate characters who splinter off are personifications of missing but essential personality traits. As I said earlier, I felt that dissociative identity disorder was the more accurate diagnosis for Alana's symptoms, especially after I "met" who lived in her head. Alana couldn't get angry, but Chloé was pure anger; Alana was unable to be insolent with and impervious to Art, so that was Roger's job; Amos, the hick who wore bib jeans, defended Alana by belittling the pompous Art. It's no wonder that she liked Amos so much: no one else had ever stood up to Art for her. I felt that these characters weren't technically different personalities, but rather a personification of the traits Alana needed to protect herself against the Art tapes.

Now that I was more informed about the disorder, my next step was to find the best way to help Alana. One approach would be to help her get rid of Chloé, Roger, and Amos by finding ways to integrate them into her main personality. If Alana learned how to express her anger, for example, she'd have no more need of Chloé. If she had her own boundaries, she'd no longer need the alternate personalities. Another approach, less ambitious but possibly more realistic, would be for Alana to keep Chloé, Roger, and Amos in her head to help fight the recurring Art tapes. We could work on strengthening her ego so that she wouldn't lose control of her alternates and let them split off. Or, as Alana put it, "I must not let the Chloé, Roger, and Amos programs turn rogue."

The ideal solution would be to get rid of the tapes, but I wasn't sure that was possible. Alana had withstood sadism and deprivation for a long period of time. People who've suffered that degree of trauma are often irreversibly impaired; they can become paranoid, mute, or psychotic and end up in institutions. I had to accept the fact that there'd be some residual damage. If babies are starved and fed later, their bones will always show the traces of the lack of food. The same is true of severe abuse. The brain will adapt in strange ways, but it won't ever be fully normal, whatever that means. (As one of my sons always says, "normal" is just a setting on a washing machine.) I needed to establish realistic goals for our therapy so that both Alana and I could feel we had succeeded.

I decided that the best solution was to assume that Alana needed the other three personalities to fight the debilitating effects of the Art tapes. We could work on strengthening her ego so that the alternates wouldn't have to go to battle for her in the outside world. We could work on coping strategies, like creating boundaries, learning to be assertive, reading her own feelings, and acting on them. That way, when the next crisis came, Alana wouldn't have an empty toolbox.

Over the next weeks we seemed to draw closer. Since Alana's suicide attempt her lovely delicateness had become a wan pallor, her freckles almost translucent. Her pale eyes looked empty, like a china figurine whose eye paint had worn off with age. "Honestly, I feel old," she said one day in almost a whisper. "The war has gone on for so long." It was unusual for Alana to bypass black comedy and irony and to admit that her life had been hard. *She'd decided to be real.*

I saw this as a step forward, and took this unguarded moment to empathize. "It must have been pure hell to have fought, and I mean actively battled, for your sanity and for your life ever since you were born," I said. "No wonder you have battle fatigue. You fought longer than any war hero ever fought."

Looking down at the floor and nodding, she said that one of her favourite songs was Don McLean's "Starry, Starry Night." "It's about Vincent van Gogh. The line that I often sing in my head is the one where he says he fought for his sanity."

I, too, liked that song. We both knew the next lines about no one listening to van Gogh's mental anguish, so I said, "I hope you know I'm listening."

"I know," she said and smiled at me. It was a wonderful bonding moment, and we sat in silence for a long time.

The following week I got a copy of Alana's hospital report, which outlined that she'd almost died, that she didn't cooperate with the psychiatrist who was sent to interview her, and that she refused to take the prescribed antidepressants. "Discharged against medical advice," it declared.

At Alana's next visit I discussed the report with her. She mimicked the psychiatrist, using an old-white-man voice: "'Well, hello there, friend. You've caused quite a kerfuffle.' What did he want me to do? Apologize? I just rolled over and faced the wall until he left." She was also offended by his calling her "friend" when he hadn't taken the time to look at her chart to find her name. (And when I called the hospital regarding Alana's follow-up, the psychiatrist didn't remember her. He had to look up her chart.)

When I pointed out that they felt she needed antidepressants, Alana said, "Yeah, well, people who try to kill themselves aren't happy. They're not getting a Nobel Prize for that diagnosis." She said she'd been forced to take too many drugs as a kid and would never consider using them now. "I'll work hard in therapy, go to kickboxing and judo, but I'm not going the drug route. Besides, I honestly feel better than I ever have in terms of my mood."

I relented, but said I wanted her word that she'd let me know if she felt suicidal again.

She agreed. "Offing myself is not in the offing, Gild."

6

IT TAKES A VILLAGE

SOMETIMES PATIENTS AND therapists hold different views on what should happen in therapy. But in the client-centred approach it's usually the patient who sets the agenda—the rationale being that the only person who knows what's most important to the patient is the patient. I'm usually an acolyte of this method, as I mentioned earlier in the book, but in Alana's case, I proceeded differently. Alana didn't want to discuss the suicide attempt; now that she'd separated from Jane, she felt that the moment of crisis had passed. I didn't. I challenged her, saying that she needed to build tools for handling emotional calamities in the future. Building these coping strategies was going to be the last leg of our therapy together. If she got backed into a corner, she'd need an arsenal to fight with. Otherwise she'd have to turn to Chloé again, and no one wanted that. Regarding the suicide, I said it would be terribly sad if she gave up on life just when she was starting to win the battle.

"Winning what battle?" she asked.

I reminded her that she was successfully growing up. She no longer needed Jane because she was no longer a wounded child who needed a mother and a father. Adult life presents many crises, and the world isn't made with neat boundaries. "Sometimes you have to excavate through rock with a dull shovel to establish your own fenced-in backyard," I said. It takes time to achieve love, sex, and maturity. "That's why teenagers are so difficult. They're trying to figure it out and they're making myriad mistakes, but hey, it's trial and error. There'll always be emotional debris along the way. Welcome to adulthood."

"I hope I get there soon because this never-never land is killing me," Alana said, looking tired but with a wry smile.

The first ego-strengthening technique we worked on was establishing boundaries. People who've had cruel parents experience difficulty in creating healthy boundaries. Alana had to learn to say no, even to people she loved. With Jane, she'd needed to tell her that "I'm a different person now, I've changed, and I don't want to be together anymore." I reiterated that it wasn't cruel to express her emotions and desires honestly. "It's just part of the messiness of life," I said.

Months after the breakup with Jane, Alana was still confused about how she could have dealt differently with the situation. I set it out as starkly as I could. "As a child, you never had the chance to set your own boundaries. By that I mean a chance to say 'No, Art, I won't have sex with you. No, Grandma, you can't sexually abuse me. No, Mom, I won't wear a frilly dress and pretend I'm Anne of Green Gables. Sorry, Gretchen, I don't want to be a seven-year-old mother today after taking LSD and being raped by Art and his friends.'"

She nodded but still seemed unsure, so I cited normal rebellious teenagers as an example. Even teenagers who have good parents don't always listen to them. Sometimes they set their own boundaries. If parents forbid their daughter to see a boy, she might do it anyway: she'll sneak out, meet him, and think nothing of it. That's how children break away from their parents. They start defying them and becoming more independent. They take their own route. "It's called growing up." Everyone she'd ever met had defied their parents at least once in their lives, I told her.

Alana leaned back against the chair in shock. She thought boundaries were selfish. She didn't know that it was Art's cruelty and narcissism that didn't allow boundaries. She had no idea that *even though Jane was a good person*, she had the right to want to break up.

For the next few months we engaged in role-playing sessions to help Alana learn how to set boundaries. We used the "here and now," as they do in Gestalt therapy, which meant acting out a scene from her present, not her past, in order to work on a problem. The problem had to do with Alana's current family life in Toronto. She was living a block away from Gretchen, who had a husband and two preschool children; they saw each other often. They also saw their mother: twelve years earlier, when she'd heard about Art's arrest and realized that he'd lost power over her and the children, she immediately returned from England to be near her daughters. She'd also come out of the closet as a lesbian, and brought Peggy, her long-time partner, with her. Now the mother and Peggy lived within five minutes of Alana and Gretchen, and they all visited frequently.

In the role-playing session, Alana wanted to address her mother's fantasy that she'd been an ever-present parent. Alana would become upset when her mom would tell Gretchen how to handle her children. "When my mother says, 'Well, I was a mother too, you know,' that enrages me. When she says things like 'When you girls were little I used to do this and that' I want to say, 'It's all untrue. Please stop, because I don't want to engage in that fantasy.'" But Alana felt that her mother, who'd been through hell herself, was too fragile to hear anything critical.

An opportunity arose during a visit with her mother, Gretchen, and Peggy. When Gretchen's toddler started to cry, Alana's mother said, "Just let him be, that's what I did." Alana wanted to say, "Yeah, for fifteen years," but she didn't. Instead, she repeated what we'd practised in my office. She told her mother that she hadn't actually been an active parent, and although she didn't want to blame her since it wasn't her fault, she also didn't want to share her parenting fantasy with her. Her mother cried, said she didn't have to listen to that "bunk," and left.

But Peggy lingered. "I know what you mean, Alana," she said. "I've noticed her doing that, and it's annoying. You were the real parent. I don't blame you. Just give her some time." Alana said Peggy's comments meant a great deal to her. And when her mother called later that week, she chatted away without mentioning the fight. Instead, they made plans to get together.

I asked Alana how she felt about her mother's call. "Shocked," she said. "I thought she'd either fall apart or never talk to me again. I'm sure Peggy helped."

When I asked her to define the difference between anger and cruelty, she said she viewed them as gradations of the same thing. I told her that learning to express anger was something else she needed in her survival toolbox.

As I'd once explained to Danny, anger has a bad reputation. It's a negotiation device that helps us stand up for ourselves, to say, in effect, "Get off my turf; you're stomping on my sense of self. Stop crossing into my backyard." Then it's up to the other person to deal with your anger—to decide whether it's a legitimate problem that requires a change in his or her behaviour. "Your mother was hurt, and then she considered it, and she hasn't mentioned her 'mother fantasy' since," I said. I emphasized that anger is a signal that someone wants to be treated differently, which is healthy; *cruelty* is when someone deliberately wants to hurt someone else. To illustrate, I said, "Cruelty would have been to say, 'Look, Mom, you didn't give a shit about us. You were a stupid teenage hooker, married a sadist, had not one kid but two, and then got out of Dodge when you could, leaving me to pay the psychopathic piper.'"

"Yeah, but honestly, sometimes I do feel like that."

"Who wouldn't, at certain moments? But you don't say it. It would only hurt her and not alter her behaviour."

As time went on, Alana began to handle more and more emotional conflict with aplomb. She gave her mother boundaries. She met with Jane to sign mortgage papers. They had to meet once a week anyway to pass Font the cat back and forth, and they managed to have a coffee together as friends. Chloé, Roger, and Amos still played inside Alana's head to help her cope with the Art tapes, but they didn't threaten to emerge again.

As our third year concluded, I realized that we'd had a dangerous roller-coaster ride. My obliviousness to her suicidal state still bothered me. I should have been more vigilant. Alana had attempted suicide before as a preteen—and according to the research, once someone has made one attempt, that person is much more likely to make another.

I once asked Alana why she hadn't told me she was thinking of suicide. She said she felt that what she'd done to Jane was so bad that I would have hated her. She felt so awful about herself that she couldn't think for one moment that I cared for her. I said, "That's an Art-thought, isn't it? He'd say I didn't really care for you—that it only looked that way because you were paying me for therapy. Just like he said you got a full scholarship only because everyone else in Prince Rupert was stupid." I told her I was sorry she'd felt so alone in her anguish, and apologized for not realizing the depth of her despair.

Psychologists have to learn from experience, and I certainly learned from my mistakes in this case. From then on I would tell my clinical psychology students about the cases in which the suicide attempt occurred just when the patient was apparently getting better. Not only does improvement require the ripping down of old defences, which is stressful, but patients who have weak egos and who've been neglected also often have no idea how to ask for help when in crisis. They don't believe they deserve extra care, so their despair goes under the radar.

Another area that caused me discomfort was my failure to pick up on the hints of Alana's possible DID. The periods of "catatonia" after university, along with the changes in her voice and manner when she described her casual sexual partner at the law firm, should have alerted me. And when she showed up at my office unexpectedly, I should have twigged and asked to whom I was speaking. However, the condition is so rare—indeed, I never saw a multiple personality before or after Alana—that it never occurred to me as a possible diagnosis.

Establishing a diagnosis is a good intellectual discipline, but it's only a guideline, not a hard and fast rule. Psychologists shouldn't make themselves slaves to the process. Everything has gradations, and sometimes people can have a touch of something and not the full-blown illness. Also, I was never sure Alana was a true DID because her alternate personalities came out only a few times under extreme duress. Clearly, Alana was on the spectrum of DID, but she was never a clear and obvious case.

Alana was making progress: she was better able to lower the volume on the Art tapes. She'd also made some gay friends, and even though she had no sexual relationships with them, she had fun socializing on a gay curling team. This camaraderie in the gay community was new to her, and a comforting revelation. When she met people she didn't like, she no longer felt trapped by them. She was able to choose her friends and detach from others.

She went through her "wild girl" stage quickly, and sex began to fizzle. A year after her "nooner," as she called it, she found it difficult to have sex with others if she hadn't been drinking because she feared they'd see her scarred genitals. She said it also set off bad memories, or triggers. She found that sexual abstinence was best for her psyche, and that since she had so much scar tissue, she didn't have much sensation during sex anyway. Alana remarked that she'd gone from the terrible twos to the teenage years and then right into menopause—all within two years!

We laughed, and I suggested that she'd finally caught up with me.

One episode signalled to me that our therapy was nearly concluded. When *Too Close to the Falls*, my memoir about my childhood, was published in 1999, Alana was captivated. She even memorized certain sections. As a therapist I hadn't talked about myself, so she relished finding out about my life just as I knew about hers. (She was particularly tickled that I too had been a weird kid.) She also found it fascinating to read about a happy childhood where parents were kind, since she'd always assumed that people who spoke of such childhoods were fantasizing. To Alana, my memoir read like an exotic fairy tale. Her favourite part was my nightly walk to the restaurant with my mother when we'd look up at the constellations and pretend we were explorers on camels. I'd written about how my mother had always listened to my six-year-old explanations of scientific and social phenomena as though they were fascinating.

Tears began to flow down Alana's cheeks as she recalled that section of my book. It was the only time she had ever fully wept in my presence. Finally she choked out, "Once Art was nice to me. I'd forgotten all about it till I read your book. He got me up in the night and told me to come outside with him and look at the northern lights. He said the aurora borealis was putting on an amazing light show." She recalled how the purple, green, and blood-red lights streaked and swirled across the sky. "Art told me the scientific reason why we had the northern lights and the myths that different tribes of the world attributed to them. Everyone from the Etruscans, who called them *wind light*, to the Chinese, who called them *candle dragons*, has described them. Anyway, we lay on our backs for a long time and watched, and then I went to bed."

Then Alana looked at me and said, with her slight, enigmatic grin, "Gild, you won't believe what I did two days ago." She paused for a long time. "I called Art. I just looked up his number and gave him a dingle."

I could hardly believe it, and was stunned into silence as she described the call. "When I said it was me, he said, 'Well, will wonders never cease. How are ya?' He was very jovial. He could be like that if he was inclined and was taking the right drug concoction. I said I'd called because I'd read a book that reminded me of the time he showed me the northern lights. He actually remembered it well and we chatted about it. Also, he plays the same computer games that I play, so we talked about going to the next levels. He didn't ask about Gretchen or anyone else. He said, 'Hey, why don't you come on out and see me sometime.' I said I was busy and he said, 'Cool, thanks for calling and good luck.' Then we hung up."

"Wow" was all I could manage to say, finally adding, "Would you ever contemplate going out to see him?"

"Not in a million years. When I told Gretchen I called him, she covered her ears and said, 'Stop! You're petrifying me.' So I dropped it."

When I asked how she felt about it now, Alana said she was glad she'd done it.

"I think it defanged him a bit in my unconscious," she said. "He's just an old broken-down alcoholic with a whisky voice and a smoker's cough. I wasn't even shaking when I hung up. I was no longer four and he wasn't the huge steaming beast that had overwhelmed me. I'm an adult now and he can't control me."

I reminded Alana that she'd been fighting Art all her life—and that when she felt particularly threatened and couldn't handle Art's tapes alone, she brought in Chloé, Roger, and Amos, and together they fought him.

"It takes a village to raise a child," she said sardonically.

How did Alana preserve her sanity? I believe that, as Viktor Frankl described in *Man's Search for Meaning*, Alana found meaning in her life. She had to look after Gretchen, and she told herself that every day. Her suffering had a purpose. It was for the betterment of someone else. She pushed away all thoughts of suicide and escape for the sake of her sister. No matter how tired she was, she never laid down her sword.

Soon after her call with Art, Alana said, "Guess what, Gild? I'm winding it up. I think I've done all I can do here. I've peaked. I used to die to get in here, but now it's just an appointment."

I agreed that we were at the end of the road. I felt happy that she'd achieved so much, but I was a bit wistful. I was very fond of Alana and would miss her honesty and wit. But mostly I'd miss her bravery. I'd wanted her to use her big brain and become a mathematician or a lawyer, but the stress was too much for her.

Those were my dreams, not hers. Plus, time was marching on. She would soon be forty. She'd kept her job at the law firm and got a big bonus each year. Chloé had never appeared again, Alana said, and the tapes were far fainter than they'd ever been. Sometimes hours would pass and she wouldn't even hear them. She no longer, as she said, "ran the programs with Chloé and Roger." She said simply, "I don't need them anymore," but admitted that Amos was still with her. She started laughing and said, "I just love that guy."

Years later, when I was preparing this book, I found Alana on Facebook and sent her a message about it. She was fine, she told me, but said she didn't want to get together because she was in a "hibernation phase." We still exchange emails, always her favourite means of communication. One of them contained some unexpected news. Alana had played violent war video games for years, along with millions of other people. Everyone who plays has a pseudonym, so the identity of your opponent isn't known. There's a worldwide ladder for success in this kind of gaming, and Alana was near the top. But there was one man who kept beating her. As Alana wrote:

He was devious, quick, and clever, and always seemed to know what I was going to do next. Then about three years ago, he stopped competing and I gained the title. (My most tawdry achievement to date.) I found out that that dude was Art. We were battling each other, just as we'd done in real life. The reason he stopped is that he dropped dead. He was found in our old house long after he died.

Alana summed up her life by saying that she still worked at the law firm, wasn't in a relationship, and lived alone with her cat, Font the Second. To my surprise, she lived in the same apartment complex as her mother and Peggy and saw them often. She was still very involved with Gretchen and her two nephews, who were in university. Unfortunately, Gretchen, who did well for many years, was now suffering more from PTSD, drug flashbacks, and other Art-related trauma. This upset Alana, who said she'd hoped she'd protected Gretchen from Art.

She spent her time on two hobbies: kickboxing and physics. She was also something of an expert on string theory and field theory, and participated in online chat groups about physics. She and Jane had maintained a close friendship, even though Font the First had passed away. Neither had had a long-term relationship since.

When I asked about her mental health, Alana said she'd learned to guard her boundaries fiercely. She needed routines, and then she would take "forays into interesting things." One of those was online courses from MIT. But when a professor once asked her to post her comment for all to see on a special forum, she declined, saying that she felt better staying on the periphery. She said she'd learned her limitations. However, no matter how small her world, she didn't "put up with any crap"—and didn't need any alternate or splinter personalities to do it.

She would hear the Art tapes only when she was very tired or doing something stressful. "But now I run the Gild tapes," she wrote. When I asked, with some trepidation, what was on those tapes, she responded after a few days:

The Gild tapes are a verbatim compilation of things you've said. The one I use most often is when you said I was a hero. I picture myself as the mythological Theseus, stabbing the giant Art-like Minotaur. When Art yells his obscenities and belittlement in my head, I tell him that people less strong than I am would be in a diaper in a back ward, believing two plus two is five. Then I tell him he's lucky I didn't kill him. Remember when you said that? I hear your voice calling him a narcissistic coward. Often Amos chimes in as well, and I can usually shut Art up.

She summarized her life this way: "I guard my boundaries like a junkyard dog, and as long as I stay in my protected scrap yard, I'm happy as a clam."

I asked what, if anything, therapy had done for her.

I would have to say it changed my life for the better in every way. First and most important to me, I don't have weird "seizures" anymore. That is HUGE, and that is thanks to your tireless work on tracking down "triggers" (such a misused and overused word these days that I can't help but eye-roll when I use it) and explaining the process to me until I got it. It's amazing how understanding what's going on in my brain when that happens has allowed me to take control, and stop my brain from pulling the master switch when something threatens to awaken memories I don't want to relive. So—although I hated every second of therapy, and was still throwing up and breaking out in rashes before sessions right up to the last year—it's the best thing I've ever done for myself.

Finally, I asked her if there was anything she would have done differently in her life.

I'd have killed Art.

MADELINE

"Mirror, mirror, here I stand. Who is the fairest in the land?"

THE BROTHERS GRIMM, "Snow White"

THE FATHER

MY LAST CASE AS A therapist proved to be one of my most fascinating—and certainly the most unorthodox. (It's surprising how often fascinating and unorthodox have gone together in my life.) Madeline Arlington was a thirty-six-year-old antique dealer in Manhattan who'd grown up in Toronto under the influence of a disturbed mother, Charlotte, and an inconsistent father, Duncan. It was Duncan who called to ask that I treat Madeline—a call that came six years after his own brief time in therapy with me. And when I look back on the errors I made in the father's, and by extension the daughter's, case, the only way I can explain it is that I was in the grip of a powerful parental transference.

Transference means several things. The first meaning is simply the strength of the relationship between therapist and patient. Or it can be, as Freud suggested, something more complicated, such as a redirection of feelings we've unconsciously retained from childhood. The patient may transfer his feelings for a parent or other authority figure onto the therapist. For instance, when I called Danny "handsome," he transferred his childhood feelings of anger toward the abusive priest in his residential school, who'd also called him handsome, onto me. Both Danny and I had to work out this transference—a process that helped us uncover his buried pain and that was crucial to our successful therapy.

There's also countertransference, where the therapist develops feelings about the patient. This usually happens unconsciously—and unconscious motives can be the most powerful and pernicious rulers of our behaviour. The problem isn't only with the initial countertransference; it's also that patients pick up on it, and learn to manipulate the therapist. This is what happened when I inadvertently transferred my feelings for my late father onto Madeline's father, who was twenty-five years my senior. And although Duncan was only briefly in therapy, and years before his daughter was, that encounter would ultimately influence my treatment of Madeline in ways that took me by surprise. That's why I'll begin Madeline's story by recounting my short but intense therapy with her father.

In 1998 Duncan Arlington, then seventy years old, called me seeking marriage counselling. As a WASP Brahmin from one of Toronto's oldest and richest families, his name was embedded in hospital-wing plaques and featured frequently in the newspapers' business and social sections. When I told Duncan I didn't do marriage counselling, he said gamely, "Good, because I'm not really married. I live with someone, and although I love her, she's a whack job." "Whack job" struck me as unusual phraseology for a man in his seventies.

Somehow I let him talk me into seeing him alone so that we could discuss the relationship. When he arrived for the appointment, though, he had his girlfriend, Karen, in tow—and, lamentably, he persuaded me to see them both. I could see why he was such a successful businessman: he had the winning combination of force without bombast. Then, before I ushered them into my office, Duncan smiled broadly, calling me "Cathy" instead of Dr. Gildiner. He reminded me of my American father, who was also an outgoing, confident, friendly businessman. He too would have immediately called me Cathy instead of Dr. Gildiner. And he would have dressed in the same tweed suit jacket with a double-starched shirt.

Karen, meanwhile, with her dark brown hair pulled back in a bun, looked astonishingly like Wallis Simpson, the American divorcée whom the Duke of Windsor had abdicated his throne to marry in 1936. But at seventy-one, Karen looked surprisingly unlike a trophy wife. She wore a navy blue Ralph Lauren blazer and riding pants, the kind with the baggy-hip sides. A septuagenarian cowgirl ensemble is an unusual outfit to wear for a first meeting with a psychologist.

In the first session I learned that Duncan had been in love with Karen in high school, and that they'd become engaged just before he went away to college. He said, as he smiled lovingly and reached for her hand, "She was the prettiest girl on the dock at our cottage and at the country club pool." But shortly after their engagement, Karen, who was unhappy about being left behind, hastily married someone else—a man who would, eventually, leave her penniless with four young children. In the hard times that followed she had several breakdowns, including shock treatments and hospitalizations. She did, in fact, look older than her years; she was gaunt, with nicotine-stained fingers and a jaded, gravelly smoker's voice.

When Duncan came home to find his fiancée married to someone else, he was distraught. Then, while visiting wealthy cousins in Martha's Vineyard, he met a spectacularly beautiful blonde named Charlotte who was staying at the house. He married her quickly, on the rebound, and only later discovered that his new wife was a poor relation who'd been sent there by her mother to bedazzle Duncan. Once she hooked the wealthy young man, he'd have to take care of her threadbare family. It worked.

Duncan and Charlotte had one child—Madeline—but over the years Charlotte had several affairs, and eventually left Duncan and her daughter for another man. In the aftermath, Duncan and Karen, then in their late sixties, reunited. They'd been living together, unmarried, for four years.

When I asked the pair to describe the major issue troubling them, Karen unleashed a torrent of invective. "Duncan is a cheap bastard who won't spend a dime," she said. "I live in a mansion that hogs one city block, but most of the rooms are closed off because he won't heat them, and the furniture is covered in white sheets. The place is falling down around our ears and he won't repair it or let me decorate it. All the decor was done by Charlotte, his previous wife, or should I say his *present wife*. It's a mausoleum to his mother's antiques and his goddamn bratty daughter, who's in the antiques business in Manhattan. You've probably heard of her—Madeline Arlington." Indeed I had, as she'd been written up everywhere as a Canadian who'd made it in New York.

Karen pantomimed taking a drag on a cigarette and then spat out the following: "So one day last year I'd had it. I just walked around the whole house and broke every one of his mother's and grandmother's antiques. The bitchy daughter, pardon my French, heard about this, flew home, called the police, and tried to have me charged. When she walked into the house I honestly thought she was going to kill me. *I feared for my life.*"

I was taken aback by what Karen had done and by the confident, almost proud way she'd described her destructive behaviour, as though she'd been Napoleon in battle. Why had such a prominent man chosen such a feral companion? It was too early in the therapy to explore these issues, so I continued gathering information by asking them both about the extent of the damage. In an even-keeled voice, as though he were describing the weather, Duncan said, "There were hundreds of things smashed. The appraisers said the lot was worth millions of dollars. Some of the pieces had been in my family for generations. Really, they belong to my daughter, Madeline. My mother left them to her. She just hadn't picked them up when she moved to Manhattan. She left them in what was her childhood home—"

"So fucking what?" Karen broke in. "Then give me a pittance to buy some clothes and take care of my horse instead of doling out pennies for each trivial necessity. Women who live on food stamps have more freedom than I do."

"I bought you three horses and a horse farm just last week."

"You bought the farm, true, but it's in *your* name and everything's left to Madeline. If you die tomorrow I won't have a thing. Until you marry me, or include me in the will, that merciless daughter of yours may not enter the house. She thinks it's *her* house to store her antiques and *I'm* an interloper. She's got a lot to learn. *She may never set foot in that house again!*"

I was also surprised that Duncan took all this abuse with such equanimity; he'd actually smiled through the tirade. When I asked him how he was handling Karen's request, he said, "Well, so far I've kept my daughter out of the house for a year, but I don't like doing it."

"*Boo-fucking-hoo!*" said Karen. "I'm not a common criminal."

Duncan turned to me and said, "Well, Cathy, there you have it—our dilemma. I can't marry Karen because I'm already married to Charlotte. And she's right: I am a cheap bastard. I refuse to give Charlotte half my estate, and that's why I won't divorce her."

"You send her a fortune every month," Karen said. "You're scared stiff of her and you still love her."

"I send her what will keep her off my back."

"You're a frightened little mouse. You let Madeline, little Miss Mini-Mussolini, rule your life."

"Well I'm not giving you the money or the marriage, but you know I adore you."

I tried to intervene during Karen's invective, but she only spoke over me. Often when people come into therapy they'll spew out their anger first, and then, in the ensuing sessions, we settle down to therapeutic work. So I let her fulminate. Karen was clearly volatile and, I suspected, slightly unhinged. Yet Duncan's unruffled, hail-fellow-well-met demeanour during her venomous rant was just as unusual.

After the couple left my office, I collapsed in my desk chair. Why had I let Karen in the room when I'd said I didn't do couples therapy? What was wrong with me?

During the next session, I began by asking why Duncan and Karen had chosen each other. I was hoping to draw out something good about the relationship so that Karen would calm down. When I asked Duncan to go first, he said they had a great sex life (Karen rolled her eyes at this), lots of fun together, and shared many childhood friends. When I suggested that Karen seemed angry, he said, "Oh, that's just talk." Then he laughed and said, "You should have met Charlotte."

It's rare for men to initiate marriage therapy, but it was Duncan who'd called out for help. He said his major concern was that his only daughter, Madeline, wasn't allowed to enter their home, not even for Christmas, while Karen's four children visited regularly. I could tell that this upset him—it was the only thing that even slightly pierced his otherwise impenetrably cheerful veneer.

"Tough noogies, Romeo" was how Karen responded. "*Choose!* Her or me." She wouldn't budge.

I tried to reframe the situation so that it wouldn't be adversarial, but both of them seemed to enjoy the sparring. The marriage counselling stalled. I chalked it up to a failed case of symbiotic needs, with Duncan withholding financial security from Karen while she withheld love from him. However, I'm not sure he ever wanted *real* love. He wanted the fantasy girl on the dock in the bathing suit. Duncan wanted his youth back.

I saw them only a few times more—and with each session they became more entrenched in their positions. There wasn't even a spark of awareness about how each of them contributed to the problem. Either they didn't want real help, or they had no idea what a real relationship was supposed to be, or I was simply woefully lacking as a marriage counsellor. It was probably a combination of the above. I realized that I was good as an advocate, but mediation of any kind was not my forte.

Three years later, in 2001 when I was in my early fifties, I had one of those "to be or not to be" moments. I decided to leave my private practice and embark on a career in creative writing. I'd been listening to others' recollections for twenty-five years; it was time to write my own story. So I gave up my office and all my professional associations and happily got to work in my third-floor garret at home. I went on to write a memoir, *Too Close to the Falls*, and then two sequels, *After the Falls* and *Coming Ashore*.

But in 2004, in the midst of writing a novel on Darwin and Freud called *Seduction*, I was abruptly plucked out of my psychotherapy retirement by a phone call. It was from Duncan Arlington, whom I hadn't seen for six years.

Duncan wanted me to take on his daughter, Madeline, as a patient. Since I was no longer in practice I offered to refer him to a colleague. He proceeded to flatter me about how much I'd helped him and then, in classic negotiating style, asked what it would take for me to agree. I explained that it wasn't a question of money; I'd left psychology for a literary career. He said, "Want to have all your books in the window at all the bookstores in Toronto? You know it's only product-placement money that puts them there." When I declined, he tried another approach: "Want me to buy a thousand books and give them to people?" *That* was tempting, but again I declined.

The next day I went to my local coffee shop and there he was, ensconced alone in a booth for four. He must have had me followed. He broke into a boyish grin, joined me in my booth, and told me that Madeline was suffering debilitating anxiety. She'd had three bouts of cancer, each a different type, and she wasn't yet forty. Meanwhile, he said, her mother, Charlotte, had undermined and demeaned her at every turn. "Believe me, my wife Charlotte makes Karen look like Mother Teresa." So I guess he did know that Karen, who still lived with him, was ferocious. (His daughter was *still*, all these years later, not allowed in the house.)

When I pointed out that Madeline lived in New York, Duncan offered to pay me for a full day's work along with travel expenses and a driver who'd meet me at LaGuardia Airport. Once again he flattered and cajoled, saying I was the only person who really understood the situation involving Karen—her destruction of the antiques and, as he called it, her "restraining order" against Madeline.

I reluctantly agreed to see Madeline for a limit of six sessions—and those six sessions would turn into four years.

There are worse things than being in Manhattan one day a week.

2

THE DAUGHTER

MADELINE WAS WELL KNOWN in certain circles as the rich young heiress who ran her own antiques business. She had a reputation as an *enfant terrible* who raced around the Hamptons at breakneck speed in a sporty, plum-colored Ferrari convertible.

Her office was in a Tribeca loft with an expensive restaurant on the first floor. The next four floors housed her antiques business; she lived in a suite on the top floor with a giant roof garden. Her grandmother had bought the building for a song in 1975 when New York was about to go bankrupt. The security guard who appeared to escort me announced my arrival on his walkie-talkie. Someone from the reception desk blasted back, "Oh, it's Dr. Gildiner. Thank God! We can't take much more. Madeline's up in her office with clients. Bring her in."

The office had high ceilings and soaring arched windows that filled the room with light. Impressively large columns were spaced out across what must have been six thousand square feet. The walls were brick and the floor was wide-plank hardwood.

Employees were running around frenetically like ants after someone had stomped on their organized home. Men who spoke an Eastern European language were unwrapping antiques from huge wooden crates while women in designer outfits, teetering on spike heels, hovered over them with clipboards to note any damage. Couriers waited for signatures. The walls were lined with floor-to-ceiling shelves that held hundreds if not thousands of antiques—each one attached by a string to a three-by-five ecru label crammed with tiny writing on both sides. Red motion-detector lights flashed when anyone walked by; to take an item off a shelf, you had to press a button to deactivate the alarm. A ladder on wheels zinged from one end of the loft to the other.

One slight man was in charge of the ladder and getting the antiques down from the shelves. He wore an Armani suit with a vest and sported a Pee-wee Herman hairstyle. Six employees stood at the foot of the ladder demanding various wares as he yelled, "Pipe down, minions! Anyone ever heard of standing in line and waiting your turn? Jesus Christ, have some civility." I later learned that larger antiques were stored on the upper floors, to which a burly black man—an artisan who did all the wood refinishing and repairs, never spoke, and always wore a Stanley Kowalski undershirt, suspenders, and camouflage pants—controlled entry with a buzzer he wore around his neck.

As I made my way to the reception desk, another male employee in a designer suit said, "Good luck, you'll need it. If she yells at you, it's just her way. Please don't abandon ship; we're sinking."

Thirty-five minutes past our appointment time, a chatty woman in dreads named Vienna took me to the inner sanctum of Madeline's office, one of the few walled rooms in the loft. Vienna—sporting a tiny miniskirt, a black tank top, and black-and-white striped tights like the Cheshire cat in *Alice in Wonderland*—was the only cheerful woman there, totally relaxed and swinging her tattooed arms as she walked. She told me how Madeline had had a tough time and that so far it had been her job to hold her together. She talked about her boss as though she cared and wasn't the least afraid of her.

Entering the office, I saw a huge desk, and behind it stood a tall, lanky brunette with her hair pulled back into a bun. Madeline was truly beautiful, with glowing, flawless skin and full bow lips like Snow White. She wore purple velvet spike heels and an amazing Prada outfit consisting of a full black taffeta skirt and a pink bolero sweater. She's the only person I've ever seen in exotic Prada clothing who's managed to carry it off. She also wore large diamond post earrings that telegraphed Tiffany's along with a diamond medallion that looked vintage. (Years later in our therapy, I commented that I'd never seen her dressed in the same outfit twice. She frowned, saying, "It's a sickness.") Madeline's makeup was odd, though: lipstick drawn past her upper lip and coming to two points above its cleft; eyebrows drawn in two thin brown lines, like a 1930s actress. Despite this anachronistic face paint, she was an arresting beauty.

Before Vienna left the room, she told Madeline she'd be holding her calls. Then, in response to her boss's anxious look: "No, I *am* holding them. *We have to do this.*"

As Madeline sat down I remarked that she didn't look much like her father. No, she said, she looked almost exactly like her mother and had her father's brains. I later discovered that Madeline had gone to Yale, followed by the London School of Economics for grad school. Then she launched her antiques business, picking up on a passion she'd developed at an early age while cataloguing her grandmother's collection. She found she loved the work, as it combined her admiration for her grandmother with the two family traits: a prodigious business skill and an artistic eye.

I then began to do a family history. Madeline told me that, as the only child of divorced parents, she lived with her father from her mid-teens, when her mother left, until she went to university. In her twenties she married a man named Joey, and they divorced nine years later.

At this point in her narration Madeline suddenly threw down her pen and said, "Can we leave this history for another day? I'll definitely do it, but I have to put out some psychological fires first." When I nodded in agreement, she looked relieved and blurted out, "I'm a wreck. I've always had anxiety and obsessive-compulsive behaviours, but now, in the last year or so, it's become debilitating. And it's affecting the whole office. If I crack up, this whole place folds."

When I asked for an example of how Madeline's symptoms were hurting her business, she replied, "I can't travel or let anyone from work travel for fear of a plane crash. Like, I *know* it will crash. I think about it all the time." She said she used to fly all over the world with her parents on vacation, and with her grandmother on buying trips without any qualms—and that although she'd always had obsessive traits, in the last few years they had escalated.

"I told everyone in this office that if you don't help me, we'll just have to close the doors." Now I understood why the employees had been so relieved to see me. I found it interesting that Madeline was so formidable in one way and so vulnerable in another. Business leaders who make it into *Forbes* magazine don't usually confess to their employees, including the security guard, that they're falling apart.

By this time Madeline was hyperventilating, so I calmly reassured her that therapy was like solving a mystery—and that together we could discover the source of her symptoms and solve the problem. She said she *had* to get better because so many people were counting on her. "It's interesting that your first concern is your responsibility to others instead of to yourself," I said. "Most people would say 'Doctor, *I* can't live like this. *My* life is torture.'"

Her response was startling. "Honestly, no one cares about me. I'm not saying that in a 'poor me' way, I'm just saying I have mouths to feed." That statement told me she had an exaggerated sense of responsibility and little self-regard.

After Madeline had outlined all her symptoms, I could see she suffered from OCD (obsessive-compulsive disorder) and anxiety. Obsessions are unwanted, intrusive thoughts that trigger anxiety—and Madeline had obsessive thoughts that she and her staff would die in a plane crash. Compulsions are behaviours a person engages in to get rid of the obsessions and reduce anxiety—and Madeline compulsively cancelled flights, which reduced her obsession about plane crashes and eased her anxiety but was crippling her business.

Although her father, Duncan, had told me she was anxious, he hadn't mentioned her disorder. Treating anxiety was my main area, but I always referred OCD cases to specialists. So I connected Madeline with a well-known OCD psychiatrist in Manhattan, and said we could try a two-pronged approach in which she could see him for her OCD and me for anxiety. It was a bit unorthodox, but I felt we had to address a lot of issues quickly. While we were discussing this treatment plan, the double doors to Madeline's office burst open and Duncan strode in, saying cheerfully, "Oh great, Cathy, you're here!"

Madeline, surprised, yelled "What the fuck are you doing here? You don't come bursting into my office in the middle of a *therapy* session. Get out! I can't come into *your* house and you think you can come bursting into *mine*?"

He didn't move. She shouted, "Seriously, or I'll call security!"

"*I'm* the one who got Cathy here," Duncan said, smiling in mock bewilderment. I saw repeated before my eyes the same strange reaction I'd seen six years earlier when Karen had ripped a strip off him.

When he pulled out a chair, Madeline raised her voice even higher: "Honest to God if you don't get out of here, I'm going to get the boys from delivery and mail you home. You fuck me up and then don't even let me have therapy without being a jerk. Translation—overbearing asshole."

"Okey-dokey." As Duncan started for the door he said, "Want to have dinner later?"

To my shock she replied, with perfect equanimity, "Okay, later." Then he left.

Madeline shook her head at me and rolled her eyes. "Sorry for the interruption. Where were we?"

It took me more than three weeks just to piece together Madeline's complicated life history. Once in a while she'd bellow into an intercom, "Starbucks emergency!" and a man whose sole job was to run to the café would go off to get huge cups of complicatedly named drinks.

Madeline told me that her mother, Charlotte, had never wanted children, but Duncan had wondered what they'd do with their money: who would they leave it to? To Duncan's horror, Charlotte, like Karen after her, said that they could spend it all. When I suggested that it was strange to want children only as financial beneficiaries, Madeline said, "Why do you think the Rockefellers had kids? You have to keep things in the family or all you've worked for just gets scattered to the wind. I mean, you hear people say all the time that they want to 'pass on the family line.' What's the difference?" She added that at least her mother had been honest: "She agreed to one kid to please my dad and grandparents, and then she shopped."

Charlotte was true to her word, devoting most of her time to shopping. She had the entire third floor of their mansion divided into four walk-in closets (one for each season) that were filled with clothes, shoes, and matching purses. She kept her furs in storage during the summer; it took a truck to return them each fall. And she redecorated constantly. When Duncan once complained, saying their furniture was fine, she slit it all with an

X-Acto knife and, as down drifted through the air like pollen, said, "Well, it's not fine now." It called to mind Karen's rampage among the antiques years later.

Madeline said her mother made her and her father's life hell in myriad ways. Charlotte was anorexic; there was little food in the house—the only items in the fridge were limes, olives, and maraschino cherries for drinks—and so they ate in restaurants. "I know it sounds unbelievable," Madeline said, "but it's true." The strange thing was that it didn't sound weird to me, since I too had grown up as an only child with a professional father and unusual mother and no food in the house; we ate all our meals at restaurants as well. Clearly, in some ways, Madeline and I were peas in a pod. That's probably why I came out of short-lived retirement to take on her case.

She went on to tell me of her mother's cruelty to her when Duncan was out of the house. Madeline would try to sneak potato chips into her room between restaurant meals; every morning when she'd round the back servant stairs to the kitchen, hoping for some breakfast before school, her mother would greet her by saying, "Good morning, monster." Then she would accuse her of skulking for food. Yet the restaurant meals were never sufficient, since Charlotte would force Madeline to say she wasn't hungry. Her mother would say, "One day when you're not a fat pig, you'll thank me."

They ate in Toronto's toniest restaurants every night. Charlotte would only chew her food and then deposit the chewed meat into a linen napkin. Then it was Madeline's job to smuggle the napkin out of the restaurant and into the garbage. One evening a waiter caught seven-year-old Madeline fulfilling her mother's request and accused her of stealing the embossed linen napkin. Duncan, shocked, asked Madeline what she was doing with it. "I had no idea what to say," Madeline told me. "I knew my mother would punish me if I didn't cover for her, and believe me, her punishments could be brutal. But I also didn't want to embarrass my father, who just said that I should tell the truth."

"That's a horrible double bind for a little girl," I said.

Charlotte blurted out that Madeline was "a little thief" who'd been caught out at school as well. The waiter opened the napkin and found the masticated food. "He looked repulsed and carried it away with two fingers." When I asked her how she'd felt, she said, "How do you think? Ashamed, betrayed, and mortified that I'd embarrassed my dad. You could hear a pin drop in the restaurant." Then she added, "Oh! I just remembered this part. Then my mother turned to the audience of tables watching this, some of whom she knew, and said, 'Never marry a man who spoils his precious only child.' *She* acted like the victim."

When the family returned home, Madeline's father came to her room to tell her that she could confide in him about her problems, and that she was a waif and needed to eat more. As he was leaving he hesitated at the door, then said she should spend some more time with her grandmother. "I think he thought I was in trouble, and he knew my mother couldn't help."

Did her dad suspect that her mom had framed her? I asked. Madeline shook her head. "No way. He usually gave my mother the benefit of the doubt. Plus, he was frightened of her. She didn't play by normal rules. My dad is smart in business. He's doubled the family fortune in his lifetime. But he had a gentleman's code. She didn't. She could smother you in your sleep, and he knew it."

When I asked why he didn't divorce her, she said, "No one in the Arlington family ever divorced. He said it was not something his family did." I filed that in the back of my mind, sure there was more to it.

After the napkin caper, Madeline began spending one day a week at her paternal grandmother's, an antique collector, whom she adored. "After she died," Madeline said, "her will left instructions to auction enough antiques to fund the construction of a new hospital wing."

"What was she like?"

"Formal. But kind and good, and she probably saved my life. She taught me everything I know." Then I asked what her grandmother thought of Charlotte. "She was always polite to my mother. But you pick up disdain by osmosis. Inscrutability is a WASP specialty."

At our next session, I could see that it was getting harder for Madeline to discuss her childhood. She refused to cry, only dabbing her eyes and claiming she didn't want her makeup "flowing all the way to Brooklyn." Her neck had large red blotches. I realized she needed some shoring up, so I asked what Charlotte had ever done that was good for her. She thought and thought about my question, and finally said that because her mother never liked her, she was incredibly hard on her. (I wondered when we were going to get to the good part.) When Madeline made her bed and cleaned her room every single day, Charlotte would criticize if things weren't perfect. "My dolls had to be lined up according to size, and if one bunny was in the wrong position, she'd say, 'What's wrong with that one? It looks ready to pounce.' So when I got to school my work was always perfect because I assumed the teachers were the same picayune taskmasters as my mother. It was just easier to do it right the first time." Madeline sat silently for a few minutes. "I was forbidden to be lazy. So I guess that means my mother gave me a work ethic."

Parents who instill a solid work ethic in their children are certainly doing them a favour, but this was different. Charlotte's cruel perfectionism didn't foster a healthy work ethic; instead, it promoted workaholic behaviour. And workaholism is another compulsion—you work because you feel anxious when you're not working. Some psychologists see it as an addiction, and certainly our modern culture has glorified it. It's not unusual to hear people say proudly that they do nothing but work. Substitute another addiction in that sentence—"I do nothing but drink," say—and it doesn't sound so virtuous.

The staff had already pointed out how driven Madeline was and how gruelling the pace at work, yet I didn't bring it up at the time simply because Madeline hadn't included this in her list of symptoms. After all, the art of therapy lies in recognizing the sweet spot: the time when the patient is ready to look at his or her pathology (advice I failed to heed in the later part of the therapy).

I didn't believe that Madeline could have achieved so much business success without someone, somewhere, having bolstered her ego. Her father was supportive at times, but he'd been unable to protect her from her mother's clutches, and had emotionally abandoned her again when Karen locked her out of her own home.

Madeline's grandmother seemed to be the most likely candidate. (She rarely mentioned her grandfather, other than to say he was quiet, kind, and constantly followed the stocks.) The grandmother, the one with the family money, took Madeline out once a week for lunch and to shop for antiques. On those occasions, Madeline said, they had an agenda, and would tick things off once they were accomplished. They also pursued antiques by travelling to different cities, where Madeline learned that her grandmother was a great negotiator. They went to New York together and discovered the art world. Along the way, the grandmother would take Madeline shopping for clothes; she'd go with her to puppet shows and Broadway productions, and she'd allow her to get whatever treats she wanted.

Madeline was amazed that she could eat as much as she liked when she was with her grandmother. Once, up at their island cottage, known as "the compound," she and her grandmother baked chocolate chip cookies together and Madeline ate three in a row. "I waited for her to call me a monster and a pig, but all she said was 'Slow down, dear. You can have as many as you want.' I thought I had to get them all in my mouth before someone took them away."

"Didn't your mother come up to the compound?"

"Never. She really didn't like my grandparents. She didn't get to be her horrible self with them. She said she was from America and that it was bad enough coming to the wilds of Canada; she wasn't going to be on an island with three prudes, a brat, and an army of mosquitoes."

"Why did she call your dad and his parents prudes?"

"Oh, well, she had this group of friends who were . . ." Madeline sighed and trailed off, looking distressed. Then, after some prompting: "Who were sort of *fast*, for want of a better word. The women all smoked, drank, and spent money to look flashy. They had facelifts in the States before Cher was even born. They got drunk at the country club and swapped spouses. One of the husbands was disbarred for spending other people's trust money. Some of them were divorced. My mother's best friend was her gay interior decorator. They always went shopping and once had to go on a, get this, 'emergency trip to Rome' to buy a certain credenza. One day I came home from school early and she was sitting on his lap with one leg on either side of him. It was then I realized that he wasn't gay."

"What a good cover."

"I know, and that was thirty years ago. No one ever said she wasn't inventive."

"How did she handle the situation?"

"She got rid of the lover right away and then called me a filthy snoop and said that—" Madeline looked down, clearly unable to go on. Her eyes filled with tears for the second time.

"What could be so bad to cause you so much pain?"

"Oh, it's bad. She said she'd tell my father that I took my underpants off and was playing sexual games with Pasqual the gardener, and that I'd started the whole thing. Then she walked out the patio doors and fired him on the spot, writing him what I assume was a big fat check." Madeline was actually very fond of Pasqual. "Sometimes he played hide and seek with me, or he'd throw me in the pool or off the diving board, or he'd sneak candy to me from his pocket. But now I started to think I'd done something dirty and disgusting with him."

When Madeline, distraught, protested, her mother said, "Good work, you little monster. You just got Pasqual fired." Then she added, raising her voice, "Serves him right for getting us that stupid mutt."

Pasqual's dog had had puppies, and when he'd brought one to show Madeline, her dad had said it was okay to keep it. With an unguarded smile I hadn't seen before, Madeline told me that it had been the happiest day of her life. The dog's name was Fred, after Fred Astaire, because her mother made him dance every night for his supper. Apparently his routine was so good that the neighbours came to see him perform. I suggested to Madeline that her mother had done the same thing to Fred that she'd done to her.

"That's right—no free lunch." Then her demeanour changed and she said enthusiastically, "I was amazed that someone could love me." She recalled how overjoyed Fred was when she came home from school. He slept in her bed at night. "I honestly think his warm body rescued me," she said. "Once when my mother lifted her hand to hit me, which she did on occasion, Fred growled at her." Madeline broke down into sobs when she told me this, and put her head down on her antique marble table.

"Why does that bring up so much pain?"

"He was the only person who ever defended me." (She always called Fred a person.)

"What about your father?"

"He'd take my side in things, but if my mother went ballistic, he never took her on. Once when she was really wrangy, I went down to the basement to sit in the tool room and eat a candy bar I'd brought home from school. I found him there eating a can of Spaghettios. I sat next to him and we ate in silence."

"She had the run of the upstairs?" I asked.

"We were terrified."

"Why was your father so afraid of her?" I'd asked this before, but I still didn't understand it. "Were his parents cruel?"

"Not at all. They were very proper, with a great work ethic, but they were also loving and very giving of their time. My grandmother spent hours teaching me statuary from a young age. She took me all over the world and we had a grand time. I could tell a fake Ming vase at thirteen, and I'm not exaggerating."

At our next session, Madeline had a big, beautifully wrapped Christmas present for me. When I explained that, for professional reasons, therapists can't accept gifts from patients, she didn't protest. I think the giant present was a test and that she was relieved when I didn't accept it. I mentally filed that away for future use as a way to discuss the notion of trust.

When I asked about her holiday plans, she said she was staying home alone. Thinking of Madeline knocking around in her massive New York City apartment, I said it must be hard, especially at Christmas, to be locked out of the home she'd grown up in.

Madeline said she'd thought her mother was a one-off, and so was amazed when her dad got together with Karen. "She has the same crazy streak as my mother, but she wasn't as focused, young, and beautiful—she had trouble carrying it off. Plus, she didn't have a family fortune to mop up after her."

When Karen began destroying the antiques, the long-time family housekeeper called Madeline, who contacted the police and then got on a plane to Toronto. By the time Madeline arrived at the house, the police were waiting in the living room, paging through magazines; the housekeeper had made them coffee. As soon as Karen saw Madeline she called her Charlotte—she was either psychotic or drunk. She had a history of both. The housekeeper told Madeline that Karen tortured Duncan, and that sometimes he had to lock himself in the bathroom while she banged on the door with pots and pans. The housekeeper showed the police the dents in the door. No one could find Duncan during this latest rampage, but Madeline knew where to look. "Again, there he was in the basement, sitting on the tool bench holding a can of Campbell's Chunky soup." When Madeline confronted him, he said that Karen would calm down and that everything would blow over. "Long story short, the police just left. In essence he took Karen's side, and I haven't been allowed back in the house since."

When I continued to probe into Duncan's behaviour over the years, Madeline explained that he seemed to feel he shared a pact with her. "He said Karen was unstable and I was strong, and together we had to make sacrifices. It was the same as the noblesse oblige speech he'd made about my mother when she would go crazy. Actually, that's not true. He would admit my mother was dangerous and could do real damage." Her father would go on to say that he and Madeline were the real Arlingtons and that

Charlotte was a stupid interloper. "It's true, she wasn't very intelligent, but she was wily and ruthless and outsmarted my dad her whole life."

In the entire therapy, I never solved the mystery of why the imposing Duncan was such a barracuda at work and yet so emotionally castrated by first Charlotte and then Karen. He spent his life in the clutches of two unloving women. It upset him to keep his daughter out of the house, yet he complied with a woman who gave him nothing in return. Madeline had said that Duncan's parents, although formal and physically undemonstrative, were not unkind. All I could think was that sometimes grandparents who are warm and kind may have been far less so when they were parents. People will often mellow in old age.

Duncan himself seemed to be emotionally obsessed with money: first its acquisition and then its use as a form of power. Although affable, he sadly reminded me of Dickens's Scrooge or George Eliot's Silas Marner. His only real love was for his daughter, but because he couldn't protect himself, he was unable to fulfill the job of protecting her.

It was the end of our first year of therapy. So much for my notion that I'd last for only six sessions! When people have experienced as much trauma as Madeline had, they don't begin to heal until they've dumped out their pain. I was there to act as a witness, to assure her that to be greeted as a "monster" every morning was cruel, and that it had nothing to do with her. I was there to help her deal with the aftermath of such a painful childhood.

3

FEAR OF FLYING

I WANTED TO SORT OUT the mystery of Madeline's fear of airplane travel. Since it hadn't been a lifelong phobia, our job was to figure out what had caused its recent onset and what would stop it.

Apparently, Madeline's assistant, Vienna, was on the same wavelength. She took me aside to say that the accountants wanted her to talk to me because the company was floundering: Madeline wouldn't let any of the scouts fly even though they had deliveries to make—some of their most expensive merchandise couldn't be shipped on its own. Vienna summarized by saying, "Sorry for overstepping my role, but it won't be long until the clients revolt. They're a bunch of entitled trophy wives or finicky museologists who want everything yesterday, if you get my drift."

Just then Madeline swept into the room, shouting, "Vienna, what are you *doing* here? Do you want Dr. Gildiner to think we're nutbars? First my father, now you? Jesus Christ, get out of here!" Vienna nonchalantly tossed her dreads over her shoulder, smiled, and said goodbye.

Madeline asked what Vienna had been saying. "She's concerned about you and the company," I began. "She's worried that your obsession about planes crashing is having a bad impact on the business. Have you been seeing Dr. Goldblatt"—the OCD specialist—"about this?"

She had—and he'd given her a big workbook in which to record her fears, part of a six-week program. "I couldn't figure out if fearing that the plane was going to crash was an obsession or just a neurotic fear," she confessed. "You see, Dr. Gildiner, when things go well, I get frightened that fate or someone will find out that I'm really a . . ." She hesitated.

"What word came to mind?" I asked.

Madeline looked surprised, blinked, and then fell back in her chair as though she'd been struck. "Monster."

"Your mother's word for you."

She nodded.

"So you feel you don't deserve to have things go well. Underneath, you feel you're a monster and that you deserve to have the plane carrying your best workers and your antiques crash."

Madeline looked confused for a moment. "Yup. This whole business is built by a monster who's a phony."

She sat silently, absorbing what her unconscious had decided to release. "You know, when I was head girl and chief prefect in high school, everyone thought I had a perfect mother," she recounted. "The other mothers would say, 'Charlotte, Madeline is such a serious girl and works so hard. How did you manage it?' My mother would just smile and say, 'Oh, I was just lucky.'"

"Did your mother have obsessions?"

"Oh, yeah, and we all had to deal with them," she said emphatically, describing how her mother dug out her eyebrows. "First she plucked them all out and then, if she was in a real frenzy, she'd pull out the hair by the roots and gouge the skin under her eyebrows with tweezers until she bled." Charlotte would have to wear sunglasses for weeks to hide the scabs. "When my father would tell her to stop, she'd say she was driven to do it by me, the monster, and by my father and his boring tight-fisted friends and family. She would scream, 'Ever heard the phrase *I'm ready to pull my hair out?* Well, that's what you two have done to me. You've ganged up on me, along with your stodgy, judgmental parents.'"

I explained to Madeline that her mother had a common disorder called trichotillomania, which is the compulsive urge to pull out (and, in some cases, eat) one's own hair. It leads to noticeable hair loss, distress, and social or functional impairment. An impulse-control disorder, it's often chronic and difficult to treat.

As I spoke I looked at Madeline's eyebrows, or lack of them. I'd been struck at our first meeting by the lines drawn on in strange arches, and I'd suspected she had the same disorder. I waited for her to say something.

Finally, after a long therapeutic silence, she asked, "What?"

"What about *your* eyebrows?" I ventured.

"I don't have that problem. I tweeze mine and they're already thin, but I don't dig them out like my mother did and leave crusty lines. Mine are a style."

I said nothing. I suspected that this was the first time Madeline had prevaricated with me. It was strange: during the entire therapy, she never once admitted that she had trichotillomania. In an article about her in a magazine, the writer commented on her "Kewpie-doll makeup," so I knew I wasn't imagining it. Yet she held fast.

I've found in therapy that it's impossible to predict why some people will admit to, or be willing to explore, a very antisocial or uncivilized act, but will refuse to acknowledge that they've committed a relatively trivial social transgression.

This was a juncture in the therapy that I had to consider carefully. I knew Madeline had tested me by trying to give me a big expensive Christmas gift, and by refusing it I'd gained a measure of trust. When we talked about it later, she described how a marriage counsellor she'd seen had wanted free evaluations for some antiques she'd inherited. And Duncan, Madeline's father, had told me he was surprised that during our sessions I never asked him about the stock market; his previous psychiatrist had started each session with stock queries. I've often found that people who've been "used" in some way as children unconsciously find therapists who repeat that pattern.

And yet trust doesn't always take you home right away. In other words, there's no point in going head to head with a client. They may confess whatever neurosis you're attempting to shed light on, but it's a Pyrrhic victory. True insights happen only when the therapist gets out of the way so that the patient is able to gain his or her own psychological knowledge. If Madeline needed to separate so much from her mother that she couldn't admit to having the same affliction, then so be it. I decided to let the eyebrow issue drop and hoped to revisit it. After all, I'd long since come to realize that therapy didn't have to be by the book. All that was really necessary was that Madeline knew I had her best interests at heart and that she could trust me to help her deal with her demons.

It seemed that every time I entered the busy Manhattan office for a session with Madeline, someone different would approach me. One week a man in a snazzy Ermenegildo Zegna suit strolled up to me, stood uncomfortably close, and spoke conspiratorially in a thick Eastern European accent. "Of course she is crazy," he said. "She works seven days a week and does not leave here until midnight. She pushes us hard as well. We are ready to quit."

"Why don't you?" I asked.

Not having expected that question, he paused. "She pushes herself more than us. Plus, she pays twice what we could make anywhere else. She makes my life a living hell, but I am loyal to her. I hope you know that she is a workaholic." Then he skittered like a crab out a side door as we heard the loud clatter of Madeline's high heels on the stairway.

"What was Zoltan nattering about?" she demanded. "He's always got some bug up his arse."

"Why do you keep all these employees who are so difficult?"

"Honestly, they give 'high maintenance' a new meaning. Would you believe, I just had to buy an air purifier for Bartal? Most of my appraisers and buyers are Hungarian. They're all neurotic—it's a national trait—but they're smart and as obsessive as I am about getting the job done right. They can study a statue for days on end. They can carbon-date till the cows come home. When you're dealing with high-end product, you need obsessive people. If you have one fake, your reputation is damaged forever."

"Are they all like Zoltan?"

"Worse. He, at least, works hard. He always has to take stomach medicine because, as he says, he gets 'the flutters,' but he keeps going. You should meet Ulrich, the Austrian, who's a world authority on Biedermeier furniture. He actually has smelling salts and takes off at least one day a week, for God knows what, and comes in on Sunday because he says he needs quiet. I don't know how I went wrong with him."

We both laughed at this, since the entire company was burgeoning with classic hysterics. Even the cleaning lady had once called out "Dr. Gildiner is here, praise God!" and then brought me an Easter cake with a Holy Card that said she was offering up a novena for me and Madeline.

When I occasionally did psychological work in industry, I often found that if a company boss had demanding, narcissistic parents, she often unconsciously hired the same personality type. Then she'd exhaust herself catering to them, even though she was the person in charge. A company is a family of sorts, and a corporate culture can be a recreation of a family dynamic.

One week Madeline arrived half an hour late for our appointment and asked whether I'd seen the newspapers. "My ex remarried this weekend." This was the first time she'd mentioned Joey, her former husband, other than when I'd collected a family history in our first weeks together. Madeline had told me that she'd married Joey, an Italian Catholic whose parents were first-generation immigrants who owned and operated a bakery, because she thought he was outside the mould of the rich WASP Toronto milieu she knew so well. She thought he would make her "more real."

Joey was always cheerful and interested in business. He was also good-looking, charismatic, an ex–football player, and, above all, not neurotic. Duncan adored him; the two men both liked planes, cars, boats, and fishing. And whenever Madeline fretted about something, Joey would say, "Don't worry, babe. It'll all be fine."

He was shrewd about global business trends. Once they were married, Joey hit up Duncan for money to buy Canadian distribution rights to a company whose products would eventually make it one of the largest in the world. It was, as Madeline said, "an impressively savvy decision." He repaid Duncan within five years.

"*Savvy* is a word you've used to describe your mother."

Madeline seemed taken aback by my comparison.

"I thought I was marrying someone who saw through her," she said. "Honestly, his dislike of my mother was his main attraction. Joey really hated her. By the time I met him she was living in Palm Beach and flying in only to get money or for various celebrations."

"Did no one else see through her?"

Madeline's eyes welled up. Despite the cruelty she'd recounted over her time in therapy, she was rarely brought to tears, so I knew that whatever she was about to describe must have been painful. She explained that she had to discuss her first boyfriend, Barry, who lived on her street and was from the same social set. They both went to private schools and belonged to the same club. The two dated for four years, from grades nine to thirteen, which was a long time measured in teenage years. She was also attached to Barry's large, happy family of five boys. The mother cooked and made big dinners; they often had family parties at their cottage. The mother was kind to Madeline, and together they made dazzling desserts that she knew Madeline liked. She described Barry's mother as warm and round and someone who didn't care about perfect makeup. "The brothers used to kid her and put their arms around her and lift her up in the air and spin her. She always said, 'Boys! Boys! Boys!' To me, it looked like heaven. She never flirted or wore suggestive clothing and spike heels around the house."

"Flirted? What mother flirts?" I asked. Now it was my turn to look surprised.

Barry thought Madeline's mother was pretty. Charlotte would walk around the house in a bathing suit and heels, smoking a cigarette. "I never had sex with Barry," Madeline said. "I didn't want to be like my mother. She'd say things to him like 'What are you and Miss Prude doing this evening? Why do your homework? Why not go out and tango?' and then she'd tango in front of him." Her father saw her flirting with Barry once and told her to knock it off, saying that no one is interested in a forty-year-old when they're sixteen.

Charlotte's response sent a chill through her daughter: "Oh, really? You'd be surprised."

Once when she went to Barry's cottage, everyone was drinking on the dock. Madeline didn't drink since she didn't want to behave like her mother. Barry, not a real drinker, got drunk and started crying, saying how sorry he was and that if he had it to do over again, he'd never have done it. Madeline knew right away that Barry was referring to having had sex with her mother. Charlotte had seduced him and they carried on for nearly a month. Madeline had been betrayed by her mother and the first love of her life. Both Barry and Madeline, who loved each other, tried to get over it, but the betrayal was too raw and that was the end of Barry.

The Snow White fairy tale describes the murderous competitiveness the mother feels when her daughter comes of age, is revealed as a beauty, *and* has youth on her side. (In the original fairy tale she's a mother, not a stepmother. They're not called the Brothers Grimm for nothing.) As Bruno Bettelheim says in his book *The Uses of Enchantment*, the mother's narcissism is confirmed by how she seeks reassurance from the magic mirror on the wall early in the story, long before Snow White's beauty surpasses her own. There is no better tale for conveying how imperilled a teenage girl can feel with a narcissistic, competitive mother. And for Madeline, there were no friendly dwarves.

The repercussions of the sexual indiscretion played out about a month after the breakup, when Madeline and her parents were dining at the country club. Her father asked where Barry had been of late; Madeline said only that they'd broken up. "My mother just kept drinking. I don't know what made me say what came next, but I was honestly crushed. Not only had I lost Barry, but I'd also lost his family. I'd learned at the foot of a master, so I said with the same arch tone my mother often used, 'It was too awkward for him to visit me after what happened. Our house is big, but no house is big enough to house *that*.'"

"My mother just laughed and shook her head as though I was insane. My father knew each of us well enough to know it was true." Duncan shook his head, left the table, and went to the men's lounge for a cigar.

Her mother didn't say a word the next morning. When Madeline got home from school that day, she got a sinking feeling when Fred didn't run barking to the door to greet her. "My mother was standing in the kitchen and said, 'I took Fred in for his clipping today. The vet said he was riddled with cancer and they had to put him down. So sad.'

"It was the only time I'd stood up to her, and then she killed Fred."

"No wonder you and your father were so scared of her." (This incident reminded me of when Art killed the family cat after Alana asserted herself.)

"My father didn't really care about the Barry thing, or most things she did, but he never forgave her for Fred. Nor did I." (When I'd read the notes from Duncan's previous psychiatrist, the doctor acknowledged that Duncan's greatest sadness seemed to be the loss of the dog.)

"I can see why not falling for your mother's charms was high on your list when finding a man to marry." Joey became a millionaire practically overnight by marrying Madeline—and using Duncan's money to set up a successful Canadian franchise. According to Madeline, he became appallingly nouveau riche and wanted all kinds of embarrassingly glitzy consumer items. As their first year of marriage was wrapping up, he complained that Madeline worked too much. He had a point. But once he got the money and the business, Joey hired managers to deal with the stores. He would get up at noon. It wasn't the work ethic that Madeline and her father shared. Plus, he was a terrible sexual partner.

"Did you confide your sexual frustration to him?"

"Many times. He just said, '*I'm* happy.' When I said we had to go to marriage counselling, he said forget it. As consolation he added, 'Honey, I never promised you a rose garden.'"

Their differences were becoming more divisive. Joey wanted to buy things like airplanes, race cars, and huge boats, which Madeline had no interest in. He refused to go on any European trips that she would have enjoyed; he wanted to go to the Grand Prix. If she didn't like it, she could stay home. Joey didn't care about her happiness or sexual satisfaction. He was, in effect, saying that now he ran the marriage and Madeline would have to tolerate it. He was the one who had the rose garden; she was left with the thorns.

Madeline's mother also cared only about herself and what she wanted. And just as she had done, Joey dismissed Madeline's needs as annoying and had no plans to meet any of them. Charlotte had snared Duncan and then spent her life spending his money; Joey had done the same with Madeline.

"No wonder Joey was on to your mother from the get-go. He recognized shared traits," I said.

"Still, I was afraid he'd leave me, so I tried to stick it out."

"Why were you afraid of abandonment? I mean we're all afraid of it, but why stay with a bad husband? You're rich, beautiful, and talented."

"First of all, I don't feel like I'm any of those things—well, maybe rich—but that doesn't count. It never made me happy."

"Do you think I'm making these traits up?" I inquired.

"No . . ." She hesitated. "Not exactly. Honestly, you're scaring me because I think I've fooled you as well."

The fear of being abandoned was a strong force in Madeline's life. She'd stayed with a bad husband for years because of it. She also feared that some of her lacklustre and disloyal employees would "abandon" her, so she overpaid them and put up with far too much. As I heard more about her childhood, I realized that her issues stemmed from years of neglect.

When Madeline was on her high school rowing team, her mother would rarely pick her up at the appointed time. She'd be the only girl left after practice, freezing at the dock waiting for a mother who'd be an hour late. "I'd get in the car and she'd say 'Well, if it isn't Miss Sourpuss. No wonder I put off picking *you* up. Who wants to be greeted with that mug?'" Because she was always the last one left, the teachers would send notes home saying they couldn't stay that long and asking that arrangements be made to pick her up. Her mother would rip up the notes so Duncan wouldn't see them, saying, 'We pay that private school a fortune. They can wait as long as it takes for me to get there. Why did they send this note home? You went mewling to them for pity, you little monster. Maybe they aren't on to you yet, but I am.'"

True narcissists, like Charlotte, never think they're wrong. When they react by lashing out, they're convinced that they're simply defending themselves against some nefarious provocation from someone trying to harm them. When they feel threatened, they go into overdrive and retaliate quickly. Narcissism can be described as a trigger-happy defence.

The next week, while still exploring abandonment, Madeline told me about her parents' six-week trip to Russia with her grandparents when she was eleven or twelve. Instead of getting a babysitter, Charlotte left her money for cabs and restaurants. "But I was too frightened to go out and clung to Fred. The house was huge, and then there was the guesthouse, green house, garage, and pool cabana."

On one occasion while her parents were away, she had dinner at her friend Lorraine's house across the street and casually mentioned that her parents were in Russia. Later, as she carried dishes from the dining-room table, she overheard Lorraine's parents talking in the kitchen. "I heard her mom say the words *neglect* and *child abuse*." Madeline knew that Lorraine's mother was a normal person and never fabricated or exaggerated. Lorraine's father said Duncan must not know Madeline was alone or he would never have allowed it. Finally Lorraine's mother asked Madeline the name of their cleaning lady and her phone number. She called her and got her eldest daughter, Asunción, who was nineteen, to stay at Madeline's house until her parents got home. "The words *child abuse* stayed in my mind," Madeline said quietly. "I think a tiny door opened that day."

One night when she was alone in the first week her parents were in Russia, it was really windy. The burglar alarm went off and the power went out. Madeline was terrified, thinking someone had cut the electrical lines and was coming inside to kill her. She was afraid to call anyone, knowing that if her mother found out she'd been "mewling," as she called it, and "turning people against her," she would have been furious. "The lights were all off in my room except for my princess phone, so I called 911. The house alarm was blaring. Fred was under the bed, shaking like a leaf." The police eventually came, with the alarm people behind them. As it turned out, the alarm had been set off when heavy winds downed some trees onto the hydro lines.

The alarm people explained to the police what had happened. The two officers wanted to talk to her parents, but Madeline explained they were in Russia for six weeks. When they asked who was looking after her, she said she was on her own. The officers exchanged glances. Frightened, and realizing she'd have to cover for her mother, she told them that a cleaning lady came in twice a week and that she could call people if she was nervous.

"Didn't the police say you couldn't stay alone?" I asked.

"No. They hesitated and then left, saying to call a neighbour if there were any problems." By this time a neighbour was outside in his bathrobe, concerned about all the ruckus. The police talked to him. Madeline saw them at a distance all shaking their heads, as though it were a bad situation.

It's interesting to consider the class differences in this child-abandonment situation. Only the *financially* needy are considered in danger. If the police officers had gone to a housing project and found children who'd been left alone for six weeks, they would have either located the parents or moved the kids into foster care. The police who came to Madeline's mansion must have somehow assumed that moneyed people have moral authority—that if they'd left their daughter alone, they knew what they were doing. After all, they were "responsible" adults. Or they may have feared exposing such neglect in a wealthy, powerful family: Duncan might have retaliated, and they had no desire to commit career suicide. So they left a seventy-five-pound eleven-year-old alone for well over a month. The incident was never reported to any child welfare authority, nor did they check on her again.

Madeline recalled how, years later, she and Joey had gone to see the movie *Home Alone*. "I had to leave because I felt like I was going to faint," Madeline said. "I was so shocked that the audience was laughing. I felt like yelling at them to stop."

"You lived it and knew it wasn't funny."

The cleaning lady's daughter met Madeline's parents at the door upon their return from Russia and told them about getting the worried call from Lorraine's mother. Once the teenager had been paid and left, Duncan was, uncharacteristically, furious. He'd assumed that Charlotte had made arrangements for someone to look after Madeline, and he demanded to know what the hell she'd been thinking. "They had a huge row and my mother said, 'When I was fifteen I was out collecting my family invitations to the Hamptons. Not only did I have to ingratiate *myself* but wrangle my

whole family a summer vacation.' Then she really started screaming, the kind of scream that goes right through you, because you
know you'll pay later: 'Who ever asked Little Lord Fauntleroy here
to do anything? Boo-hoo! All she had to do was eat dinner at a
restaurant. I would have been thrilled to have my boyfriend over,
but not her. She has to call the police and every Tom, Dick, and
Harry in Toronto just to make me look bad. Jesus Christ Almighty.
Save me from the two of you.' And she stomped upstairs." Duncan
yelled up after her that there was a huge difference between eleven
and fifteen years of age. Plus, he pointed out, what had happened
to Charlotte as a child wasn't what he wanted for his child.

"She said over her shoulder from the landing, 'If you're so god-
damned concerned about your precious baby, why didn't you get
her a babysitter? Key word: *baby*.'"

After hearing that story and many others like it, I asked Madeline
whether she felt she'd been parented by a mother who had set out
to destroy her or a mother who simply had no parenting skills.

She sat for a long time, reflecting. Finally she said, "It was probably a combo. I'm not sure if she wanted to destroy me. I don't think
I was that important to her. But, in terms of parenting skills, I know
she came from a mother as bad, if not worse, than she was." I was
surprised to learn that Madeline had never met her maternal
grandmother. Charlotte told her that she'd been a devious whiner
whose husband hated her, left her with Charlotte, and refused to
see either of them again. He had money but wouldn't give them a
penny. Even Duncan had made a point of saying that Madeline
wasn't to go there, and that his mother-in-law wasn't welcome in
their home. "That was unusual," Madeline told me, "since he never
laid down any laws unless it had to do with money. I have no idea
what she did, but it must have been bad."

———

At our next session, Vienna accompanied Madeline into her office and said, "I don't know what's going on here therapy-wise, but the accountant told me to tell you that if people don't start flyin' out with product, we'll be flyin' into bankruptcy." Madeline looked at Vienna as though she wanted to throttle her. Ignoring her, Vienna continued: "Hey, you told me not to let you shove this under the carpet. So, Dr. G., we are in crisis mode."

"Vienna, get out!" Madeline shrieked.

"Okay, okay, I'm leaving." Vienna smiled her broad smile, saying, "Dr. G., I loved your book" as she backed out of the room, pulling the double doors shut.

Madeline looked at me, slightly defeated. "Vienna's right—I'm losing customers and money. I have to deal with the flying phobia. But I'm working on it with Dr. Goldblatt and doing my exercises, and I *am* managing to calm my heart rate a bit."

"I guess when people get on a plane and leave you, it brings up a lot of feelings. Last week we discussed the abandonment you felt when your parents went to Russia. Abandonment is a powerful feeling, and people will do a lot to avoid it—even put their business at risk."

"No, it's not the abandonment," Madeline replied. Then she sat silently thinking for a good five minutes. "Again, it's the monster theme. When things are good I feel like I'll get punished. I'm a monster and people will find that out, and even if they don't then bad things will happen because monsters don't deserve success." Then she hesitated and added, "Or happiness."

"Is this all from your mother, or have you done something that's made you feel like a monster all on your own?"

She turned red. "How did you know that?"

I remained silent. Then, when she didn't offer anything, I said, "One thing I know is that we all do things we're ashamed of.

Shame erupts when you violate some taboo. Anyone who says they haven't suffered shame either hasn't lived or else is lying."

Madeline folded her arms in front of her and looked down at the desk. "I slept with one of the men in my delivery department while I was still married. It went on for about a month, five years ago. I hate myself for it. I was as bad as my mother."

"Let me see: your husband used your dad's money to establish a business then didn't go to work, and paid no attention to what you enjoyed. He bought big costly things you had no interest in, like speedboats and planes. He never did a cultural thing you liked. He refused to have mutually satisfactory sex, and when you said you were unhappy he basically told you he didn't care."

"Please don't justify it or I'll stop believing in you as a psychologist."

"I'm not justifying infidelity. I'm only saying that an affair is not an unusual response. You did all you could to let Joey know that you wanted things to be different. You wanted to go to marriage counselling. He refused, so you went on your own for a few sessions. You laid your cards on the table and he basically said, 'So what? I don't care about your feelings.'"

Madeline still didn't look convinced. So I said, "By the way, who does he sound like?"

She looked blank.

"He spends money like water and actually says he doesn't care if you're happy. When you mention a work ethic, he calls you a stick-in-the-mud."

"My mother. *Holy fuck*, I never saw it. They're so superficially different and hated each other so much that I missed it. Jesus Christ, I'm a cliché. *I married my mother.*"

I had alluded to this similarity before, but clearly it hadn't sunk in. Sometimes patients have to see and hear things from many angles, many times, before their unconscious will release it to their conscious minds. That's one of the reasons why therapy can take a long time.

"How are Joey and your mom different?"

"Joey is so affable. Everyone likes him."

"So is she to others. Both of them have many superficial friend-ships but no real friends."

"I felt I couldn't leave him. I had to stay for nine miserable years."

"Just like you couldn't leave your mother. You were a child. She was all you had. You bonded to indifference and, at times, her cruelty. Your job was to endure it and to protect her from detec-tion."

"Oh my God, that's what I did for Joey! When his store man-agers would call wondering where he was, I'd cover for him while my heart sank. When he said he was out with the boys, I knew it wasn't true and that he was carousing, but I never took him on. I was terrified he'd leave me."

"Like your mom did when she went to Russia, or left you alone after rowing and field hockey and eventually for good, with another man. You couldn't leave Joey. You were bonded to his own cruelty and indifference."

"*Cruelty?* That's an exaggeration. He was never cruel."

"When someone says they don't care if you're sexually satisfied and they don't care if you want to go to nice restaurants instead of car races, they're at least indifferent and unkind. He was nice when you were dating and until he got your dad's money."

"He *did* pay that back to my dad."

"Sure, but without him he never would have had those millions to take advantage of that business opportunity."

"Maybe men just don't care if women are happy?"

"I don't think you know what kindness is, or what's normal for a spouse to do for his mate."

"My dad was kind."

I explained to her that, clearly, Duncan was a much better father than Charlotte was a mother. I believed he did genuinely love her. "But he wasn't there for you when you needed him," I pointed out. "He was also fearful, and for reasons I don't understand, bonded to cruel and unloving women." When he should have been defending Madeline against her mother, he was hiding in the basement tool room with her. And now he was siding with the enemy again. "Madeline, you're not allowed in your own home, where Karen destroyed your grandmother's antiques. Your father stood by Karen; he betrayed you again. It's not surprising that you're having these symptoms now." I said that she'd survived one betrayal by Duncan with her mother, but the second one, with Karen, had proven to be too much. It was like breaking an ankle in the same spot twice. No wonder she was psychologically limping.

But Madeline wasn't focusing on what I was saying about her father's betrayals. She was still stunned to realize that no matter how hard she'd tried to get away from her mother, she'd wound up marrying a clone of her.

"I felt I couldn't leave Joey. I thought it was my duty to stay." She sat silently for a minute. "You know what's going through my mind?" She grimaced. "I might as well say it. Who else would want to be married to a monster but another monster?"

"Mr. Monster marries Mrs. Monster," I said, and she nodded in agreement.

"But at the very least, you wanted to have decent sex. So you had an affair. I'm not advocating it, but you were feeling desperate."

"Exactly. I *was* desperate. I can't believe I chose *that* guy. He plays darts, for God's sake!" It had started one night when they were both working late; the product had to go out early the next morning, and he was the packer. "We ordered in food and he made a pass. He was kind and cared whether I had a good experience. A few weeks later, when I said it was over, he said he was going to kill himself and all other kinds of hysterical inanities."

When I asked if she'd turned to anyone to help her deal with this, to my surprise she said yes: she'd turned to a Russian museologist named Anton, who worked with her and whom she trusted. "Anton is the most normal person here, which isn't saying much. He found me crying in my office. I dumped out the tawdry story. I told him I was a filthy slut and hated myself. He said it wasn't true and that Joey was the true cipher and I should cut my losses and get rid of him *tout de suite* by paying him off or doing whatever it took to get rid of him." Anton dealt with the shipper by calling him in and telling him he'd have to leave if he ever mentioned it again to Madeline or anyone else. If he didn't stop carrying on, he'd be fired. Then Anton assured Madeline that the shipper wouldn't kill himself—that "Romanians always say that." Moreover, he said, even if he *were* fired, the shipper was terrified of the police and immigration officials and so would never call a lawyer.

In the end, Anton had been right. The shipper returned to normal; he was still working there. (I wondered if he was the guy who brought us our coffees.) Then Madeline took the next step. "I told Joey we were finished. He barely blinked, and didn't balk when I suggested he'd been paid a lot over our years of marriage." They divorced, and less than two years later he remarried "an Italian girl who never would have expected to have a say in anything, least of all sex."

One of the things I love about being a therapist is that, as things become clearer to patients, mysteries unfold and psychological clues, or revelations, emerge. The big picture comes into focus. That's not as easy to achieve as it sounds, especially since the patient herself is part of that picture.

For Madeline, the first revelation was that deep down she believed she was a monster, and that monsters don't deserve happiness. So it followed that, in her mind, if things were going well they'd sooner or later be ripped away—which accounted for her worry about planes crashing.

The second revelation was that Madeline, like so many of us, had married a version of her difficult parent, firmly believing she'd married the opposite. Madeline, old-guard WASP, chose Joey, a working-class Italian Catholic, and discovered that once the class veneer was peeled away, Joey had the same traits as her mother. Like Charlotte, he was narcissistically self-involved, lazy, unkind, and duplicitous.

Third, we confronted Madeline's history of abandonment and revisited the terror of her being "home alone."

It was time for Madeline to weave these three themes together and discover why she remained in narcissists' clutches, both within her family and at work. We needed to piece the information together into a new narrative that would help Madeline step away from her crippling symptoms.

4

YOU GET WHAT YOU GIVE

IN THERAPY YOU CAN deal with symptoms forever, but nothing changes until the bedrock issue is exposed. In this case, Madeline's mother was at the root of the problem; she had deliberately instilled in her daughter the belief that she was a monster.

At our next session, Madeline was shaking with fright when she told me that Charlotte, who now lived in Florida, had called to invite her to visit. The last time she'd flown there, her mother had "forgotten" to pick her up at the airport and Madeline had to search out her address in the phone book. When she'd finally arrived at Charlotte's condo, understandably miffed, her mother said, "Why do we have to start out angry? Usually you take twenty-four hours to hate me."

Same old song.

I wondered why Charlotte was in Florida year-round: "No one wealthy lives in Florida full time," I said, "unless she's on the bad end of a divorce and all she got was the winter vacation home."

"You're close. My mother had affairs while she was married to my dad, and she didn't do a lot to hide them. There were always too many cigarette butts in the ashtray and men who were 'just visiting.'" When Madeline was fourteen, Charlotte got involved with a married man named Jack who belonged to their club. He was rich and sleazy—a real estate developer, alternately flush with cash and in the red, involved in what Madeline skeptically referred to as "bridge financing." When they met, Jack was fiftyish and Charlotte was around thirty-five. Charlotte left Duncan for slimy Jack, but neither parent ever sought a divorce. Madeline remarked that she was now thirty-six, the exact age her mother had been when she'd left her father.

The separation had occurred more than twenty years ago; Jack was seventy now and had prostate cancer, among other things. Meanwhile, Charlotte was stuck as a caregiver—not, I assumed, a natural role. When I noted my surprise that she'd chosen an older man, Madeline said, "He was everything my dad wasn't. He was exciting, racy, moved with a fast crowd. Travelled to Monaco to gamble, was handsome in a soap-opera-star kind of way."

And both Jack and Charlotte were capable of being under-handed. Duncan's family had a condo in the same complex in Palm Beach as Jack's family. When Madeline's parents were still together, Charlotte used her as a decoy for their trysts. "I was dragged by my mother to the condo where Jack lived with his then-wife. She and Jack would touch hands under the table and play footsie, and my mother would pull antics like saying to his wife that our children should get together and play tennis. His kids were in their mid-twenties when I was fourteen—it was ridiculously embarrassing. And if I didn't act excited about her shenanigans, she'd call me a bump on a log and say, 'Madeline, you're the one who admired Jack's boys' tennis-playing and wanted me to ask if you could play with them. For heaven's sake, say something.'"

Jack's three children never spoke to him after he left their mother and lost his money, which was pretty well simultaneous. Charlotte told Madeline that Jack's kids were cruel when she called them to say he had cancer—they didn't even call back. Madeline said, "Note to self—they're really solicitous toward the mother."

"Makes you wonder what kind of father he was," I mused. "You get what you give."

Madeline sat up straight and put her coffee down. "Say that again?"

"You get what you give."

She said it aloud slowly, as though it were another language. "*You get what you give.*" Then she said it louder. "You get what you give!" She leaned back in her chair. "Well if *that's* the rule of relationships, then why do I give so much to my mother?" Madeline pointed out that whenever Charlotte called she'd always try to be there for her, and would send flowers for each special occasion. Yet her mother remembered nothing and gave her nothing in return.

I asked Madeline why she persisted. She had no idea why, she said, but then admitted that she was still frightened of her mother. "She's somewhat declawed because I can always leave, but cats have more than claws at their disposal."

When I suggested trying to free-associate to this notion, Madeline grumbled that she wasn't in Freud's office. "I know it may seem hokey to you," I said, "but sometimes the unconscious is dying to come out, if only you give it some breathing space. Why don't you picture pushing away all your defences and just sit with the question 'Why am I still nice to my mother?' And then see what floats into your mind."

Madeline wasn't someone who wore her heart on her sleeve. After all, she'd had to be tough or she would have been destroyed— she could have succumbed to anorexia, drug addiction, psychosis, or any number of disorders. She exhibited that same toughness when fighting her internal battles. Much to her credit, she stepped into the firing line, closed her eyes, and put that question to herself.

After a minute or so, tears streamed over her perfect makeup. Finally, chocking with sobs, she said, "I was nice every time because I thought maybe *this* time she'll love me. I thought I just hadn't found the right combination of things to do. There was always the next time. Just one morning I wanted to come down the stairs and have her *not* say 'Good morning, monster.' If I worked hard enough, I'd find how to make her love me."

"There isn't a child on earth who doesn't want a mother's love," I said.

Crying and frustrated, she yelled, "*Morons* get their mother's love! Joey never did one thing for his mother. Even when he got money, he didn't buy a new oven she needed for the bakery. Yet whenever she saw him her face lit up. And Barry just had to walk in the door for his mother to stop whatever she was doing and kiss him. She'd ruffle his hair and ask him about his day. All he ever did was grunt in response. Yet he was adored."

While drying her eyes, she looked at me and asked, "What did I do wrong?"

"Did your mom love anyone?"

"*Maybe* Jack. He told her how beautiful she was all the time. So who knows? She stayed with him. However, she's in her fifties now. Where can she go?"

"She was with your dad for fifteen years. Did she love him?"

"She couldn't stand him. You know what's weird? *He* loved *her.* If she ever threw him a bone, like taking his arm in public, he'd beam. I learned to long for her love, just as he did."

"Love is hard to understand. Look at that play *Who's Afraid of Virginia Woolf?* The wife tortured the husband, cuckolded him, and still he loved her."

"It's weird you mention that because my father and I once saw that play on Broadway, and neither of us thought the wife was so bad." We both laughed at that.

"It's strange that your father would continue to long for your unloving mother, especially since, as you say, he had such decent parents. But it's not at all odd that you wanted her love. That's what any child, or any animal for that matter, wants from its parent. It's innate."

To bring the point home, I told Madeline about some studies done on gorillas at the Toronto Zoo. Gorillas are known to be good parents in the wild, but in the zoo, they wouldn't even procreate. First they were depressed, and exhibited obsessive ritualistic behaviours. Madeline perked up at the mention of obsessions. The male gorillas had no interest in sex—they sometimes exhibited copulative behaviour, but not with a partner.

The zoo wanted the females to get pregnant, so they brought in a male gorilla that had been raised by its mother in a troop (in the wild, gorillas live in groups comprising one adult male along with adult females and their offspring) and knew what to do. But the female gorillas that hadn't been raised by their mothers or in a troop were terrified of the male when he tried to copulate with them; they thought they were being attacked and fought back furiously. They'd never seen sex in a troop, but more importantly they'd never seen sexual foreplay, and determined that it was a form of aggression.

At their wits' end, the zookeepers called in an animal behaviourist, a friend of mine, who decided to artificially inseminate the gorillas. Most gorillas aborted, but a few finally got pregnant and actually gave birth. The first mother to give birth immediately killed the newborn. She eyed the infant as though it were a foreign object she had excreted: as soon as it began moving, the mother looked alarmed and then beat it to death. The veterinarians and behaviourists were taken aback.

These female gorillas had never attached to their mothers, nor had they ever seen bonding in a troop. They'd never witnessed a birth or seen an infant gorilla, and it frightened them.

For the next births, the animal behaviourists were in a quandary: they wanted the mother to bond with the baby but didn't want to run the risk of her murdering it. So they opted to take the baby at birth and have a familiar female zoo assistant role-play bonding with it in front of the mother, hoping the mother would imitate the bonding behaviour. The woman held and cuddled and fed the baby gorilla, but its mother paid little attention. (Sometimes she'd even look on as if to say "Better you than me.") When they tried to gradually introduce the baby to the mother gorilla, she would swat it away.

The sad thing was that the baby would continually crawl back to her mother, trying to bond. The mother almost killed the baby by swatting it away. Yet the baby wouldn't give up. Tragically, the baby had to be separated from its mother just as the mother had been separated from her own mother—a multigenerational dysfunction that we see again and again in human cases.

Madeline commented that the mother gorilla had been cruel. I explained that the female had no idea what a mother was supposed to do, since she herself never knew her mother. She didn't even know it was her own offspring, or what that meant. And maternal instinct is complicated: it's a combination of instinct and an early socialization that has to include attachment.

"I told you my mother's mother was so bad that my father wouldn't let her in our house," Madeline said. "She stayed in bed all day and basically pimped her daughter, not letting her come home unless she had some invitations from important people. I once asked my mom whether her mother was sick, and she said, 'She was rich, then poor, and then a snake.' My mother was never one to confide anything. She might give you one line, and then if you asked more, she'd just say, 'Mind your own beeswax.'"

We sat there for a few minutes. Then I said, "It's hard to be an only child. If you had brothers and sisters, you'd probably have seen how unloving she was, or one of them might have helped you and maybe been a substitute parent for you." (I was thinking of how Alana had protected her younger sister.) "But you were alone with your dad. The two of you were in the basement, eating scraps of food, terrified of Charlotte and yet hoping to be loved by her. Unfortunately, your father acted like a frightened child instead of a protective parent."

"Okay, okay, I can see that she couldn't *love* me, but why did she *hate* me and call me a monster?"

"Why did the gorilla hit the tiny baby gorilla and no other one?"

Madeline was silent for a long time. "The infant wanted what she couldn't give."

"Bingo. You blew your mother's cover. Remember when you overheard your friend's mother and father whispering the words *child abuse*? You were only asking for normal love and not to be abandoned. Your mother must have seen other mothers and how they behaved with their young. She had to have some idea, albeit buried, that she wasn't fulfilling her job description."

"You're right, because she couldn't stand Barry's mother. She called her an overprotective hausfrau who was making her kids into babies. She called all the mothers we knew smothering and incapable of discipline. I sort of believed her."

"Deep down did you believe it?" I asked, trying to push this further.

"I did and I didn't. I thought the kids were babied, as she said, but I also *wanted* to be babied. Now I'm realizing that Barry's and the other moms were just loving mothers, and mine wasn't. As Dr. Goldblatt would say, I've reframed *babying*, which is bad, as *loving*, which is good."

I agreed. "Your mother didn't buy the babying story either. At some unconscious level, every time she saw you, she knew she couldn't do the job of mothering you."

Madeline looked off into the distance for a long time. "It's *so* hard to believe it wasn't me," she said. "Is there anyone she could have loved?" She looked confused, still grappling with the idea that her mother's cruelty wasn't her fault. This was an important moment in the therapy, and I wanted to help her clarify the question.

"Not someone who wanted *real* love, affection, warmth, and empathy," I replied. "She was so wounded by her own mother and abandoned by her father that she didn't have what was needed to pull it off. She's a narcissist, or a psychopath, or both. But those are just labels." (There is great debate in the psychology world over whether narcissists and psychopaths are born that way or made. It's part of the ongoing nature/nurture debate.) "The point is, Charlotte lacked the tools for motherhood, yet was somehow expected to do the job."

Madeline looked at me sadly and said, "For the first time in my life I almost feel sorry for her."

Therapy is a lot like growing a tree. For the first few years there appears to be no major growth, but by the third year, after the roots have established themselves and can support the trunk, the tree shoots upward. Madeline had had several important revelations about her behaviour. One was the rule of human nature: *You get what you give.* That phrase galvanized her. She'd had no idea that she had the right to give her mother only what she received from her—which was precious little.

The second revelation occurred when her unconscious released the idea, or the false belief, that her mother would love her only if she were totally perfect. Of course, that wasn't true. Her mother was incapable of loving her, and being perfect wouldn't alter that fact. That insight helped to free Madeline from trying so hard to please her mother.

The most important revelation of the year was that her mother, like the captive gorilla, wasn't capable of love. She'd never been mothered herself, and she had no role model. Many psychologists believe that narcissistic personality disorder occurs at a very young age, probably before the age of two. The child is neglected or traumatized and learns that the primary caregiver cannot be trusted to provide for his or her needs. The child becomes emotionally stunted at the age when the trauma occurs, unable to experience more mature emotions such as gratitude, remorse, empathy, or love.

A huge weight was lifted from Madeline's psyche when she realized it wasn't her fault that her mother didn't love her—that Madeline wasn't an unlovable "monster" but rather that her mother could not love.

The final revelation arrived when Madeline found the answer to her earlier question: "She may not love me, but why does she hate me and call me a monster?" Madeline was a symbol of failure to Charlotte, who knew, unconsciously, that her daughter needed what she couldn't give. And so the mere sight of Madeline repelled her, for it reminded her of her own inadequacy—after all, no one likes what they don't do well.

Armed with those insights, Madeline was able to disrupt her usual pattern of behaviour. She stopped visiting Charlotte in Florida. She also stopped trying so hard to please wealthy female customers (mother figures) who were also perpetual malcontents. Instead, she drew up new contracts that laid out specific goals, and then wouldn't tolerate their attempts to change the terms of the contract or otherwise manipulate her.

When you go from fearing your mother to feeling sorry for her, it usually means you've travelled a long way toward recovery.

5

THE BENDS

MADELINE'S FOURTH YEAR of therapy would prove to be extremely tumultuous for both of us. I would make a big mistake as a psychologist, one that I would pay dearly for.

Madeline had started to be on time for her appointments and arrive with a list of things to cover. But at one session she looked panicked and shouted out the door, "Coffee, *now*! Jesus, what do I have to do? Clean the floor and crate the orders as well?" She threw her papers on the table and said, "These are unfilled orders. One has to get to the Getty Museum in L.A. by Thursday. I want to send Anton with it because it's crucial, but I'm sure the plane will crash. *When is this going to get better?*"

It seemed as if Madeline had relapsed into crippling anxiety and that her ongoing obsession about plane crashes had intensified. "Well, there are three options," I replied. "One is to let him fly and then live with your anxiety; another is to take medication so that the business can function; and the other is to work on it in therapy. If I were you, I'd take medication simultaneous with the therapy."

Madeline was frustrated with the slow pace of therapy and dismissive of the idea of taking drugs for her anxiety. "Medication is out. I don't want to be my mother. She took everything in the book, on top of booze, and still does. My father drinks his fair share as well, but still manages to function. He's in his seventies and still works sixty-hour weeks and the younger guys can't keep up with him." After a long silence, she put her head down on the desk and mumbled, "My body can't take much more."

I looked at her tall, lithe frame and wasn't quite sure what she meant. She was every inch a powerhouse in some ways and yet so damaged in others. Finally, she said she'd had four cancers, and that not one of them was related to any other. At twenty-one she was diagnosed with breast cancer, at twenty-eight thyroid cancer, at thirty-five endometrial cancer. Now she had melanoma.

I just shook my head. I'd known about the first three cancers from her father, of course, but I wondered why it had taken so long for Madeline herself to tell me about them. When I asked what she thought had caused these unrelated cancers at such a young age, she said, "Well, honestly, I like to be scientific and read up on everything, but I think my immune system got used up as a kid and I don't have a thing left to fight with. Don't bother asking the obvious question: 'Then why don't other kids who had harpies for mothers have a hundred cancers?' *I don't know*." She sat tapping her pencil. "All I know is that I have to have a kidney X-ray next week, and I just know it will be cancer." When I asked Madeline whether she believed this was one more way the universe had of punishing her for being a monster, she brightened and said, "Glad you're *finally* understanding me." Then she deadpanned, "I guess God said 'Breast cancer isn't enough, let's give her thyroid cancer. Then let's work our way down so she can't have children.'"

"Would you have wanted children?"

She looked wistfully out the window. "I would have liked it to have been my choice. The cancer did save me from having kids with Joey. So I guess there is a silver lining."

"Is it God that's punishing you or is it fate?"

"It's what my mother said: 'The world will find out about you and you'll have an awful life. Monsters can't hide.'" (Madeline did a great imitation of her mother's Boston accent.) "Mind you, I don't believe that as much as I used to. But all these unrelated cancers are a lot to deal with."

I asked how Charlotte had reacted when Madeline got her first cancer at twenty-one. Instead of answering the question, she went into how her mother had left her dad when she was in her mid-teens. Charlotte and Jack moved to New York City, where he started a new business, and spent the winters in Florida in a house Duncan had inherited from his parents but then gave to Charlotte. "Life was way better without her," Madeline recalled. "My dad and I went out to dinner. He kept up with the PTA meetings and came to my games and even came to Ottawa for my debating team competition. We had a live-in housekeeper, Nelcinda, who was organized, loving, and kind. I'm very attached to her, and she came with me to New York years ago."

I wondered why Madeline had ignored my question. So I asked it again. She shook her head as though it was hard to have to remember; I could tell by her face that she didn't want to go there. "My father told her and she sent a Hallmark card. I can still remember it had purple violets piled in a small white wagon. Inside it said 'Get well quick' and was signed *Charlotte*."

"Not 'Mom'?"

"Nope."

When Madeline developed endometrial cancer fourteen years later, Charlotte came to visit her in the hospital. "I was shocked when I saw her. My dad was there; he stayed with me most of the time. She breezed in wearing a pink dress and pink shoes, saying, 'Duncan, your secretary said you'd be here.' Then she expressed her sympathy to me in one line." When Madeline asked why she was so dressed up, Charlotte said that she and Jack, who was waiting in the car, were in town for a wedding. "Then she presented my dad with divorce papers and left. Whenever she needed money, she threatened divorce. By the way, they never divorced. She just wanted to serve him with the papers in person as the law required and then get out. She never intended to visit me."

When I said that had to be disappointing, Madeline remarked, "Only because, as I'm discovering in therapy, kids never give up hope. I honestly think that now I *have* given up. She's like a hollowed-out pumpkin. Her mother emptied her pulp and then carved a smile on her face. If she'd been unattractive, she'd be a psychopath in some local jail."

"If you honestly feel that way—and I think it's a fair assessment—then why do you cling to her monster moniker?"

"I don't believe it *logically*. I was a symbol of what she couldn't be: a mother to her child. She hated me for that. Still, it's been my *only* definition."

"What about your father?"

"Do you know, he comes here to New York every week and does work for my company on international trade and tariffs. I'd rather pay someone. Honestly, it would be less hassle."

"He does everything but let you in his house."

"*Exactly*."

"The big question is, does his fear of psychopathic, narcissistic women mean he doesn't love you?"

"I feel he loves me. You can be totally fucked up and still love your kid. Anton asked that same question. I've been talking to him late at night as we work."

"He sounds like the first person you've confided in."

"Yeah. He was here for the Joey marriage, the affair, and my mother's stupid visits with her friends. She likes to show off my success because it reflects on her as the 'perfect mother.' She always used to say things to me in front of her friends that indicated I was doing a job for some famous client. Vienna calls her a 'starfucker.'"

"Anton saw this whole circus?"

"Yes. We kidded that his father was as bad as my mother, so we both had to be on our toes." She went on to say that Anton was a smart and sensitive person, but that his poor English held him back. He lived with his brother and spoke only Russian at home. Madeline, rarely one to be effusive, told me how talented he was as a museologist—he could date almost any statue within five years of its origin. Apparently, to be a museologist you had to not only know the history and craftsmanship of hundreds of forms of beauty; you also had to have a talent, or an eye, for them. She said Anton had recently caught a fake six-hundred-year-old porcelain Ming vase that Christie's and she herself had missed.

Jumping to the crucial details, I asked if he was single. Madeline said he'd been married briefly in his twenties while still in Russia and was now divorced. When I asked if she cared for Anton, she replied that she hadn't had sex with him. They worked well together, she said, even if they weren't the same type and travelled in different circles. Anton had a Ph.D. from the top university in Moscow, and associated only with the huge Russian community in New York. Madeline praised his artistic sensibility, and compared his mind to a catalogue. "Once, on a site visit, he saw an empty nook in a client's foyer and said, 'How about the blue Finnish chest we got several years ago in that Estonian estate sale?' He's always spot on." She added that Anton had absolutely no financial sense, and that she couldn't let him price anything or go near the books. I suggested that if it was business sense she wanted, she could have stayed with Joey. We both laughed at that.

When I arrived the following week, Madeline looked very tired. Vienna, who was directing the Starbucks deliveryman to put the coffees on the desk, said, "Before I leave, I'm telling Dr. Gildiner a few things that are on my mind."

"Vienna, you're overpaid to do very little but annoy me. Please leave."

"Nope. Dr. Gildiner, I don't think Madeline will tell you that the reason she has dark circles under her eyes is that she's worked for 678 days straight. I know because I've been here as well. That would give anyone cancer. I'm worried about her. She has to take some time off."

"You've been paid, and you bring your son in every weekend."

"I'm not complaining; I *care* about you. Ever heard of caring? Man!" With that, she strolled out.

I took my cue from Vienna and reminded Madeline, a walking encyclopedia on cancer causes and treatments, of the theory of immune system overload. If a person is continually stressed, the stress uses up the immune system and there's nothing left to fight cancer. (Research has shown that children who suffer abuse are about 50 percent more likely to get cancer than other children.)

Madeline protested that the rest of the staff had been at work every day as well. Then she corrected herself, saying that evenings and weekends it was only she, Anton, and sometimes Vienna and her son. She smiled a rare smile and added, "We're like a little family. Jacques, Vienna's nine-year-old, is a lot of fun; he's interested in the work and has a natural eye." Anton taught him a lot, and had even gone with Vienna for Jacques's interview at a private arts school that Madeline was paying for.

"Anton sounds like a really good man. And it's odd how his name comes up every week."

"He's a new immigrant. Sometimes, for a break on the weekends, we walk to Starbucks. He has to point to the size he wants.
He can't even get the sizes straight."

"What a tragedy. Wow! I get it now. You should have told me
that earlier," I deadpanned.

She laughed. "Okay, that is sort of minor."

"You're going to have to come up with something a little worse
than that before we dismiss Anton, the one loyal man in your life."

"Jesus Christ, all right already. Here's my full disclosure. Why
would he want me? I'm grouchy, I scream, I've failed at relationships, I'm riddled with cancer, and I'm so neurotic it's pathetic."

"Why does he stay?"

Madeline said he was well paid and employed in a field where
jobs were scarce. She sat silently for a minute and then smiled in
a way that made her face look radiant. "One thing I like is that
when he leaves every night, he touches my head and says,
'*Spokóynoy nóchi moy zavetnyy odin.*'" When I asked what that
meant, she said, "I don't know. Probably goodnight."

Thinking it was a long phrase for goodnight, I looked it up on
my phone as we sat there. As I was searching, I said, "Strange you
never asked him what that meant or looked it up. I mean, you're
a woman who knows the value of the yen every day and can decipher a contract in seconds. Someone says this every night and you
never ask?" I found the phrase and read it aloud: "*Goodnight, my
cherished one.*"

Silence. She sat looking at her desk for a long time, her non-
brows furrowed. Finally she shouted, "Holy shit!"

Her face looked crumpled, devastated. The mystery was coming
together.

But this is when I made a grave error: I overinterpreted. "You
don't want him in an airplane, right?" I began. "You're a monster,

and you think he'll be taken away from you. His plane will crash. It's too frightening for you to lose someone who's as kind, good, and caring as Anton. Is this overwhelming fear your bizarre way of telling yourself that you love Anton?"

Madeline yelled "Fuck off!" and stomped out of the room, teetering in her multicolored Manolo Blahniks.

Minutes later Vienna tore in and said, "What happened here? Major meltdown. Madeline is jamming a lot of paper through the shredder and told me to tell you therapy has permanently concluded. There's a check in the mail."

It was so typical of Madeline and her family to say, even during an emotional cataclysm, *The check is in the mail.*

I declined the chauffeured ride to the airport and wandered around the streets of New York, admiring the spring dazzle as I cut through Central Park: azaleas had just bloomed, dotting the meadow with pink; forsythia bushes, usually so nondescript, had burst out into butterscotch-yellow flowers all along their stems; fallen blossoms were strewn along the paths as though I were at my own wedding.

There was no point in asking where I'd gone wrong with Madeline's case. It was obvious. I, a veteran therapist, had made a rookie mistake: I'd shown off what I knew. Now *there* was a Minotaur I should have slain long ago.

I'd been trying to push Madeline's therapy along at too fast a pace and was overinterpreting. I saw that she cared for Anton and didn't want to lose him. She didn't feel she deserved him. All the memories of her mother telling her she was a monster resurfaced. Her obsessive thought patterns took over, and no one from the firm could board an airplane. Her plane-crash obsession was obscuring her fears of real attachment. Anton was a good man who cared for her and only told her so in Russian. He shared her love of art, beauty, and hard work. Would her obsessions overwhelm her very real feelings for Anton?

Madeline's meltdown illustrates the nature of obsessions: they're essentially defence mechanisms that protect patients from looking at what really terrifies them. Madeline *said* plane crashes terrified her, yet as a child she'd flown all over Europe without a palpitation. This obsession was new and had surfaced after she fell in love with Anton. What really terrified Madeline was loving and being loved. "Love" had spelled abandonment, disappointment, and betrayal for her. She had a mother who did cruel things to her and then said, "I'm only doing this because I love you." Her father loved her but had chosen two narcissistic psychopaths over her welfare. As Elie Wiesel says, "Silence encourages the tormentor, never the tormented." Her husband, Joey, turned out to be a slightly more affable version of her mother.

Madeline had fought so hard just to stay alive. She took *herself* to the hospital for all four of her cancers. How could she lower her defences to love someone? Love was too great a risk, one that terrified her. She took constant risks with her company, but she'd been groomed to succeed in business. She'd never failed at it, and her father and grandmother had praised her for her artistic eye and financial acumen.

If you've been told you're a monster, and then you fall in love with someone, you believe that that person will not return your love. No wonder Madeline thought it best to keep a lid on her feelings for Anton.

My first mistake was presenting something (love of Anton) as a good thing when Madeline perceived it as terrifying. Second, Freud was no fool when he discovered and labelled defence mechanisms. Our unconscious needs are strong—so strong that they can overwhelm us. We all desperately want to be loved. Madeline was no exception. Yet whenever she'd tried to be loved and give love, it only caused her pain. Her mother called her a monster; her father locked her out; Joey didn't care about her. She couldn't risk the pain of another failure in love. Now that she loved Anton, she feared losing him in a plane crash. In reality, she felt she didn't deserve love. All her obsessions about travel concealed her longing to be loved, but also her fears about being loved. It causes great anxiety to want something desperately while at the same time feeling terrified of it. It's a constant isometric exercise for the mind.

Plumbing the unconscious is a bit like deep-sea scuba diving. You can't rise to the surface too quickly. You have to come up gradually and acclimatize or else you'll get the bends. Madeline had gotten the psychological bends. I'd tossed off too much painful material too quickly. Her defence, evident in her terror of air travel, was so important to her that she was willing to lose thousands of dollars a month and put her business in jeopardy. That's how much she wanted to protect herself from her feelings of love. Love means vulnerability; people who love you can also hurt you. Making oneself vulnerable is the ultimate in bravery. It's scary, and that's one of the reasons why therapy can take a long time. A patient has built up defences over a lifetime, and a therapist can't just rip them off; they must be peeled off slowly. In this case, the problem wasn't the length of time Madeline had spent in therapy, as five years is enough. It was my sudden, rushed overinterpretation that was wrong.

When therapists make a mistake, they must examine their own motives. I knew that I had my own set of impulse-control issues— but that my office helped me don the therapist's full metal jacket. In Toronto, I had what I called my "detached chair." Here in New

York, though, I'd bowed under Duncan's pressure to treat his daughter and succumbed to the non-psychological needs (fear of bankruptcy, work pressure, etc.) of others at Madeline's workplace.

Another factor was that I identified too strongly with Madeline. I, too, had been an only child. My mother was never cruel, but as she herself said, motherhood was not her forte. If it hadn't been the 1950s, when women were expected to stay home, she probably would have been an academic. My mother, like Madeline's, said things like "I'd rather put hot pokers in my eyes than host a seven-year-old's birthday party." So I arranged all the parties and ordered the sandwiches and cake, just as Madeline had done. I understood from the inside out how she'd had to grow up before she was ready. I remember being shocked as a child when my friend's mother said my mother was neglectful. I thought she just minded her own business, as I assumed all mothers should.

When Madeline had read my memoir *Too Close to the Falls*, she was touched because our lives were similar in so many ways. Neither mother ever made a meal. Neither had food in the house. Yet whereas my mother was supportive whenever I was criticized, Madeline's was destructive. When the nun at school chastised me for "trying to be funny and the centre of attention," my mother said, "Well then, let Sister Agnese entertain the class. Honestly, that nun wouldn't know a comedian if she fell over one."

I sat down on a bench in Central Park next to a doctor in his greens. He was still wearing his operating-room hairnet, so he must have walked straight across from Mount Sinai Hospital. His hands were folded between his knees and he was looking down at his feet, which were shod in red clogs. I said, "Operation gone badly?"

"Lost one of a set of twins."

Although the scale of the tragedy was different, I said, "I just lost a patient as well. I'm a psychologist."

"They both were a good size and had strong heartbeats going into delivery. One just wasn't ready. I still don't fully understand what went wrong. What happened to yours?"

"I was fired. Mission aborted."

"How so?" he asked.

"Sometimes people aren't ready to learn things about themselves, just as babies aren't ready to come out. It's all in the timing."

"You got to keep going," he said, stretching his arms above his head as we both stood up to leave.

I'd now walked miles from Tribeca, and fully realized I'd made a mistake. There was no undoing it. I thought about calling Madeline, but that was my need; it wasn't the best thing for her. I'd helped her in some ways. Now it was best to withdraw and hope that the wound I'd opened would heal.

A check was indeed delivered the next day by international courier, with no note. Only Madeline would pay for same-day international delivery just to get me off her hands.

6

REVELATIONS

THE MORE I THOUGHT ABOUT Madeline's case, the more I wondered how I'd gotten into such a bizarre labyrinth. I turned to one of my mentors, Dr. Milch, a professor of psychiatry who was among the best therapists I'd seen. I'd spent many hours observing his tapes of sessions with patients and watching him in person through a one-way mirror. He was now in his eighties, a German Jewish refugee who'd come to Canada via New York in the 1930s. He was one of the last of the greats who'd worked with, and often quoted, the founders of psychoanalytic theory. I liked to think we had a special bond, so, even though he was retired, I called to ask him for advice. Dr. Milch agreed to meet me at his home.

I sat across from him in his book-lined study and recounted the whole case, from its unusual beginning to its international check delivery. Then Dr. Milch summarized in his thick accent: "So, *Liebling*, you told this man, Duncan, that you did not do marriage counselling, then you agreed to it. You told him to come alone, he brought his girlfriend. He would not allow his daughter in her own home, but you chose to focus on the cruelty of the disturbed girlfriend instead of the father. Then you refuse to see his daughter in therapy, as you have left private practice. He follows you to a restaurant, stalking you, and there you agree to fly to New York once a week, to her workplace. You do not even demand that she come to you. It seems to me that this case was doomed from the outset, before you even met the patient. Why have you broken every rule for this man—a man you hardly knew?"

I felt stunned. I'd realized from the beginning that I had experienced a countertransference to Duncan, but I hadn't fully credited its impact. Duncan actually looked a bit like my father; he spoke with the same American brashness; he wore the same starched shirts. And just like my dad, he was a charming businessman. Dr. Milch made me understand the insidious effect of this countertransference: I'd failed to explore thoroughly why Duncan had emotionally abandoned his daughter. I had no idea why he could run a business with hundreds of employees across the country and yet have to hide in the basement when his ninety-pound wife lost her temper. The major questions remained: Why did he still love—or rather, remain adolescently infatuated with—such a cruel woman? And why had he repeated that behaviour with Karen?

I had solved none of this, nor had I *really*, in my own unconscious, held him responsible for it.

Dr. Milch reminded me that I had twenty-five years of experience as a psychotherapist, had taught at the university level, and had supervised psychology students. For me to have made such a countertransference signalled that there was trauma or at least some level of disturbance in my relationship with my father. I assured the doctor that we'd had a wonderful relationship, and that as a child I'd worked happily by his side in his drugstore.

But Dr. Milch didn't pull any punches. He said he wanted to describe what my unconscious felt about my father. "He was a very successful, smart, and well-liked man until he began to lose his mind when you were a young teenager. Then he embarrassed you by doing strange things, like driving the car into restaurants and missing the drive-through. He lost all the family money through bad investments, and then you and your mother were left destitute. In fact, you owed money. You had to get two jobs while in high school. He betrayed you by leaving you, and then abandoned you with a mother who couldn't cope. He basically said, 'You are fourteen, but now you pick up the ball and run with it.'"

I argued with that assessment, saying that my father had had a brain tumour when I was a young teenager, and so none of that was his fault. Dr. Milch held up his hand in a *stop* gesture. He pointed out that the unconscious never cares for the facts. "It only knows what abandonment *feels* like." He emphasized that the unconscious doesn't acknowledge the reality (the fact that my father had an inoperable cancer and died), but it does acknowledge the emotional impact (I was abandoned). My unconscious had registered the fear of having to take over a fractured, poor family. "While Madeline's parents abandoned her by going to Russia, your father abandoned you at the same age through death." I nodded in agreement.

Dr. Milch said, "Now, knowing this, you tell me what Duncan meant to you."

I thought for a long time and finally got it. "He represented my father when he was a success and on top of the world, before the brain tumour. I wanted to recreate that time. I bonded to the fun and lightness of Duncan—which was the same as my dad's."

He agreed. "You wanted to freeze time, when you were the adored daughter of a loving, successful father."

I saw that I'd played the role of the daughter who wanted to please instead of the therapist who had boundaries and who explored her patient's pathology. Clearly, I should have come to Dr. Milch earlier. People can't overcome all the issues in their past on their own; I'd been wrong to think I was above needing help. Although the good thing about being a seasoned therapist is that you've seen it all and have gained wisdom, the bad thing is the complacency this can breed.

Another connection came to light for me much later, in the process of writing this book. Although it's unusual for girls to be raised by their fathers, each of the women I'd chosen to write about—Laura, Alana, and Madeline—had been brought up mostly by her dad. I didn't realize this until long afterward. It came as quite a shock: out of the thousands of women I've treated in therapy, I unconsciously chose three who were, in one important respect, raised as I was. No wonder I identified with them. It's a perfect example of a psychologist being ruled by her unconscious and not realizing it.

Thirty-six days later, Vienna called and booked an appointment at our regular time. "Man," she said, "we all went through hell here. Will debrief when you arrivé." (Vienna said *arrive* with a French accent, as in *arrivé*. She often peppered her speech with approximations of French.) "It's a new world here in good ol' Tribeca. We've had systems analysts, consultants, computer guys in, and even the walls are getting redone. Changes ga-lore!"

After I'd arrived, Madeline stomped into her office dressed in Armani—with gold Bulgari studs glinting, hair in a French twist, eyebrows on and lips pointed. She sat down and said, "Okay, so you were right. It was hard to hear. I had to act. If I crumbled whenever I heard something frightening, I'd have been drooling in a straitjacket by the time I was nine.

"I was deathly ill for a week. Suffice it to say every orifice was active. But I survived, got up, and made a list of what had to be done." Then, in a staccato blast, Madeline began reading from a pink leather monogrammed clipboard with a leather bow. "Point one," she said. Madeline had called in IT consultants, who advised her to create a digital inventory system accessible to all employees. She'd hired people to design a better website, and was now employing people in China and Hungary to scout for the company. "Everyone here has to take courses in what the fuck they're supposed to be doing," she said. "The entire library is being recatalogued. In short, *I am learning to delegate.*"

Madeline said she was sick of not trusting anyone. She and Anton were fed up with staying at the office until midnight while her highly paid associates, claiming that only she really knew the merchandise, went off to dinner. Now, she said, they could learn or get out. She'd kept them on only because she'd thought she was a monster and no one else would work for her. "They're all paid more than any museum would pay them, so they can fucking well start earning it."

I nodded and started to respond, but Madeline cut me off. "Dr. Gildiner, you've said enough," she told me. "This is my session."

She read on: "Point two: I had a complete meltdown and hyperventilated so much I had to breathe into a paper bag. I learned how to do that in grade eight." Then her voice cracked, but she pushed ahead. "Oh yeah, I told Anton I loved him." (I wanted to know his reaction, but I knew better than to ask.) "And I told him he'd *better* love me. He said he did.

"Point three: new regime. He moved into my loft. I told my father that Anton and I were in love. I didn't want to hear one word about how he wasn't my type. My type have been assholes who drove Maseratis. Anton has a bike and fucking reads books. He sends money to his mother." (Fortunately, Duncan said that as long as she was happy, he was pleased for her.)

All business flights were back on, Madeline continued, and in fact they were running thirteen flights that week. Still, she said, she sometimes cried telling Anton not to crash. He would hold her, reassuring her that she wasn't a monster (and pointing out that he had a greater chance of getting killed by walking to

Starbucks). Madeline had also informed the whole staff that although business was full steam ahead, they'd have to deal with her anxiety until it settled down. She never worried about the customers—she could always handle them.

She and Anton were flying to Palm Beach with some Meissen china and she'd decided not to visit her mother. "I'm doing what you said—I'm 'giving what I got.' She'd only forget to come to the airport or say something awful about Anton. I can take it. But I want to protect him. He doesn't deserve it."

Madeline put up her hand like a stop sign in my face. "I know you want to say 'Neither do you.' I'm working on it, okay?"

She hadn't been able to keep any solid food down; Nelcinda, her lifelong housekeeper, was making her baby food. "*But I will do this*. Terror can't stop me. I wore flats today because my legs are shaking so much. I was like a newborn calf in high heels. Anton told me to stop wearing them—he said they're putting holes in the floor and in his heart when he sees how they hurt my feet."

Finally, it was my turn to talk. "I'm sorry that I overwhelmed you in our last session," I said in apology. "It was my mistake."

In a dry, matter-of-fact tone, Madeline waved it off. "No big deal. I have been terrorized by a master. I've had to make battle plans all my life." Then, archly, she added, "It's my forte."

Madeline's declaration perfectly fit the definition of a hero, according to Bruce Meyer, the author of *Heroes: From Hercules to Superman*. "In its most refined sense, the heroic can be defined as that moment in a narrative when the forces of life make a stronger assertion than death," he writes.

Madeline had been so frightened after that last session, her legs had been trembling so much that she'd had to switch to flats. Yet she still strode into battle. This was a woman who'd been traumatized by emotional abuse since birth and had held on for dear life. She wasn't an adult who fought one battle and defeated an enemy; she'd been a little girl who fought every day for her sanity—and whose enemy was her own mother. She had to smuggle the uneaten meat out of the restaurant, cover for Charlotte's affairs, endure the betrayal of her mother sleeping with her first boyfriend, and bear being called a fat pig when she was emaciated and wanted a meal. She was called a monster when she was just being a child who wanted her mother's attention. She'd been abandoned for weeks on end. And her father couldn't help her; he was as frightened as she was.

Once, when she was eight, Duncan turned to her in the car and said, "Madeline, how are we going to make it?" Part of Madeline's fear of Charlotte was picked up from Duncan's own fear of her. Not only did she have to take care of herself; she had to take care of him.

Yet Madeline did it all. Much to her father's chagrin, she rejected the family fortune, giving her trust-fund checks to cancer research. Her grandmother had bequeathed Madeline her Tribeca building and her antiques, but other than that, she lived only on her own money. Madeline had built a huge business that far eclipsed the value of her grandmother's antique collection. She worked long hours and never once said "I'm rich, I don't need to work. I've had four cancers before forty. I think I'll rest." If that's not a hero, then who is?

That week when Madeline had her meltdown—or, as she put it, "when I went fucking postal"—changed her forever. Of foremost importance, she declared her love for Anton. The two of them have had a great relationship ever since—I never heard one worry, or even an ambivalent word, about it again. Sex, love, and intimacy were all there. They shared the same interests and work ethic. It helped that Anton had been a friend before he was a lover.

I was leaving Madeline's office once and had just gotten into the limo for the airport when a tall, lanky, strikingly handsome blond man knocked on my tinted window. He gave me a thumbs-up sign and a beautiful full smile. When I didn't roll down the window (even gorgeous blonds can shoot you in New York), he mouthed, "I'm Anton," and the limo drove off. He reminded me of Baryshnikov, but with longer legs. Typical that Madeline had never told me how good-looking he was. When I saw her again, I mentioned it. She looked derisively at me and said, "I may be neurotic, but I don't have bad taste."

Madeline referred to the therapy sessions we had after her meltdown as the "post-apocalypse." In religious terms, the apocalypse involves a sudden vision of the heavens opening and revealing their secrets—secrets that make it easier to understand earthly realities. And for Madeline, everything did become easier. One change followed another, with me bearing witness.

Anton and Madeline began to take Sundays off and then to travel to Europe for pleasure. They went skiing in Aspen, taking Vienna's now-teenage son with them. She forgave her father, and he would fly into the city for weekly dinners with her and Anton.

It had been more than four years since I began travelling to New York City, through de-iced wings and garbage strikes, to work with Madeline for two hours a week. I now knew everyone in the company. When I began to recognize certain kinds of bone china, I knew I'd been there long enough.

Madeline's mental health wasn't perfect at the end of our therapy, but a therapist has to know when the bulk of her work is done. It's a bit like parenting, in that you have to know the difference between support and dependence. When I looked at where we'd started, despite mistakes along the way, I was proud of our work. Like all former prisoners of war who suffer from post-traumatic stress disorder, Madeline could still regress. When she's tired, stressed, has a trigger, or is facing some adversity, her symptoms, mostly workaholism, can resurface.

The biggest hurdle was overcome when Madeline and Anton were able to fly in a plane together. He'd wanted to show her St. Petersburg's Hermitage Museum along with his other beloved spots in Russia. What's better than seeing the wonders of the world through the eyes of someone you love?

During our final therapy session, as I drank my venti nonfat decaf latte, Vienna came in and threw her arms around me, crying. They'd miss me, she sobbed. Madeline, ever the dry wit, said, "Don't worry, with my luck, she'll be back."

People who are wealthy are assumed to have it all, and so are often misread or misjudged. A magazine journalist once described Madeline as "haughty" because she didn't smile or make eye contact. If she'd been poor, she might have been described as "shy." The journalist's assumption could not have been more wrong. Madeline didn't make eye contact because she was frightened of any form of intimacy or attention, and she hadn't smiled because her mother had told her that when she did, she looked like a "dancing hyena with purple gums."

Madeline is my hero. I think of her as a prisoner of war who was brainwashed in her own home. She had a mother who was a narcissistic psychopath who put up a good front. Sometimes it's harder to have a mother like Charlotte, who was socially accepted in the community but privately cruel to her child, than it is to have a parent who's obviously insane and regarded that way by the community. At least with the latter, the child can learn that the abuse is nothing personal.

In her five-star prison, Madeline was repeatedly told she was a monster, that she was spoiled, grumpy, lazy, and fat. In reality she was pretty, president of her class, a tennis champion, head girl. When I saw her childhood pictures, she looked like a stick-figure drawing wearing a fancy party dress. Yet, like all children, Madeline believed her mother's depiction of her. On the rare occasions when she'd point out her successes, Charlotte would say that only *she* knew the real monster who was Madeline.

In every way, Charlotte instinctively knew how to brainwash her daughter. Psychologist Margaret Singer, an expert on brainwashing, lays out the ground rules in her book *Cults in Our Midst: The Continuing Fight Against Their Hidden Menace:*

1. *Keep the person unaware of what is going on and how attempts to psychologically condition him or her are directed in a step-by-step manner.*
   Madeline's mother called her a monster every morning for all the years she lived with her.

2. *Systematically create a sense of powerlessness in the person.*
   Every child is powerless, while every mother is all-powerful. That power structure is built into the nuclear family. Charlotte was so powerful that her husband, who supervised hundreds of employees, cowered in the basement with his daughter.

3. *The group manipulates a system of rewards, punishments, and experiences in order to promote learning the group's ideology or belief system and group-approved behaviours.*

There were two competing ideologies in Madeline's home. The father stood for truth, civilized behaviour, and the primacy of the social contract. (One major omission, however, was in not protecting his daughter from a predatory mother.) The mother laughed at the father's rules, labelled his lack of promiscuous behaviour "prudish," and called Madeline "a baby" for not having slept with her teenage boyfriend. Charlotte termed her own psychopathic behaviour "fun" and Duncan's ethical behaviour as "boring and stodgy." Charlotte was more ruthless, and therefore her ideology won in the home. She could have brainwashed the Manchurian candidate and made it stick.

It had been fourteen years since I'd seen Madeline and twenty since I'd seen Duncan. I'd kept track of her business ventures through various magazines and had seen one glorious picture of her in a floor-length Gucci gown holding the arm of Anton, dressed in his tuxedo. They both had huge smiles that beamed out of the Who's Who column about a hospital charity ball.

In our email correspondence, Madeline told me she was still living happily with Anton, that her cancers hadn't returned, and that she'd become closer to her father. Karen had become senile and had to be admitted into a nursing facility; Madeline was once more allowed into her childhood home. She'd learned to forgive her father for his inability to stand up to her mother and Karen. He tried to make it up to her, and she let him.

Although Madeline's mother was more benign than she'd been when younger (psychopaths tend to burn out), she hadn't really changed her stripes. Often psychopaths do not do well in later life, since they've failed to build long-term relationships, one of the major purposes of human existence. Charlotte had been beautiful, rich, and had enjoyed her husband's social position. However, her later live-in mate, Jack, had died penniless. She'd lost her looks through age, smoking, drinking, tanning, and lack of exercise. Suddenly, to no one's surprise, she wanted to spend more time with her daughter. Madeline didn't trust this newfound friendliness, and did only what was required of a dutiful daughter. Both she and her father gave Charlotte money but refused to do much more. They'd learned how to protect themselves. As Madeline said, "Thank God for therapy and call display."

EPILOGUE

*I remembered that the real world was wide, and that a
varied field of hopes and fears, of sensations and excitements,
awaited those who had courage to go forth into its expanse,
to seek real knowledge of life amidst its perils.*

CHARLOTTE BRONTË, *Jane Eyre*

THIS HAS BEEN A BOOK about people I consider to be psychological heroes. It's true that they bear emotional battle scars, but they *did* make it. I chose to concentrate on those who succeeded, those who emerged from troubled backgrounds without an addiction or a crippling mental illness. I've always opted for inspiration over tragedy. (When I was nine years old I read all the available copies of *The Diary of Anne Frank* in my local public library, hoping to find one where Anne didn't die at the end.)

Arnold Toynbee, a philosopher of history, informs us that the first job of a hero is to be an eternal, or universal, man or woman—meaning that through a singular act of bravery, a hero is perfected and then reborn. The second job of a hero is to return, transfigured, to teach us, the uninitiated, the lessons he's learned. And so this book is my way of hailing these five conquering heroes, of having them tell their terrifying but rewarding tales. Each had to slay a different Minotaur, each used a different weapon, and each employed different battle strategies.

These five people may at first have seemed vastly different, yet when the economic and cultural layers were peeled away, their unconscious needs were strikingly similar. They all needed to feel loved in order to live better lives.

What Laura, Peter, Danny, Alana, and Madeline can teach us is that we can *all* be heroes. They exemplify Thomas Hardy's words in his poem "In Tenebris II": "If way to the Better there be, it exacts a full look at the Worst." They show us how to dig into our own psyches and shine a light on those parts that lie in shadow. They found what was in those dark corners, dragged it into the light, and confronted it. By striking out heroically on an unknown path, they sought change, and persevered in the face of obstacles. They remind us that it is possible, although not always easy, to overcome our fears, to break out of our self-imposed boundaries where we mistake confinement for security. Finally, these heroes inspire us by showing that all self-examination is brave.

These five courageous psychological warriors made an indelible impression on me when they were my patients. I still think of them often. I hope their bravery will inspire you in the same way.

ACKNOWLEDGMENTS

Thanks to the heroes in this book who never gave up and fought on, giving me inspiration. Without them, there would be no book. Not only were they heroes, but they generously agreed to share their stories. Thanks to my first readers, Jon Redfern and Linda Kahn. They set me on the right track.

I'd like to thank my tireless agent, Hilary McMahon, not only for suggesting necessary changes, but for finding a perfect home at St. Martin's Press. I'd like to thank my editor, Elisabeth Dyssegaard, for her untiring efforts to make this the best book it could be. I'd also like to thank Jennifer Enderlin, the publisher, Katie Bassel, in publicity, Danielle Prielipp, in marketing, and finally Laura Clark. None of these jobs were easy to do from New York City during the Corona Pandemic of 2020. But they all did them with ingenuity and grace.

Finally, I'd like to thank Michael, my husband of forty-eight years, who has always listened to my ideas as though he has never heard them before—an acquired talent.